Future Interaction Design II

Pertti Saariluoma · Hannakaisa Isomäki
Editors

Future Interaction Design II

 Springer

Editors

Pertti Saariluoma
Department of Computer Science
 and Information Systems
University of Jyväskylä
Finland
ps@jyu.fi

Hannakaisa Isomäki
Information Technology
 Research Institute
University of Jyväskylä
Finland
Hannakaisa.Isomaki@titu.jyu.fi

ISBN: 978-1-84996-775-4   e-ISBN: 978-1-84800-385-9
DOI 10.1007/978-1-84800-385-9

British Library Cataloguing in Publication Data
A catalogue record for this book is available from the British Library

Springer Science+Business Media
springer.com

Contents

The Human Modes of Being in Investigating User Experience 191
Hannakaisa Isomäki

Contributors

José J. Cañas Department of Experimental Psychology, University of Granada, Granada, Spain, delagado@ugr.es

Dimitris Charitos Laboratory of New Technologies in Communication, Education and the Mass Media, Department of Communication and Media Studies, National & Kapodistrian University of Athens, Athens, Greece, vedesign@otenet.gr

Neil Charness William G. Chase Professor of Psychology, Pepper Institute on Aging and Public Policy, Florida State University, Florida, USA, charness@psy.fsu.edu

Gordon Fletcher Salford Business School, University of Salford, Salford, England, G.Fletcher@salford.ac.uk

Anita Greenhill Manchester Business School, University of Manchester, Manchester, England, A.Greenhill@manchester.ac.uk

Anne Honkaranta Department of Computer Science and Information Systems, University of Jyväskylä, Jyväskylä, Finland, anne.honkaranta@it.jyu.fi

Hannakaisa Isomäki Information Technology Research Institute, University of Jyväskylä, Jyväskylä, Finland, hannakaisa.isomaki@titu.jyu.fi

Tiffany S. Jastrzembski Psychology Department, Florida State University, Florida, USA, tiffany.jastrzembski@mesa.afmc.af.mil

Petra Kohler Daimler AG, Division of Data and Process Management, Ulm, Germany, petra.p.kohler@daimler.com

Juha Lamminen Department of Computer Science and Information Systems, University of Jyväskylä, Jyväskylä, Finland, julammin@cc.jyu.fi

Mauri Leppänen Department of Computer Science and Information Systems, University of Jyväskylä, Jyväskylä, Finland, mauri@cs.jyu.fi

Antti Oulasvirta Helsinki Institute for Information Technology [HIIT], Helsinki University of Technology and University of Helsinki, Helsinki, Finland, antti.oulasvirta@hiit.fi

Sebastian Pannasch Institute of Psychology III, Dresden University of Technology, Dresden, Germany pannasch@applied-cognition.org

Hanna Parkkola Department of Computer Science and Information Systems, University of Jyväskylä, Jyväskylä, Finland, hanpark@cc.jyu.fi

Pertti Saariluoma Department of Computer Science and Information Systems, University of Jyväskylä, Jyväskylä, Finland, ps@jyu.fi

Antti Salovaara Helsinki Institute for Information Technology (HIIT), Helsinki University of Technology and University of Helsinki, Helsinki, Finland, antti.salovaara@hiit.fi

Sakari Tamminen SOBERIT, Helsinki University of Technology, Helsinki, Finland, sakari.tamminen@hut.fi

Kaisa Väänänen-Vainio-Mattila Human-Centered Technology (IHTE), Tampere University of Technology, Hervanta, Finland, kaisa.vaananen-vainio-mattila@tut.fi

Heli Väätäjä Human-Centered Technology (IHTE), Tampere University of Technology, Hervanta, Finland, heli.vaataja@tut.fi

Teija Vainio Human-Centered Technology (IHTE), Tampere University of Technology, Hervanta, Finland, teija.vainio@tut.fi

Boris M. Velichkovsky Institute of Psychology III, Dresden University of Technology, Dresden, Germany and Kurtchatov Research Centre, Institute of Cognitive Studies, Moscow, Russia, velich@applied-cognition.org

Introduction: The New Interaction Design

Pertti Saariluoma and Hannakaisa Isomäki

Human interaction with machines, devices, and information systems has become commonplace in nearly every aspect of contemporary Western life. Yet this everyday human-technology interaction has become problematic because the performance capacities that underlie the technologies are being introduced or changed with increasing speed. For example, while the recent trend toward the ubiquitous use of information systems utilizing high technology, such as real-time simulation and multiple sensorial interaction functions in three-dimensional interfaces, could open new use possibilities—allowing people to make or achieve new things in varying situations with new technologies—it remains unclear whether people can and want to adopt these new use possibilities. Or, perhaps more accurately, it is unclear how quickly people will accept these new possibilities.

As a result, interaction design now faces a crucial period in terms of capitalizing on new design possibilities that would solve contemporary problems in an efficient manner. Failure to seize new design possibilities, at the very least, delays the realization of such solutions. But such delays could also result in negative implications for individuals and societies. The pace at which societies and organizations change as the result of technological advances also raises concern for variations in future use scenarios, underscoring the need for interaction research to find its true form in adequate time to positively influence the design use potentialities. This means that even though interaction design is practical in nature, the process benefits greatly from providing enough time and space to consider how current design possibilities might affect, and be affected by, the future challenges of the field, the nature and application of possible solutions to these challenges, and even the very foundations of the interaction design field.

Contemporary interaction design must no longer reflect only the immediate solution to a current challenge. Investigating future challenges and potential means of solving them forms an essential aspect of current interaction design, implying that future interaction design processes must be constructed upon the foundation of past and present experiences and thus, by extension, current design decisions may have profound implications on future designs and applications.

This book presents papers by experts in interaction design research who view the issues at play in interaction design from diverse perspectives. Yet despite the variety of topics and approaches to interaction design, there are some issues and characteristics that are fundamental and which are necessary to understand in order to advance the field. These include, among other things, the implicit and explicit preconceptions that designers use in problem solving.

One might think that the reason for slow development in some areas of scientific research or delays in application to practical use result from a lack of good new ideas: Solutions to problems take time, and thus the process does not proceed as quickly as one might like. However, an alternative perspective could be proposed: Old ideas, assumptions, and preconceptions within the field impede or prevent interaction designers from approaching novel problems in a way conducive to finding innovative solutions. For example, it is not uncommon in interaction research for designers to apply everyday folk psychology as the basis for analyzing the human behavior component of a problem when attempting to solve that problem. This practice limits the accurate understanding of the human role in interaction design as well as inhibits the development of new science-based methods of interaction design. The continuation of such practices means that designers are addressing psychological issues with assumptions that fulfill neither scientific criterion of reliability or validity.

Why is it so natural—and thus commonly practiced—to rely on everyday assumptions in interaction design when, for decades, it has been demonstrated that folk psychology cannot replace, or even approach, the value of scientific research in accurate understanding of the human mind? The answer is quite simple: Designers' intuition has served them acceptably in the past. But the technological environment is changing and becoming more demanding, and this has ramifications for the future.

The application of information and technologies—the designs of products and the products themselves—can be seen as the result of argumentative chains. At each stage in the design process, a number of important decisions must be made concerning, for example, the engineering of the product as well as the interaction processes. Each detail of the new product must be thought through for current and future implications. For the most part, these decisions are based on solid, scientifically based design knowledge and well-tested procedures.

Mathematics and the natural sciences provide a wealth of information that designers draw on to predict the performance of their designs. Practical engineering is built upon the laws of the basic sciences of physics and chemistry, following the laws of nature in applying this knowledge to address design restrictions (Pahl, Beitz, Feldhusen, & Grote, 2007). Engineering designers use scientific standards in calculating the forces at play in a new technology, for example, adjustable friction drive, so that they can know in advance of the actual construction of their product how that product will perform in reality (Pahl et al., 2007). Science makes it possible for engineering designers to secure their designs against most errors.

Yet, somehow, interaction design is quite different from engineering design in that, quite often, interaction decisions along that argumentative chain are not based on explicit scientific grounds. Instead, decisions are frequently made on intuitive grounds. Traditionally, the knowledge of interaction design has been based on good and best practices, which is not entirely bad in that it does safeguard the design process to some degree (Cooper, Reimann, & Cronin, 2007; Nielsen, 1993). In fact, the "it feels right" approach is the surprisingly common way of finding interaction design solutions. This means that many popular procedures undertaken in interaction design today rely on folk psychology and rather loose methodological practices, rather than on reliable knowledge about the human mind and human behavior. The scientific practices of technical design do not seem to have migrated to the field of interaction design.

As a result, the foundations for interaction design remain quite intuitive. Of course, even scientific knowledge relies, to some extent, on intuition (Nagel, 1961; Saariluoma, 1997). It is not possible in most design processes to scientifically resolve every step in a chain of arguments, and therefore all scientific truths have intuitive limitations. Yet even with these limitations, the application of scientific traditions—with all their methodological reliability, empirically tested results, and carefully analyzed theories—provides the best protection against errors. Even Euclid's *Elements*, a paramount example of a carefully constructed scientific whole, had intuitive limitations. The rise of non-Euclidian geometries illustrates that Euclid's *Elements* contained tacit limitations—unfounded intuitions—that limited its scope, even if it did not make it incorrect (Non-Euclidian Geometry, 2008).

Therefore, the ultimate intuitiveness of scientific knowledge does not mean that these carefully built scientific systems are insignificant or replaceable by commonsense knowledge, but rather that designers do operate within an environment that acknowledges that there is no absolute security against errors, even when their decision points are supported by scientifically grounded research. Rather, the limiting function of intuition can best be observed in the fact that designers cannot solve practical problems in the absence of suitable scientific knowledge. Because intuition is an essential and unavoidable element in scientific knowledge as well as design solutions, and because scientists and designers face the reality that they often cannot find scientific information to complete or close the argumentative chains, they should not simply close their eyes to the possible roles of intuition in science and design, but rather learn how to live with and address these scientific limitations and the need for intuition in specific cases. It is evident that the correct way of living with intuition is not to accept it at face value, as is done in folk psychology within interaction design. Intuition is not problematic because it is necessarily incorrect, but rather because the designer *does not know* whether it is true or false (Saariluoma, 1997). Therefore, reliance on intuition substantially raises the risks of error and/or failure. It has become quite apparent that designers, in most cases, must give up their reliance on intuition as the foundation for decision making, and replace their approaches to understanding the human component with investigated and argued knowledge, thus making the design process evidence based.

In many ways, design processes are constructive and they do differ in nature from basic scientific theories. The fundamental goals for constructive thinking are practical, with the ultimate criterion for the validity of the construction being practicality, not truth. If a construction works and users can safely reach their own goals by using the product, then the product is valid. While this reality makes interactive design processes somewhat different from scientific research processes, it does not eliminate the ongoing possibility that the intuition that underpins the construction incorrect for a particular use situation.

Reliance on intuition, such as folk psychology, makes interaction design a vulnerable area within the industrial design field. The belief that designers understand the human mind because they are themselves human is a very risky perspective. Psychologists, who studied the human psyche through their own experiences, gave up this practice long ago because they realized that investigating one's own mental processes resulted in very little concrete knowledge advancement. Fundamentally, their goals of openness, replicability, and objectivity were endangered (Watson, 1918). Moreover, vast areas of psychological research, such as unconscious processes, were totally outside the psychologists' ability to investigate properly within themselves. Freud (1933/2003), who introduced many psychological processes to the public, studied other people, and not himself. The rationale for the psychologists' decision to go beyond their own experiences and intuitions in advancing their understanding of the human mind and their field of study applies equally to interaction design. The field must abandon subjective practices.

A question may arise in the minds of some readers regarding what the practical consequences of intuitive interaction design are. If, as noted earlier, the ultimate goal of interaction design is usable and practical products that people can interact with in an acceptable manner, why should the interaction design industry invest time and energy in new types of practices when the old ones seem to work reasonably well? The answer is that the implications of and consequences for an intuitive basis for decision making in design simply shifts the problems of use to the consumer. Products not developed within the reliable scientific understanding of the human mind and behavior can result in the consumer having to battle hours with devices that do not quite fit their needs, their cognitive and behavioral abilities, or their interests and desires. This is especially true for users who do not fit the "average user" stereotype. As the chapters within this book will indicate, the human condition and the environment play important roles in the design, application, and use of technologies, as well as affect the way designers research and fashion design solutions for contemporary challenges. Products designed poorly as the result of intuitive approaches within the design process mean that the technologies will not be as responsive to the human need as they could be, and that the human may be less inclined to use or adapt the technologies as they might have. Turning new inventions into real innovations takes more time, and is less secure in its outcome, when the design process is built upon folk psychology or intuition. This reality, in turn, adds to the time and expense involved in the design, development, and implementation processes. Indeed, the concepts "working," "working well," and "working excellently" are quite distinct, and have implications beyond the immediate product.

When all is said and done, it becomes quite clear that one's own perspectives and conceptions can limit the advancement of interaction design. Reliance on intuitive concepts of the human mentality and how that plays out in human behavior during interaction contexts is simply a mindset, but one with great risks for hampering true technological development. This development is not endangered by the absence of new ideas but rather the fixation on old practices. The adoption of new practices—scientifically based and viewed with an inquisitive mind—not only brings about the reality of more secure and accurate decisions within the argumentation chain, but also introduces the practicality of new ideas in problem solving. These are essential for advancing the field of interaction design.

In this second volume of *Future Interaction Design* a number of forward-looking papers are presented. Each author attempted to foster the theme of replacing intuition in research with science-based research practices. This collection of papers provides a look at knowledge drawn from different schools of human research and helps advance a versatile perspective on finding new scientific ways to cope with the human role and function in technological interaction and interaction design.

Neil Charness and Tiffany Jastrzembski analyze gerontechnological factors in interaction design. They consider various age-related changes in and challenges to human performance, as well as the underlying psychological mechanisms. They also apply the goals, operators, methods, and selection rules (GOMS) architectural model to demonstrate the differences in performance between younger and older adult users. In this way, Charness and Jastrzembski present an experimental analytical approach that points toward a more holistic vision, a transition essential for practical design processes.

Petra Kohler, Sebastian Pannasch, and Boris M. Velichkovsky address, with new cognitive studies, two classical problems inherent in groupware systems design. First, they investigated the spatial orientation and coordination of attention by group members interacting within traditional (in-person) and technology-supported distributed work conditions. The enhancement of technologies allowed the members of distributed work groups to better follow the shifts in their remote colleagues' attentional focus in order to successfully maintain distributed work processes. Second, they explored the emotional consequences of replacing a human being with an avatar in virtual collaboration.

José Cañas presents a new approach for interaction design that underscores the mutual dependency between the human cognitive and interface functions.

He argues that it is necessary to implement usability methodologies that, on the one hand, could be used to evaluate the user experience interacting with the prototypes as it develops, and on the other hand, could anticipate any conditions of interaction in future scenarios. This second aspect is crucial if future systems are to be truly innovative.

Pertti Saariluoma, Hanna Parkkola, Anne Honkaranta, Mauri Leppänen, and Juha Lamminen discuss the nature of user psychological knowledge and analyze the process of developing respective ontological solutions for information systems. They maintain that the actual design process is organized around action models, and propose an action-related ontology that designers can consider in looking for psychological knowledge that can provide the scientific backbone for the design actions for information systems.

Antti Oulasvirta explicates the problems researchers face during experimentation in field conditions. He examines the theory of quasi-experimentation as an alternative conceptualization of causality, control, and validity, particularly with respect to the threats to experimental validity in human-computer interaction (HCI) studies conducted in the field. As new technologies provide various possibilities for mobility to users, field experimentation is an essential methodology in the future. Therefore, the accuracy of the methods should be ensured.

Kaisa Väänänen-Vainio-Mattila, Heli Väätäjä, and Teija Vainio present a new view on user experience within a service society. They explore the nature of a specific technology, Web 2.0 services, from the user's perspective, and define a new concept of service user experience. They then analyze the applicability of user-centered design principles for the service development life cycle and discuss users' new roles in that dynamic activity. As a result of their study, they present a summary of service user experience design opportunities and challenges.

Dimitris Charitos focuses on mobile location-based technologies, which have generated much interest in industry today. He discusses various technical approaches to outline locative media and their roles in current and future information and communication technology (ICT) societies. These new developments shall change the way designers and users have traditionally viewed urban space and human presence within that space. Consequently, new ways to think about and address the network society are explored.

Antti Salovaara and Sakari Tamminen present novel criticism towards technology acceptance models. They maintain that the concept of acceptance is too simplistic since users are prone to invent new uses of technology (the process of appropriation) instead of just accepting or neglecting the single purpose of a certain artifact, thus leading to suboptimal design solutions. Therefore, they advocate that technologies should be examined from the point of view of appropriation rather than simply one-directional acceptance.

Anita Greenhill and Gordon Fletcher provide exemplars of the influence of digital artifacts upon cultural experiences. According to their analysis, the cultural aspect of user experience is essentially future-oriented. Digital artifacts themselves resist any stability of meaning by being continuously disassembled and reassembled into new meaningful settings. These artifacts extend this complexity by accelerating and extending cultural relationships both temporally and geographically, resulting in a wider range and number of potential and actual relationships in an expanding context of technology usage. Through these contextual connections, new technologies incorporate multiple parameters of power, meaning, and cultural knowledge.

Hannakaisa Isomäki argues that a holistic view of the human being is needed to provide the appropriate theoretical foundations for user experience analyses in diverse contexts. She introduces a theoretical holistic framework for understanding user experience in terms of the fundamental human experience involving physical, organic, mental (cognitive, emotional, volitive), social, and cultural modes of being. From a holistic point of view, the very nature of human action may be seen through the concepts of the various modes of being, each contributing to some extent to a continuum of an active process within which the human as a whole is actively experiencing ICTs. Consequently, recognizing user experience necessitates insight into the human modes of being and their implications within the dynamic affordances that emerge between people and ICTs.

Acknowledgments The editors wish to acknowledge their gratitude to Barbara J. Crawford, who has admirably, accurately, and patiently taken care of copyediting all the texts.

References

Cooper, A., Reimann, R., & Cronin, D. (2007). *About face 3: The essentials of interaction design*. Indianapolis, IN: Wiley.

Freud, S. (2003). *Outlines of psychoanalysis* (H. Ragg-Kirkby, Trans.). Harmondsworth, UK: Penguin. (Original works published in 1933 and 1941.)

Nagel, E. (1961). *The structure of science*. New York: Harcourt.

Nielsen, J. (1993). *Usability engineering*. Boston: Academic Press.

Non-Euclidean Geometry. (2008). Retrieved from Wikipedia on March 20, 2008, from en. wikipedia.org/wiki/Non-Euclidean_geometry

Pahl, G., Beitz, W., Feldhusen, J., & Grote, K. (2007). *Engineering design*. London: Springer.

Saariluoma, P. (1997). *Foundational analysis*. London: Routledge.

Watson, J. (1918). *Psychology from a behaviorist point of view*. Chicago: Lipcott.

Gerontechnology

Neil Charness and Tiffany S. Jastrzembski

Abstract We define and describe the new field of gerontechnology, assess the challenges facing academics and practitioners in designing technology products for older users, and provide some practical advice. We review expected age-related changes in perception, cognition, and psychomotor performance and suggest principles for accommodating such changes with better design. We introduce parameters for using goals, operators, methods, selection rules (GOMS) modeling techniques to improve the design process and provide an example of such modeling for a mobile phone task.

1 Gerontechnology

Our goals for this chapter include describing the new field of gerontechnology, assessing the challenges facing academics and practitioners in designing technology products for older users, and providing some practical advice based on existing research. We also stress the potential benefit of modeling techniques in improving the design process and provide an example of a mobile phone design.

1.1 History and Definition of Gerontechnology

Although technology is as old as the first human who fashioned a tool, the field of *gerontechnology* is of very recent origin. The term apparently originated from the Technical University of Eindhoven in the Netherlands in response to its creation of an interdisciplinary program, the Institute of Gerontechnology (Harrington & Harrington, 2000). One of the earliest definitions was by Herman Bouma: "The study of technology and aging for the improvement of the daily functioning of the elderly" (Bouma, 1992, p. 1). Research in this field also falls under several other labels, such as human factors and aging (e.g., Charness & Bosman, 1992; Fisk,

N. Charness (✉)
William G. Chase Professor of Psychology, Pepper Institute on Aging and Public Policy, Florida State University, Florida, USA
e-mail: charness@psy.fsu.edu

P. Saariluoma, H. Isomäki (eds.), *Future Interaction Design II*,
DOI 10.1007/978-1-84800-385-9_1, © Springer-Verlag London Limited 2009

Rogers, Charness, Czaja, & Sharit, 2004), and gerotechnology (Burdick & Kwon, 2004), though the term gerontechnology has some advantages (Charness, 2004). The field has continued to mature over the past decade and has its own society, the International Society for Gerontechnology,[1] and a journal, *Gerontechnology*.[2] Nonetheless, given how young the field is, many of the answers to critical questions about design principles await empirical evidence from the research laboratory. As will be seen, general guidelines can be offered from basic knowledge about aging phenomena. However, we need much more research to make sound design decisions for older users of technology.

The above definition for gerontechnology provides an agenda for both academics and practitioners. Gerontechnology must rely on both traditional lab-based experimental studies of the aging process and of technology use, as well as field-based studies that attempt to implement technological solutions to mitigate age-related declines in abilities. Both approaches are necessary to permit appropriate feedback and cross-fertilization between researchers and practitioners. At the same time, this field can and should draw on existing research on disability and that of inclusive design (also known as universal design[3]), given that disability rates increase strikingly after 65 years of age, as seen in Fig. 1.

Similar increases in disability with age can be seen in other developed countries (see United Nations, Statistics Division, 2007), though declines in

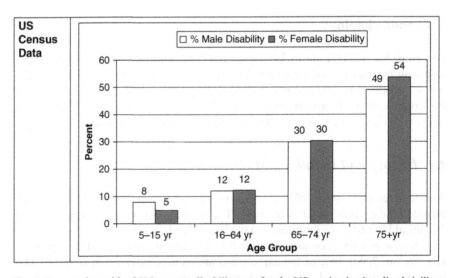

Fig. 1 *Top panel* provides 2005 percent disability rate for the US noninstitutionalized civilian population age 5+. Data source is the US Census Bureau (2005). *Bottom panel* provides disability prevalence for private households in the UK. Data from Health Survey for England, 2000–2001 (Official Document Archive 2, n.d.)

---

[1] http://www.gerontechnology.info/

[2] http://www.gerontechnology.info/Journal/index.html

[3] http://www.design.ncsu.edu/cud/about_ud/udprinciples.htm

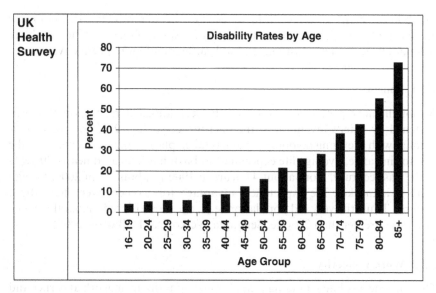

Fig. 1 (continued)

old age are seen occasionally in less developed countries, perhaps because of a "survival of the fittest" phenomenon (few persons reached old age in these countries at the time of the survey). However, as the United Nations site indicates, direct comparisons across countries should not be made because of very different definitions of disability. Given the sharp increase in disability after age 65, we will use that age to define older adult in this chapter. Elsewhere, our research team has discussed issues in design for older workers, those aged 40 + who are in the paid labor force (Charness, Czaja, & Sharit, 2007).

However, we need to be aware that the 65 + population should be segmented into multiple subgroups. Young-old adults, age 65–74, have very different needs and wants than do middle-old adults, age 75–84, as in turn do the old-old adults age 85 +. Those in good health have different needs than those with multiple disabilities. One of the challenges for designers is to provide individual solutions that appeal to a particular older adult. Unfortunately, older adults are more variable than younger adults by virtue of their having been shaped by and having shaped their environments much longer. So the challenge is to find robust solutions to perceived needs in the face of increasing variability.

1.2 Older- Adult Demographics and Capabilities

There have been striking increases in longevity in the past century in developed countries that, coupled with declines in fertility, have led to aging populations. However, increased age is associated with normative changes in many human capabilities, many of which lead to declines in adaptability. Technological advances offer the promise of compensating for some of these declines, enabling older adults to lead not just longer, but healthier and more productive, lives.

1.2.1 Longevity

Although most people are aware of the technological revolution that was hastened by Intel's invention of the microprocessor in 1971, not everyone is familiar with the aging revolution that has taken place in the past century. In the US, for instance, average life expectancy at birth has increased nearly 30 years in the past century, from about 47 years in 1900 to about 77 in 2000, though there is a marked life expectancy advantage for women over men (about 6 years). Thus, the very old population (e.g., age 85 +) is predominantly female by a ratio greater than 2:1 (He, Sengupta, Velkoff, & DeBarros, 2005).

1.2.2 Work Longevity

There has been a long-standing trend for men to retire from work at earlier and earlier ages since the establishment of social welfare systems, such as the US social security system. As a result of the implementation of such a safety net, men's labor market participation rates in the age 65 + range fell from about 46% in 1950 to 16% in 1985. However, that trend has reversed in the past decade with rates rising slightly to near 19% in 2003 (He et al., 2005). As a result, the median age of the labor force is rising with values of 35 in 1978, 39 in 1998 and projections of 41 in 2008 (Bureau of Labor Statistics, n.d.). This trend has implications for the design of office equipment.

1.2.3 Perceptual Capabilities

There are predictable age-related changes in vision and hearing, two important senses for interacting with technology artifacts. Vision is degraded for a number of reasons. Foremost, by their mid-40s, most adults develop a condition known as *presbyopia*, the inability to focus effectively on near objects. Presbyopia results primarily from changes in the lens, which becomes larger and less flexible as it adds layers of crystalline cells over time (much as an onion grows larger by adding layers). This change can be alleviated in part with external lenses, bifocal lenses in particular for those already nearsighted. However, such lenses create other challenges in terms of field of view at a given focus strength and in terms of seeing objects at intermediate distances. Problems can arise, for instance, in work settings when older workers must shift their gaze back and forth between the screen and a document on their desk. There are other changes too that degrade vision, such as the yellowing of the lens that makes it more difficult to perceive short wavelength light (the blue-to-green part of the spectrum). Also there is increased scatter of light in the optical media (e.g., from "floaters" in the vitreous humor) that makes glare more of a problem.

Hearing also undergoes negative age-related changes. By the decade of their 50s, many older adults, particularly men, begin to suffer from *presbycusis*, a reduced ability to hear high -frequency sounds. This change is usually due to loss of the hair cells in the cochlea, with differential loss for encoding high-pitched sounds, including critical speech sounds such as the "s" sound, making it increasingly more difficult to perceive speech correctly. Further, older listeners are more disrupted by background noise that can mask critical auditory signals. The result of these and other changes can be seen as reducing the signal/noise ratio for encoding environmental events (e.g., Welford, 1985). That is, older adults confront an increasingly difficult-to-perceive environment.

1.2.4 Psychomotor Capabilities

Another normative change for older adults is loss in precision in motor control. This again can be seen as having a "noisier" motor control system. Thus, for aiming tasks, unless they are willing to accept their own slowed movements, older adults can be expected to have a higher "index of difficulty" for Fitts' law (e.g., Welford, 1977), meaning that they will need larger targets or smaller distances to move (movement amplitudes) to show equivalent performance to younger adults. As an example, such imprecision in movement may make accessing and clicking on small icons on computer screens difficult to accomplish. Choosing a better input device can minimize age differences in performance (Charness, Holley, Feddon, & Jastrzembski, 2004).

1.2.5 Cognitive Capabilities

The cognitive system also changes in predictable ways with age. In general, older adults show a knowledge advantage over younger adults for what has been termed "crystallized intelligence" (Horn, 1982). That is, they are more likely to be able to answer successfully questions dealing with definitions of words, or knowledge of facts. Such an advantage is usually maintained until their 60s or 70s. Conversely, older adults are very likely to have difficulty solving novel problems or performing new procedures, a decline in what has been termed "fluid intelligence" (Horn, 1982). Adults in their 20s typically perform best on these types of test items.

From an information- processing perspective, notable changes take place in functions such as working memory, the processes that support storing and manipulating limited amounts of current information (Baddeley, 1986). Thus, older adults will be disadvantaged by having to store and process large amounts of new information, such as in using an automated telephone menu system that has too many alternatives at each level in the menu structure (Sharit, Czaja, Nair, & Lee, 2003). There is also evidence that older adults are more impaired in tasks that require that they divide attention across multiple input channels (e.g., Hartley, 1992). Similarly, there is evidence that older adults are more prone to being distracted by irrelevant information (Hasher, Stolzfus, Zacks, & Rypma, 1991).

However, the most striking change in performance is general slowing in information-processing speed (Salthouse, 1996). Older adult will typically take 50–100% longer to respond than younger adults in speeded tasks. However, this same slowing parameter holds for learning rates in self-paced learning environments (e.g., Charness, Kelley, Bosman, & Mottram, 2001). Thus, much more time should be allotted for training older adults to use technology, though knowledge, particularly breadth of experience with software, is an important mediating variable (Charness et al., 2001; Czaja et al., 2006). Training should capitalize on existing knowledge when possible.

1.2.6 Anthropometrics and Physical Fitness

A variety of changes in body dimensions and capabilities also are associated with aging (e.g., Kroemer, 2005; Steenbekkers & van Beijsterveldt, 1998). Muscular strength generally diminishes with increased age, though functional strength is often hindered more by normative onset of disease processes such as arthritis, which can make movement and force generation a painful process. Height diminishes in response to changes in bone structure and disc degeneration in the spine, more so for women than men, in part because women are more prone to bone loss (osteoporosis) than men. Many of these changes begin to occur in middle age or later, and some are associated with reduced work ability in job settings (e.g., Ilmarinen & Louhevaara, 1994; National Research Council, 2004), though strength loss can be mitigated partly by maintaining appropriate exercise routines. Thus, devices designed for an aging population should make minimal demands on strength, dexterity, and reach capability.

2 Technological Innovation

Although longevity clearly accelerated in the 20th century, the pace of technological innovation has also shown spectacular growth. A good example is found in the field of computing. Within a period of about 50 years, we have witnessed the migration of computing from mainframe systems in institutional settings to microcomputer systems in many households in the developed countries. With the invention of the microprocessor in 1971 by Intel, it became possible to build personal computer systems that could sit on a desktop. With the invention of Ethernet protocol, it became possible to link these systems through networks. With the invention of the http protocol and the Web browser, it became possible to disseminate and display information no matter what operating system the computer ran. An even more impressive example of the rapid spread of technology is afforded by the mobile phone, with many developing nations building telephone networks solely around mobile devices rather than wired landline systems. Modern mobile phones were introduced in the mid-1970s, and it has been estimated that there were 2 billion users by 2005 (GSM Association, 2005).

2.1 Principles of Design for Older Adults

In this section we provide an overview of design principles from the perspective of technology use, and focus particularly on human–computer interaction. More detail can be found in Fisk et al. (2004). Technology products can play an important role in maintaining independence in old age when disabilities strike (e.g., Mann, Ottenbacher, Fraas, Tomita, & Granger, 1999). Computers and the Internet can even help with many of the tasks defined as instrumental activities of daily living, such as shopping, using transportation, financial management, telephone use, and so on, as noted in Charness (2005). However, many current technological systems make undue demands on older users, particularly given the trend toward increased miniaturization seen in devices such as mobile phones.

A useful framework for understanding the relationship between users and technology systems is offered in Fig. 2, from the Center for Research and Education on Aging and Technology Enhancement (CREATE; Czaja, Sharit, Charness, Fisk, Rogers, 2001).

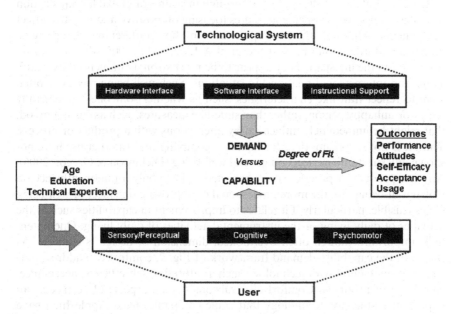

Fig. 2 Framework for understanding the demand/capability balance between systems and users. Technological systems with hardware, software, and instructional components make demands on a user's sensory/perceptual, cognitive, and psychomotor capabilities. The degree of fit determines outcomes such as performance with the system, attitudes toward the system, self-efficacy, as well as acceptance and use of the system. Different users have different educational and technical backgrounds and are of different ages, all of which affect their capabilities

Users bring differing capabilities to the operation of technical systems, such as their perceptual, cognitive, and psychomotor abilities. Technological systems make demands on those capabilities when people interact with hardware components, software interfaces, and training materials. Age is a potentially powerful individual difference variable that directly and indirectly (through education or technical experience) affects user capabilities (e.g., Czaja et al., 2006). The degree of fit between user capabilities and system demands affects the many aspects of the interaction with a system, including short- and long-term usage patterns and attitudes toward the system.

2.2 Ethics of Design

One useful principle for ethical design is encapsulated in the physician's Hippocratic oath: "First do no harm." Good design is intended to improve the comfort, safety, and efficiency of a product or process. Particularly in the design of products for work environments, efficiency and safety seem to be given strong emphasis. In the aging world, the top-level goal that might be envisioned for products and processes is to improve quality of life.

Quality of life is usually evaluated through measures of global life satisfaction as well as subjective well-being measures focusing on positive and negative affect components. Although these components can show differential change (e.g., Kunzmann, Little, & Smith, 2000; Steverink & Lindenberg, 2006), they are mostly stable across the life span. They appear to be most strongly influenced by health status and interpersonal relationship situations. Such well-being measures often seem to reflect trait-like characteristics, such as whether someone is a generally happy or unhappy person, rather than state-like measures, such as current mood, that might be immediately influenced by interactions with a product or process. Thus, it is not surprising that, for instance, computer and Internet use have not shown any substantive effects on general well-being (Dickinson & Gregor, 2006). Any one product or process can be expected to have only a minor influence on global well-being. So, the more modest goal of improving one facet of well-being seems feasible, particularly if it relates to improvement in capabilities such as the activities of daily living or the instrumental activities of daily living. One potentially important, though often overlooked, dimension of design is comfort. As shown in the capability-demand framework of Fig. 2, comfort can address outcomes of interaction with technology such as attitudes, self-efficacy, acceptance, and usage of products. Comfort also subsumes some aspects of aesthetics, an important feature for technology that some companies (e.g., Apple Inc.) have shown to be critical in product success.

There is a dearth of empirical work on ethical concerns in design. Some scenario studies have been conducted by Caine, Fisk, and Rogers (2006) on privacy concerns in high-tech aware-home environments. A group of 25 older adults were shown a variety of cutting-edge technologies that tracked people using video technology. The camera systems presented information to the viewer about the occupant either as full video images, as point-light images, or as images that distorted people into blobs so only presence and general movement in a room was depicted. Twelve scenarios were devised to describe the monitoring situation as one where the older occupant possessed varying levels of physical and mental impairment. Acceptability of these different levels of monitoring was measured under these different occupant capability scenarios. Older adults were willing to trade off privacy for the benefits of monitoring, suggesting that they engage in cost-benefit considerations with well-differentiated views on privacy. Privacy protection is often seen as one of the primary concerns for the design of active (or passive) monitoring systems for older adults. Ethical design would be expected to respect privacy rights. However, there is apparently variability in older -adult desires for privacy.

2.3 Design for Input/Output Devices

We now attempt to provide some general guidelines, followed by illustrative examples. Broad principles to consider include minimizing steps for users, adopting consistent layout of elements for controlling a device, and ensuring adequate visibility of control elements. Given that older adults have noisier perceptual and psychomotor systems for interacting with devices, they are more likely to make errors, particularly when forced to respond quickly. Minimizing steps is an important principle to observe to maximize the probability of the older adults being able to complete a complex procedure in error-free fashion.

As an example, consider the simple task of entering text associated with a phone number on a mobile phone. The user must be successful at quite a few subtasks. He or she must locate the desired character on the keyboard if unfamiliar with the keyboard, monitor the phone display to detect any button press errors (slips of the finger from the intended key), and complete keystrokes to generate an alpha character before a time-out period that moves the cursor position to a new position in the word string (e.g., a time-out of between 1–1.5 s).

The chance of completing an entry in error-free fashion diminishes with each step in the procedure if there is a constant probability of error on each step. More precisely, if there are N steps with each having the probability p of failure, the probability of success equals $(1-p(\text{failure}))^N$. If $p = .05$ (95% success rate at each step), then by the 13th step the probability of completing all these steps without error is only $p = .5$. Minimizing steps is a very good principle to observe when designing a product.

Consistency in layout is also a very important principle, particularly for older adults who learn new information more slowly. To the extent that design can draw on *population stereotypes*, such as pushing a switch upward to turn on a light or pushing it downward to turn it off (e.g., in North America), this also will aid older users. By consistency in layout, we mean that control elements should always appear in the same spatial location, minimizing the need to search a display to find a control. For instance, in software interface design, one should have icons or menus appear in customary locations (such as at the top and in consistent left-to-right order, depending on cultural norms). Many modern operating systems for computers provide automated tools to programmers for conforming to such guidelines (e.g., window element controls).

Another important consideration in design is to ensure adequate visibility of controls that are to be used in indoor environments. Lighting is often below optimal levels in homes, and can be particularly problematic for older adults (Aarts & Westerlaken, 2005; Charness & Dijkstra, 1999). Most work environments do have reasonable luminance levels (typically 100 cd/m^2 reflectance from paper-based reading materials) but designers working in such environments should not assume the existence of similar luminance levels in people's homes or in public buildings because those levels may be more in the range of 30 cd/m^2 (Charness & Dijkstra, 1999). Having adequate contrast (foreground/ background ratios) for words and symbols, or physical controls such as buttons and switches, is particularly important in low- light environments.

2.3.1 Input Devices: Positioning

Positioning devices can be classified into those with direct positioning and indirect positioning characteristics. For pointing tasks, direct positioning devices, such as placing a stylus or finger on a touch -screen device (e.g., a personal digital assistant [PDA]) or light pen on a CRT device, should be preferred to indirect positioning devices, such as a mouse or trackball. A trackball should be preferred to a mouse when using indirect positioning because the trackball can help with double-clicking tasks given the separation between positioning (using the ball) and clicking (using the keys) functions, thereby counteracting the effects of tremor. With indirect positioning devices, people must learn to map control in one plane with movement in a different plane, and older adults in particular have difficulty with this mapping (Charness et al., 2004; Murata & Iwase, 2006). However, it is difficult to set rules because the nature of the positioning task is crucial to determining which device might be optimal (e.g., Rogers, Fisk, McLaughlin, & Pak, 2005). Additional research is required to offer specific advice on a variety of the design challenges that arise.

2.3.2 Input Devices: Data Entry

Many devices require alphanumeric input from the user, and common devices such as keypads and keyboards are typically offered. Many older adults do not have typing skills (this will change with future cohorts of older adults), although they may well be familiar with number placement conventions used in keypads for telephony devices. Also, many older adults can suffer from arthritis, which makes typing or key pressing painful. Ensuring adequate key sizes and spacing between keys, and providing appropriate tactile and auditory feedback about the key press, can help older adults interact with keyboards successfully. Alternative input techniques to consider, where feasible, include speech recognition and handwriting recognition. There is some evidence that, at least for native

English speakers, speech recognition software is robust with respect to older - adult use (Jastrzembski, Charness, Holley, & Feddon, 2005).

2.3.3 Output Devices: Visual

Given the changes in vision with age, it is critical to ensure legible characters for reading. Emissive devices should be preferred to passive/reflective ones, given the problems with lighting in homes. Backlit devices are particularly helpful here and, because of their higher contrast ratios, modern LCD displays should be preferred to CRT devices. Letter sizes for alphanumeric text should be at least 0.6 degrees of visual angle or greater. (Your thumb at arm's length approximates 2 degrees of visual angle.) For printed materials, choose a font size of at least 12 points in x-height (the height of the character x) for letters. Consider flashing messages that serve as warnings, though do not flash so quickly that the message cannot be read.

2.3.4 Output Devices: Auditory

Try to keep sound signals in the 500–1000 Hz range, given the decline in ability to hear high frequencies with age. Although homes are generally quiet places, it is useful to recall that there is greater masking of target sounds by ambient noise in older adults, so if there are critical alarms to be sounded, be sure that they are of adequate intensity (e.g., at least 60 db). If evaluating the direction of a sound is important and you must use sounds with fundamental frequencies above 2000 Hz (for miniature devices using small oscillators), then try to prolong the warning sound for at least 0.5 s to permit localization by changing head position. Consider providing redundant sources for warnings, such as visual and tactile (vibration) channels in addition to auditory channels. If you need to use speech output, keep speech rates to 140 words per minute or less, and prefer male voices for conveying information given their lower pitch, but female voices for capturing attention. Avoid the use of synthesized speech (e.g., Roring, Hines, & Charness, 2007), preferring the generation of prerecorded human-pronounced words when a limited vocabulary is sufficient.

2.4 Design for Interface

Older adults are less likely to use advanced technological devices than younger adults (Czaja et al., 2006), so they cannot be expected to know many of the conventions adopted for interfaces. Hence, designers need to be careful to educate older users about interfaces, for instance, that there are scrolling options that enable the user to see other parts of a virtual screen that is larger than the actual screen display. Similarly, standard graphic user interface operations are not necessarily going to be immediately comprehended, such as how to resize windows. Older users may not expect or know how to make use of help systems or search capabilities. The mental models of how systems work may be based on simpler technological artifacts (typewriter rather than word processor). Hence, it is particularly important to provide appropriate training materials or tutorials, and to use standard layouts in a consistent fashion across a user interface.

2.4.1 Speed of Operations

Because older adults process information more slowly, standard assumptions about the time required to complete operations before a time-out in the system need to be examined carefully. See below for the case of mobile phone technology and text entry. Typically, the designer should allow for 50–100% more time to complete operations than is the case for younger users.

2.4.2 Navigation Through Menu Structures

In part because of declines in working memory capacity, older adults are more likely to get lost when searching through complex menu structures (e.g., Mead, Sit, Rogers, Rousseau, & Jamieson, 2000). Hence, it is critical to provide navigation tools that can assist users to be aware of where they are and how to backtrack without having to restart from the top of the menu structure. Particularly when there are different modes within a system (e.g., navigating, text entry), it is important to alert the user so that mode errors are avoided.

A common choice point for menu design is how to assign items in terms of breadth or depth of a menu structure. With a visually presented menu structure, breadth is typically preferred to depth as a means of reducing working memory demands. However, greater breadth is often associated with more visual search. Given reductions in working memory and the older adult's greater reliance on environmental cues (also known as environmental support; Craik, 1986), breadth is generally to be preferred to depth for visual menu structures. However, for auditory menus (e.g., automated voice response systems on telephones), for cases where the user does not know in advance the target item to select in a menu, depth should probably be preferred to breadth. Too many alternatives can overtax working memory capacity, though a recent thesis suggests that when the user can employ an updating strategy to guess the likely alternative to select, greater breadth is preferable (Commarford, Lewis, Smither & Gentzler, 2008). Nonetheless, navigation difficulties often arise with deep menu structures, so providing appropriate navigation prompts is essential. Eventually, people do learn menu structures from systems that they interact with frequently. It is important to consider whether you are designing for novice users or experienced users in your choice of menu structure and navigation aids.

2.4.3 Compatibility Issues

Because older adults are likely to have greater crystallized knowledge, designers should try to take advantage of such knowledge. For instance, population stereotypes in North America often signal increase and decrease in consistent ways. Upward, rightward, and clockwise motions are usually associated with increasing a value. The opposite directional movements usually decrease a value. Stimulus-response compatibility that draws on these assumptions should be preserved. In displays where buttons are used to respond to screen layout of alternative responses, spatial mapping compatibility should be preserved, such that alternatives map to neighboring buttons. Sometimes, for example, automated teller machine buttons do not match the number of alternatives offered on the screen or have inconsistent positioning of options to buttons. Not having a one-to-one correspondence between these features can confuse the user.

Often it is necessary to use words to label menu items. Choosing appropriate labels is always a difficult task when the designer is familiar with jargon but older adults are not as familiar. Confronting a novice user with options such as the old DOS message "abort, retry, fail" is practically guaranteed to lead to a bad result. On the other hand, assuming nontechnical interpretation of common language terms can run into difficulties as well. A classic example is the instruction to "press any key to continue," where an unsophisticated user searches vainly for a key with the label "any." Instead, use specific instructions, such as "press the enter key to continue."

2.4.4 Documentation Issues

Older adults are more likely to seek help and ask questions when using novel technology than are younger adults. Hence, having explicit documentation and well-designed help systems should lead to greater success in use. Similarly, it is important to provide older users with appropriate feedback about their actions (or failure to act at a choice point). Older adults are more likely to make errors in using new systems than younger adults, who have superior experience and more sophisticated mental models of systems. Therefore, it is critical to ensure that error messages are informative (e.g., use plain language that can be found in the manual or help system), and that the system is robust with respect to error correction so that the user can recover without having to restart their task from the beginning.

2.4.5 Adaptive Displays

Because different user groups are unlikely to be equally well served by the same interface arrangements, some degree of adaptability should be offered. For instance, well-designed Web sites provide users with the option of resizing text,[4] thereby accommodating those with low vision. However, it is unwise to assume that if the interface is adaptive, users will necessarily choose the most efficient variant. There are all too often a bewildering set of possibilities for modifying interfaces. User preference and performance may not match up (e.g., Charness et al., 2004). Instead, usability testing should be adopted to offer reasonable default settings based, perhaps, on querying the user about his or her experience level.

---

[4] See, for example, http://www.seniorhealth.gov

2.5 Training Considerations

There are very few technological products or services that do not require some amount of training. Hence, it is worthwhile to consider the training needs of older adults.

2.5.1 Design for Training

Older adults learn new material more slowly than younger adults, perhaps twice as slowly (Charness et al., 2001). Therefore, more time needs to be allocated to training programs and, if possible, self-paced training should be arranged. As well, it may be helpful to provide general guidance about the process to be trained, given that older adults may have poorer mental representations of the task to be performed. However, conceptual training (trying to establish a deep understanding about task performance) may be less effective than procedural training (step-by-step instruction; Mead & Fisk, 1998), particularly when time is constrained for training or the user may not be expected to use the system on a regular basis. In general, meta-analyses, such as Callahan, Kiker, and Cross (2003), have indicated that techniques that work well for younger workers also work well for older ones, though having self-paced training and training in smaller groups may be particularly helpful for older adults.

2.5.2 Organization of Training

Some important features of training include the schedule of training (e.g., massed versus distributed practice), and the components of training (part-task versus whole- task training). In general, it is better to space training sessions to promote better retention rather than to mass practice on a procedure to be learned. Such spacing may also counteract the buildup of fatigue in older learners. Keeping sessions to 30–45 min in length and building in rest breaks may be helpful. Also, later training sessions can act as refresher sessions for earlier ones if old tasks are tested along with newer ones. If such review is not possible because of time constraints, then providing memory aids (e.g., note cards) for earlier task processes can be useful.

When tasks involve complex procedures, it is usually helpful to train task components rather than training the whole task at once, though this depends on specific task characteristics. Sometimes it is useful to provide the user with a road map of the process to be mastered so that they can appreciate the ordering of operations before they attempt to train on the components. The type of instructional media needs to be matched to training needs. Simple verbal instructions may work well when the procedure is temporally organized (e.g. "hold down the control key and then press the b key to make the character bold"). Pictorial guides are to be preferred when spatial information needs to be conveyed (show a figure that identifies the icon that needs to be clicked to transform the selected text into italics).

Ideally, training procedures could be adaptive, so that what is presented to the learner depends on their mastery of earlier trained components. However, intelligent human or computer tutors are often needed to be able to "debug" faulty knowledge that is responsible for poor performance. For such systems to work effectively there needs to be informative, constructive feedback available to the learner. Given that older adults tend to ask questions more often than younger adults, having accessible, responsive trainers is essential.

The area of training is a challenging one for the field (see Charness & Czaja, 2006). Although there are sound general principles to draw on, the field needs to refine these principles in order to develop the variety of different training packages required for the diverse set of products that are entering the consumer market.

2.6 Principles of Usability Testing with Older Adults

Even when principles for design are followed carefully in building a technology device, some usability testing is usually necessary to ensure that the product performs as expected with the target user group. Usability principles revolve around five interrelated features: Learnability, Efficiency, Memorability, Errors, and Satisfaction (LEMES). In our context, a useful mnemonic for LEMES is Let Every Mature Elder Succeed.

Learnability refers to the ease of learning, often assessed by the time that it takes a new user to reach a given level of proficiency in device use. Criteria of error-free performance and time to carry out a task are both typically evaluated to assess learnability. Of course, older adults are often a very diverse group in terms of capability for learning, so, as Alan Welford (personal communication, October, 1985) pointed out years ago, they make a superb panel for usability testing. They often show the flaws in a design sooner than more able younger adult samples.

Efficiency indicates the extent to which users can quickly achieve a representative set of task goals with the product. Can they do so without undue frustration, fatigue, or dissatisfaction? Usually efficiency is measured once users have become at least moderately proficient with a product. If there are similar products on the market, efficiency can be assessed by comparative testing.

Memorability is the opposite of forgetting. A product's memorability is determined by the ease with which a product can be used after some time away from initial training or use. Many products are not used on a daily basis, but they must be easy to remember how to use when needed. A good example is a safety-related product, such as the fire extinguisher. In general, older adults do not exhibit much faster forgetting rates than younger adults, though those who learn more slowly apparently do forget a bit more quickly (MacDonald, Stigsdotter-Neely, Derwinger, & Bäckman, 2006).

Errors are a critical feature of product use. Obviously, the design should minimize error rates but, given their inevitability, their negative consequences should also be minimized. Obviously, some errors are more critical than others and catastrophic failures should be designed out. Usability testing often focuses on identifying when, where, and why errors occur. Categorizing errors into types, using a taxonomy, such as that proposed by Reason (1990), is a good first step in trying to eliminate errors. Some important categories are slips (actions not intended, such as when the wrong button is pressed inadvertently), mistakes (action was intended, but the user selected a wrong action), and mode errors (product is in a state that does not permit achievement of a goal, and the state must change first).

Satisfaction with a product or device is usually assessed with questionnaires and rating scales administered after the product has been used. A potential concern is that older adults and younger adults may not use rating scales in the same way, so cross-age comparisons can be problematic for an overall satisfaction measure. It may be better to ask users to evaluate different aspects of product use and incorporate that information into the design process so that improvements can be reached on the various dimensions of product use in iterative fashion.

Usability testing involves a variety of techniques, from passive observation of users interacting with a prototype device, to gathering think- aloud protocols taken during product use, to questionnaires and interviews administered after use. Often product design features are tested initially via focus groups, where small groups of potential users (e.g., 6–12) are brought together and given scenarios about potential product features and asked to comment on them. See Fisk et al. (2004) for more details. The goal is to derive insights about the nascent device in terms of the dimensions for usability (LEMES), and make appropriate modifications to enhance user performance.

Classical usability testing tends to focus on efficiency and safety issues but does not do a good job of addressing other important aspects of a product such as comfort or enjoyment. Often usability testing procedures employ one-item rating scales for enjoyment, ease of use, or satisfaction in an effort to evaluate that aspect of a product. However, paired comparisons of different product models may be a more effective way to evaluate enjoyment and aesthetics. As well, even very successful commercial products, such as Apple's iPod, are probably not very enjoyable to use for complete novices until they become efficient in using the product's interface. So, aesthetics or enjoyment may need to be evaluated over an extended period of use.

3 Simulation as a Supplement for Usability Testing

Simulation as a method of modeling human performance, particularly cognitive performance, has about a 50-year history, starting with the computer simulation work of Newell and Simon on theorem proving in the late 1950s (described in Newell & Simon, 1972). Simulation modeling expanded from serial symbolic process modeling to parallel neural net modeling in the late 1980s (McClelland & Rumelhart, 1988). Current influential models, such as Adaptive Control of Thought (ACT; Anderson, 1996), State Operator and Result (Soar; Newell, 1990) and Executive Process/Interactive Control (EPIC; Meyer & Kieras, 1997) have a hybrid structure, consisting of both parallel and serial components. A virtue of these more complex simulation models is that they account for both low-level performance features of behavior (speed, accuracy) and higher- level cognitive features such as perceived workload. We look at one type of modeling system here.

3.1 The GOMS Modeling System

One of the most popular modeling tools in human–computer interaction is GOMS (Card, Moran, & Newell, 1983), a model that has also served as a foundation for higher -level architectures. It stems from their seminal book, *The Psychology of Human-Computer Interaction* (Card et al., 1983), which meshed psychology with a human engineering approach to offer a quick, first-approximation, informal modeling tool for designers to deliver reliable, quantitative predictions of human performance. Typical parameter estimations of human information processing were culled from empirical psychological literature to construct a simulated user with known capabilities and limitations (dubbed the Model Human Processor), which could then be used to model routine, technology-related tasks, specifically described at the grain of key-strokes and mouse movements.

The basic ingredients for description of tasks depended on a simplified cognitive structure consisting of four components: Goals, Operators, Methods, and Selection rules (GOMS). Rationale for this structure hinged on the principle that the model human operator efficiently pursues goals according to constraints on knowledge, ability, and task situation, so that high-level goals are then decomposed into subgoals and units tasks and expressed in the form of very basic motoric actions, such as depressing a key on a keyboard or using a mouse to move a cursor a fixed distance on a screen to acquire a target. Actions serve as the end result of a chain of mental operations that engage perceptual and motor processors around a cognitive processor, and each processor possesses its own cycle time (e.g., 100 ms), storage capacity, and decay rate, gleaned from the psychological literature. Many tasks lend themselves well to GOMS-level decomposition, as routine tasks often have nested goal states that can be reduced to initial states, subgoal states, and final states (John & Kieras, 1996).

GOMS relies on a fairly orthodox model of human information processing involving different memory systems (iconic/echoic, short-term, long-term) and laws of human performance (e.g., Fitts' law, power law of practice, as described in Card et al., 1983), that help the model provide reliable quantitative and qualitative predictions of routine, human performance across different design specifications or task scenarios. The underlying philosophy behind GOMS and other human-computer interaction (HCI) cognitive architectures is to provide engineering models of human performance. Models of this ilk are distinguished from traditional, psychologically oriented cognitive models in several key ways: (a) they seek to optimize a priori predictions; (b) they are usable and useful for both practitioners and researchers; (c) they apply to real-world, relevant tasks; and (d) they are approximate to handle a task at the minimal level needed to describe it.

The goal of many simulation modeling exercises is to estimate the time it would take to carry out a task under different design specifications, and comparing alternative designs is one of the most obvious uses of the GOMS technique. Due to the nature of the model's output, the most efficient design may be selected by comparing alternate designs for estimated completion times on representative tasks that a user may carry out. Furthermore, GOMS analyses may provide a rationale for why one design is more user-friendly (e.g., requires less working memory strain or requires fewer visual fixations) or more satisfying (e.g., buttons are easier to navigate as a function of size), or why one design feels more sluggish than another (e.g., the overall pathway analysis is longer or requires more time to complete than another). Since GOMS analyses are able to make a priori predictions of performance, they can be performed not only on existing systems already developed and in use, but they may also be utilized early in the design process to evaluate notional, simulated designs, before they are ever implemented or even prototyped. Such modeling holds the promise that low-level design decisions may be made without having to test actual users and, further, such first-approximation modeling efforts have been consistently validated across a variety of real-world tasks and have the potential to serve as the building blocks of more formal computational cognitive process models, such as Adaptive Control of Thought-Rational (ACT-R; e.g., John, Prevas, Salvucci, & Koedinger, 2004).

3.2 GOMS Modeling Parameters for Older Adults

GOMS modeling is predicated on a normative user, the so-called Model Human Processor, which in turn is based on data collected almost entirely from college undergraduates. However, older adults vary in important ways from younger adults, as seen above, thus what is seen as an optimal, user-friendly environment will likely change in the future (Koncelik, 1982). Hence, to implement GOMS modeling in older user populations, the parameter estimates for the simulated user need to be modified. Charness and Bosman (1990) made an early attempt to estimate Model Human Processor parameters for older adults, but due to the sparseness of the cognitive aging literature at the time, estimated values for some parameters were probably unreliable. More recently, Jastrzembski and Charness (2007) updated these parameters by means of meta-analyses to construct a simulated older user. With proper application to the human engineering field, these basic perceptual, motor, and cognitive building blocks (see Fig. 1) can inform designers as to what products would suit the older user in the earliest stages of design and help create better environments for older users.

Some fairly straightforward predictions are possible from Table 1. It is worth noting that estimates for cognitive, motor, and perceptual processor cycle times are nearly twice as long in older than younger adults. In GOMS modeling, such cycle times are iterated quite often when a task is modeled, and hence tend to dominate in predicting response times. Thus, a good rule of thumb would be to predict that, when using the same strategy for performing a task, older adults will typically take 1.5–2 times as long as a younger adult (e.g., Fisk et al., 2004).

However, task components will skew the estimates for response time, so, for instance, when eye movements play a weighty role, old–young differences may be considerably smaller, given the much smaller 1.2:1 ratio observed for saccade duration. As aptly stated by Welford (1958),

> Where age changes do impinge upon performance some relatively trivial factor may often be limiting what can be done, so that comparatively small changes in the task could bring it within the capacities of older people...and would benefit both young and old. (p. 287)

Table 1 Information processing parameter estimates for younger and older adults and their old-to-young ratio

Parameter of interest	Younger adult estimate (Card et al., 1983)	Older adult estimate (Jastrzembski, 2006)	Ratio of old to young
Duration of saccadic eye movements	230 ms (70–700)	267 ms (218–314)	1.2
Decay half-life of visual image store	200 ms (90–1000)	159 ms (95–212)	0.8
Cycle time of the perceptual processor	100 ms (50–200)	178 ms (141–215)	1.8
Cycle time of cognitive processor	70 ms (25–170)	118 ms (87–147)	1.7
Cycle time of the motor processor	70 ms (30–100)	146 ms (114–182)	2.1
Power Law of practice constant	0.4 (0.2–0.6)	0.49 (0.39–0.59)	1.2
Fitts' law slope constant	100 ms/bit (70–120)	175 ms/bit (93–264)	1.75
Effective capacity of working memory	7 items (5–9)	5.4 items (4.9–5.9)	0.77
Pure capacity of working memory	2.5 items (2.0–4.1)	2.3 items (1.9–2.6)	0.92

Note. Numbers in parentheses represent the range for younger adults and two standard deviations of means for older adults (see Jastrzembski & Charness, 2007).

Clearly, designers may use these estimates to inform design of critical pathways and ultimately help minimize performance differences between young and old.

Another straightforward prediction is that older adults will show steeper improvements with practice than younger adults, given the higher value for their learning exponent and the likelihood that they have more to gain with continued effort. Designers may apply this to guidelines or recommendations for use, so that older adults may be made aware of how much practice will be needed to become proficient in a given task.

In summary, by estimating typical perceptual, motor, and cognitive parameters for the older adult, designers may be provided with a tool to optimize design specifications that suit the environment to the older user. If better modeling occurs, it is likely that older adults will feel more comfortable participating in this technology-laden society, be more likely to test out newer technologies as they arise, and be more likely to adopt new technologies that could, in theory, allow them to live independently longer, communicate with friends and family more easily, or take care of routine tasks digitally. It is also arguable that designing with the older user in mind may in fact produce better designs for people of all ages, as modifications to aid the older individual may also ease task demands for others.

3.3 Example Modeling for Mobile Phone Tasks

Jastrzembski and Charness (2007) validated the above parameters by developing GOMS models for mobile phone tasks for younger and older adults using two different mobile phones with distinct hardware and software differences to evaluate menu hierarchy structure, integration of information across screens, screen and text size, button sizes and locations, and critical pathways to successfully complete each task. These hardware and software differences helped determine how perceptually, motorically, and cognitively taxing each device was with regard to users of different ages.

Jastrzembski (2006) also extended the capability of GOMS modeling to predict error rates, rather than simple task completion times alone, using base error rates on operations in a less complex mobile phone task (a text messaging task) to estimate those in a more complex one (an appointment-scheduling task). An example decomposition of a simple dial-a-number task is shown in Table 2.

In user testing, 20 younger and 20 older participants were familiarized with each phone, shown the procedure, and required to practice the procedure until it became consistent (see Jastrzembski, 2006, for details). This extensive orientation and practice procedure was necessary for validation purposes, as GOMS modeling applies not to novice users who usually are problem solving in order to accomplish tasks, but to experienced users for whom the activity is routine.

Table 2 GOMS task analysis for mobile phone #1 in the dial-a-number task

Assumptions: In default mode the user is holding the phone in the preferred hand, dialing with preferred thumb.	Operator	Time young	Time old	Total young	Total old	Button press number
Goal: Dial number (268-413-0734) and send call.						
Method: Press numbers and hit green call button.						
Step 1: Fixate first chunk of numbers on paper (first 3 numbers)	F	230	267	230	267	
Step 2: Encode first 3 digits	3 C	3(70)	3(118)	440	621	
Step 3: Fixate keypad	F	230	267	670	888	
Step 4: Decode first chunk	C	70	118	740	1006	
Step 5: Fixate first digit	F	230	267	970	1273	
Step 6: Dial first digit	M	70	146	1040	1419	1
Step 7: Fixate second digit	F	230	267	1270	1686	
Step 8: Dial second digit	M	70	146	1424.8	1980	2
	Fitts	84.8	148			
Step 9: Fixate third digit	F	230	267	1654.8	2247	
Step 10: Dial third digit	M	70	146	1824.8	2568	3
	Fitts	100	175			
Step 11: Fixate second chunk of numbers on paper (second 3 numbers)	F	230	267	2054.8	2835	
Step 12: Encode second 3 digits	3 C	3(70)	3(118)	2264.8	3189	
Step 13: Fixate keypad	F	230	267	2494.8	3456	
Step 14: Decode second chunk	C	70	118	2564.8	3574	
Step 15: Fixate first digit	F	230	267	2794.8	3841	
Step 16: Dial first digit	M	70	146	2964.8	4162	4
	Fitts	100	175			
Step 17: Fixate second digit	F	230	267	3194.8	4429	
Step 18: Dial second digit	M	70 0	146 0	3264.8	4575	5
	Fitts					
Step 19: Fixate third digit	F	230	267	3494.8	4842	
Step 20: Dial third digit	M	70	146	3697	5219	6
	Fitts	132.2	231			
Step 21: Fixate last chunk of numbers on paper (last 4 numbers)	F	230	267	3927	5486	
Step 22: Encode last 4 digits	4 C	4(70)	4(118)	4207	5958	
Step 23: Fixate keypad	F	230	267	4437	6225	
Step 24: Decode last chunk	C	70	118	4507	6343	
Step 25: Fixate first digit	F	230	267	4737	6610	
Step 26: Dial first digit	M	70	146	4955.5	7016	7
	Fitts	148.5	260			
Step 27: Fixate second digit	F	230	267	5185.5	7283	
Step 28: Dial second digit	M	70	146	5281.3	7475	8
	Fitts	26.3	46			

Table 2 (continued)

Assumptions: In default mode the user is holding the phone in the preferred hand, dialing with preferred thumb.	Operator	Time young	Time old	Total young	Total old	Button press number
Step 29: Fixate third digit	F	230	267	5511.8	7742	
Step 30: Dial third digit	M	70	146	5740.3	8165	9
	Fitts	158.5	277			
Step 31: Fixate fourth digit	F	230	267	5970.3	8432	
Step 32: Dial fourth digit	M	70	146	6188.8	8838	10
	Fitts	148.5	260			
Step 33: Return with goal accomplished	C	70	118	6258.8	8956	
Step 34: Fixate green send button	F	230	267	6488.8	9223	
Step 35: Press green send button	M	70	146	6558.8	9369	11
Total time				6.59 s	9.37 s	

Note. In the Operator column, F refers to an eye fixation, M refers to a motor processing cycle, Fitts refers to the amount of time added to the motor processing cycle to press a button with a movement to a target of a given width and distance from the starting position, and C refers to a cognitive processing cycle. Highlighted cells represent activities that have overt responses, here a key press. Other steps represent assumed activities. Such activities could become observable, for instance, if eye-tracking equipment were used to examine fixation durations.

Users were timed and evaluated for accuracy as they carried out the task across multiple trials. The GOMS model captured human performance very success-fully for both younger and older users, as seen in Fig. 3, for the time estimates plotted for each of the 11 required keystrokes.

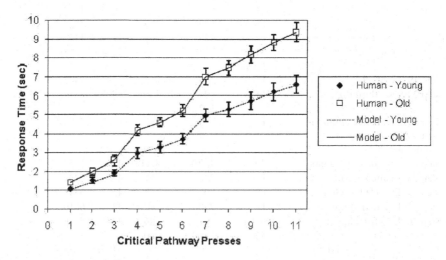

Fig. 3 GOMS model fits for mobile phone #1 in the dial-a-number task. Standard error bars (+/− 1 SE) are given for the human data

However, contrary to the popular belief that designing with the older user in mind will create better designs for users of all ages, data from Jastrzembski (2006) revealed that phone-specific factors, such as the default time-out value for screen cursor movement after a keystroke (during text entry), had different effects on younger and older errors that were predictable from GOMS modeling. If the time-out value was long enough to accommodate older users, for instance, younger users made more errors due to impatience, and the system undoubtedly felt sluggish to them as a result. If the time-out was shorter, slower older users made more errors when they pressed keys too slowly and the cursor moved ahead before they had completed the number of repetitions on a key necessary to select their desired alphanumeric character.

Each phone had design strengths and weaknesses that made them superior for one task and inferior for another in ways that were also predictable using the GOMS technique. For instance, the miniaturized keypad on one phone was superior for performance in a simple dialing task for users of all ages, but performed very poorly on more complex tasks requiring fine motor control and precision. This exercise showed that using GOMS to build models was both enlightening and very successful in evaluating existing mobile phone devices across specific tasks.

In sum, using predictive models to simulate trained users is a powerful approach to testing design specifications. Although Jastrzembski and Charness (2007) investigated usability of existing products, simulations may also provide a valid means of testing prototype models with hypothetical critical paths for younger and older adult populations.

4 Perspectives on Development of Gerontechnology over the Next Few years

Although gerontechnology has made a promising start, there are several critical challenges ahead. Much of the modeling activity emphasizes speed of processing. However, older adults are more likely to be concerned with accuracy than speed, so modeling needs to be extended to predict errors and designers should try to minimize their occurrence. Also, more effort is needed to identify the individuals and environments that can benefit the most from gerontechnological interventions.

4.1 Optimizing Design for Time or Errors?

It can be relatively expensive (time, money) to conduct usability testing for every possible new product. Also, not all firms have the capability to do such testing (or even know where to turn to outsource such testing). Hence, modeling and simulation offer an effective technique for choosing among possible designs early in a design process. As Jastrzembski (2006) demonstrated, if specific tasks with a product can be analyzed at the level of keystroke-based behavior, it is possible to use a GOMS-style model to make predictions that match human performance fairly closely on both time and error bases. However, there is a need for much more theoretical work to supply reliable human performance parameters from existing data, as well as for creating better models of error generation. So, it seems likely that the research community and the practitioner community would both benefit from the development of easier-to-implement modeling techniques.

Much of the theoretical work in the psychology of aging has been aimed at understanding performance in speeded tasks using prototypical cognitive psychology paradigms. However, the ecology of everyday activities for older adults seems to be dominated not by an emphasis on completing tasks quickly, but rather by ensuring that tasks are performed in error-free fashion. A good example is medication adherence behavior (e.g., Park & Jones, 1997), which emphasizes taking prescription drugs in the right amounts at the right time of day. You need not take them as quickly as possible within a short time limit (with the exception of acute medical emergencies), but you do have to take them in the right amount. Here problems with prospective memory, the ability to plan for future actions (Einstein, McDaniel, Smith, & Shaw, 1998), may dominate the performance function.

Similarly, when designing transportation systems for aging populations, it would be useful to have better estimates for how long it takes an aged adult to cross a street safely, in order to set appropriate signal durations for pedestrians, yet be mindful of the need to ensure a smooth flow of vehicles through streets. Errors in these tasks (walking, driving) can lead to tragic consequences. Vehicle crashes result in over 40,000 fatalities annually in the US and older drivers and pedestrians are disproportionately affected (Evans, 2004).

4.2 Critical Design Environments

Work, health, and home environments are important venues where good design can make a difference for older users. For a variety of reasons, but mainly to ensure that pension systems are able to meet the pressures of so-called baby boom cohort retirements, people will likely have to work longer before becoming vested in pension systems such as social security. In the US, the age of entitlement for a full pension has already moved from 65 years old to 67 for those born after 1960. Hence, work environments need to accommodate age-related changes in human capabilities in order to ensure that older workers remain productive. A good example is the cleaning industry, where in the EU about 50% of the workers are older women, aged 45+ (Louhevaara, 1999). Reorganization of work and design of better tools can provide a safer work environment. Although there is little relationship between age and productivity (e.g., McEvoy & Cascio, 1989; Sturman, 2004; Waldman & Avolio, 1986), rapidly changing workplaces may imperil older workers who tend to learn new skills more slowly. An aging work force will necessitate attention to design for hardware, software, and training.

As well, given the accelerating cost of health care systems to governments (and employers in the US), it is pretty evident that individuals are going to become more and more responsible for managing their own health and particularly the management of chronic diseases that develop in old age. Health care is migrating away from hospitals and into homes, given the cost differential between inpatient and outpatient care. Older adults will be required to learn to use fairly sophisticated medical devices at a time when their abilities are waning. Poor fit between user capabilities and system demands could literally lead to life-and-death situations for patients. A large-scale study in the US suggested that poor system design characteristics may be contributing to about 95,000 unnecessary deaths every year in US hospitals (Kohn, Corrigan, & Donaldson, 2000). Hence it is apparent that health care product and environment design are going to be crucial areas for gerontechnology.

Finally, the desire to remain in a familiar home environment is a goal for many elderly adults. Smart home technology (e.g., Berlo, 2002) or, as it is also called, aware- home technology (Mynatt, Melenhorst, Fisk, & Rogers, 2004), is going to grow in importance for maintaining independence at home in old age. As Mynatt et al. (2004) argue, homes can become coaches for older adults for tasks ranging from medication adherence to food preparation. Another approach is to offer smart robotic assistants to aging residents (e.g., nursing home robots that provide medication advice; Matthews, 2002), though so far only robotic cleaning units have seen much commercial success in the US.

5 Summary

Gerontechnology is a new approach to melding basic research on aging phenomena with the application of research findings to design more effective products. It requires the cooperation and collaboration of a variety of disciplines—such as psychology, human factors engineering, and design—to ensure that products meet the needs of an aging population. We have outlined some of the normative changes that occur as people age. We also provided some guidelines for design. We also argued that some of the short-term goals for this discipline should include extending our knowledge of basic human performance parameters as a function of adult age, emphasizing design for error-free performance over speeded performance, and developing easier-to-apply modeling and simulation techniques. Even with better simulation techniques, there will still be a continuing need to do usability testing, particularly for products that incur high costs when errors occur, such as in the health care field.

Acknowledgments This research was supported by NIA 1 PO1 AG17211-07 to the Center for Research and Education on Aging and Technology Enhancement (CREATE), and by SSHRC to Workforce Ageing in the New Economy (WANE).

References

Aarts, M. P. J., & Westerlaken, A. C. (2005). Field study of visual and biological light conditions of independently-living elderly people. *Gerontechnology, 4*, 141–152.

Anderson, J. R. (1996). ACT: A simple theory of complex cognition. *American Psychologist, 51*, 355–365.

Baddeley, A. (1986). *Working memory*. New York: Oxford University Press.

Berlo, A. V. (2002). Smart home technology: Have older people paved the way? *Gerontechnology, 2*, 77–87.

Bouma, H. (1992). Gerontechnology: Making technology relevant for the elderly. In H. Bouma & J. A. M. Graafmans (Eds.), *Gerontechnology* (pp. 1–5). Amsterdam: IOS Press.

Burdick, D., & Kwon, S. (Eds.). (2004). *Gerotechnology: Research and practice in technology and aging*. New York: Springer.

Bureau of Labor Statistics, U.S. Department of Labor. (n.d.). Working in the 21st century. Retrieved March 26, 2008 from http://www.bls.gov/opub/working/chart2.pdf

Caine, K. E., Fisk, A. D., & Rogers, W. A. (2006). Benefits and privacy concerns of a home equipped with a visual sensing system: A perspective from older adults. *Human Factors and Ergonomics Society Annual Meeting Proceedings, 50*, 180–184.

Callahan, J. S., Kiker, D. S., & Cross, T. (2003). Does method matter? A meta-analysis of the effects of training method on older learner training performance. *Journal of Management, 29*, 663–680.

Card, S. K., Moran, T. P., & Newell, A. (1983). *The psychology of human-computer interaction*. Hillsdale, NJ: Lawrence Erlbaum Associates.

Charness, N. (2004). Coining new words: Old (Greek) wine in new bottles? (Reply). *Gerontechnology, 3*, 52–53.

Charness, N. (2005). Age, technology, and culture: Gerontopia or dystopia? *Public Policy & Aging Report, 15*, 20–23.

Charness, N., & Bosman, E. A. (1990). Human factors and design for older adults. In J. E. Birren & K. W. Schaie (Eds.), *Handbook of the psychology of aging* (3rd ed.; pp. 446–463). San Diego, CA: Academic Press.

Charness, N., & Bosman, E. A. (1992). Age and human factors. In F. I. M. Craik & T. A. Salthouse (Eds.), *The handbook of aging and cognition* (pp. 495–551). Hillsdale, NJ: Erlbaum.

Charness, N., & Czaja, S. J. (2006). Older worker training: What we know and don't know. AARP Public Policy Institute (Report #2006-22). Washington, DC: AARP. Available online at http://www.aarp.org/research/work/issues/2006_22_worker.html

Charness, N., Czaja, S. J., & Sharit, J. (2007). Age and technology for work. In K. S. Schulz & G. A. Adams (Eds.), *Aging and work in the 21st century* (pp. 225–249). Mahwah, NJ: Erlbaum.

Charness, N., & Dijkstra, K. (1999). Age, luminance, and print legibility in homes, offices, and public places. *Human Factors, 41*, 173–193.

Charness, N., Kelley, C. L., Bosman, E. A., & Mottram, M. (2001). Word processing training and retraining: Effects of adult age, experience, and interface. *Psychology and Aging, 16*, 110–127.

Charness, N., Holley, P., Feddon, J., & Jastrzembski, T. (2004). Light pen use and practice minimize age and hand performance differences in pointing tasks. *Human Factors, 46*, 373–384.

Commarford, P. M., Lewis, J. R., Smither, J. A-A., & Gentzler, M. D. (2008). A comparison of broad versus deep auditory menu structures. *Human Factors, 50*, 77–89.

Craik, F. I. M. (1986). A functional account of age differences in memory. In F. Klix & H. Hagendorf (Eds.), *Human memory and cognitive capabilities: Mechanisms and performances* (pp. 409–422). Amsterdam: North-Holland.

Czaja, S. J., Charness, N., Fisk, A. D., Hertzog, C., Nair, S. N., Rogers, W. A., et al. (2006). Factors predicting the use of technology: Findings from the Center for Research and Education on Aging and Technology Enhancement (CREATE). *Psychology and Aging, 21*, 333–352.

Czaja, S. J., Sharit, J., Charness, N., Fisk, A. D., & Rogers, W. (2001). The Center for Research and Education on Aging and Technology Enhancement (CREATE): A program to enhance technology for older adults. *Gerontechnology, 1*, 50–59.

Dickinson, A., & Gregor, P. (2006). Computer use has no demonstrated impact on the well-being of older adults. *International Journal of Human-Computer Studies, 64*, 744–753.

Einstein, G. O., McDaniel, M. A., Smith, R. E., & Shaw, P. (1998). Habitual prospective memory and aging: Remembering intentions and forgetting actions. *Psychological Science, 9*, 284–288.

Evans, L. (2004). *Traffic safety*. Bloomfield, Michigan: Science Serving Society.

Fisk, A. D., Rogers, W. A., Charness, N., Czaja, S. J., & Sharit, J. (2004). *Designing for older adults: Principles and creative human factors approaches*. Boca Raton, FL: CRC Press.

GSM Association. (2005). Worldwide cellular connections exceeds 2 billion [Press Release]. Retrieved March 26, 2008, from http://www.gsmworld.com/news/press_2005/press05_21.shtml

Harrington, T. L., & Harrington, M. K. (2000). *Gerontechnology: Why and how*. Maastricht, The Netherlands: Shaker.

Hartley, A. A. (1992). Attention. In F. I. M. Craik & T. A. Salthouse (Eds.). *The handbook of aging and cognition* (pp. 3–49). Hillsdale, NJ: Erlbaum.

Hasher, L., Stolzfus, E. R., Zacks, R. T., & Rypma, B. (1991). Age and inhibition. *Journal of Experimental Psychology: Learning, Memory & Cognition, 17*, 163–169.

He, W., Sengupta, M., Velkoff, V. A., & DeBarros, K. A. (2005). *65 + in the United States: 2005*. (US Census Bureau Current Population Reports, P23-209). Washington, DC: U.S. Government Printing Office. Retrieved on October 20, 2006, from http://www.census.gov/prod/2006pubs/p23-209.pdf

Horn, J. L. (1982). The theory of fluid and crystallized intelligence in relation to concepts of cognitive psychology and aging in adulthood. In F. I. M. Craik, & S. Trehub (Eds.), *Aging and cognitive processes* (pp. 237–278). New York: Plenum Press.

Ilmarinen, J. & Louhevaara, V. (1994). Preserving the capacity to work. *Ageing International, 21*, 34–36.

Jastrzembski, T. S. (2006). The model human processor and the older adult: Validation and error extension to GOMS in a mobile phone task. Unpublished doctoral dissertation. Psychology Department, Florida State University, Tallahassee, Florida, USA.

Jastrzembski, T. S., & Charness, N. (2007). The Model Human Processor and the older adult: Parameter estimation and validation within a mobile phone task. *Journal of Experimental Psychology: Applied, 13*, 224–248.

Jastrzembski, T., Charness, N., Holley, P., & Feddon, J. (2005). Aging and input devices: Voice recognition is slower yet more acceptable than a lightpen. *Human Factors and Ergonomics Society Annual Meeting Proceedings, 49*, 167–171.

John, B. E., & Kieras, D. E. (1996). Using GOMS for user interface design and evaluation: Which technique? *ACM Transactions on Computer-Human Interaction, 3*, 287–319.

John, B. E., Prevas, K., Salvucci, D. D., & Koedinger, K. (2004). Predictive human performance modeling made easy. In *Proceedings of the SIGCHI Conference on Human Factors in Computing Systems* (pp. 455–462). New York: ACM Press. Available at http://portal.acm.org/citation.cfm?doid = 985692.985750

Kohn, L. T., Corrigan, J. M., & Donaldson, M. S. (Eds.). (2000). *To err is human: Building a safer health system.* Washington, DC: National Academy Press.

Koncelik, J. A. (1982). *Aging and the product environment.* New York: Van Nostrand Reinhold.

Kroemer, K. H. E. (2005). *"Extra-ordinary" ergonomics: How to accommodate small and big persons, the disabled and elderly, expectant mothers, and children.* Boca Raton: CRC Press.

Kunzmann, U., Little, T. D., & Smith, J. (2000). Is age-related stability of subjective well-being a paradox? Cross-sectional and longitudinal evidence from the Berlin aging study. *Psychology and Aging, 15,* 511–526.

Louhevaara, V. (1999). Cleaning in the European Union. *Työterveiset,* special issue [online], 2/1999, 13–14. Retrieved September 16, 2007, from http://www.ttl.fi/Internet/English/Information/Electronic + journals/Tyoterveiset + journal/1999-02 + Special + Issue/06.htm

MacDonald, S. W. S., Stigsdotter-Neely, A., Derwinger, A., & Bäckman, L. (2006). Rate of acquisition, adult age, and basic cognitive abilities predict forgetting: New views on a classic problem. *Journal of Experimental Psychology: General, 135,* 368–390.

Mann, W. C., Ottenbacher, K. J., Fraas, L., Tomita, M., & Granger, C. V. (1999). Effectiveness of assistive technology and environmental interventions in maintaining independence and reducing home care costs for the frail elderly: A randomized trial. *Archives of Family Medicine, 8,* 210–217.

Matthews, J. T. (2002). The Nursebot Project: Developing a personal robotic assistant for frail older adults in the community. *Home Health Care Management Practice, 14,* 403–405.

Mead, S., & Fisk, A. D. (1998). Measuring skill acquisition and retention with an ATM simulator: The need for age-specific training. *Human Factors, 40,* 516–523.

Mead, S. E., Sit, R. A., Rogers, W. A., Rousseau, G. K., & Jamieson, B. A. (2000). Influences of general computer experience and age on library database search performance. *Behaviour and Information Technology, 19,* 107–123.

McClelland, J. L., & Rumelhart, D. E. (1988). *Explorations in parallel distributed processing: A handbook of models, programs, and exercises.* Cambridge, MA: MIT Press.

McEvoy, G. M., & Cascio, W. F. (1989). Cumulative evidence of the relationship between employee age and job performance. *Journal of Applied Psychology, 74,* 11–17.

Meyer, D. E., & Kieras, D. E. (1997). A computational theory of executive cognitive processes and multiple-task performance: Part 1. Basic mechanisms. *Psychological Review, 104,* 3–65.

Murata, A., & Iwase, H. (2006). Usability of touch-panel interfaces for older adults. *Human Factors, 47,* 767–776.

Mynatt, E. D., Melenhorst, A. S., Fisk, A. D., & Rogers, W. A. (2004). Aware technologies for aging in place: Understanding user needs and attitudes. *IEEE Pervasive Computing, 3,* 36–41.

National Research Council, & Committee on the Heath and Safety Needs of Older Workers [USA]. (2004). *Health and safety needs of older workers* [D. H. Wegman & J. P. McGee, Eds.]. Washington, DC: The National Academies Press, Division of Behavioral and Social Sciences and Education.

Newell, A. (1990). *Unified theories of cognition.* Cambridge, MA: Harvard University Press.

Newell, A., & Simon, H. A. (1972). *Human problem solving.* Englewood Cliffs, NJ: Prentice Hall.

Official Document Archive 2 [UK]. (n.d.). Comparison of survey estimates of disability prevalence among adults (rates per 100), by age. Retrieved September 24, 2007, from http://www.archive2.official-documents.co.uk/document/deps/doh/survey01/disa/disa50.htm

Park, D. C., & Jones, T. R. (1997). Medication adherence and aging. In A. D. Fisk & W. A. Rogers (Eds.), *Handbook of human factors and the older adult* (pp. 257–287). San Diego, CA: Academic Press.

Reason, J. T. (1990). *Human error.* New York: Cambridge University Press.

Rogers, W. A., Fisk, A. D., McLaughlin, A. C., & Pak, R. (2005). Touch a screen or turn a knob: Choosing the best device for the job. *Human Factors, 47,* 271–288.

Roring, R. W., Hines, F. G., & Charness, N. (2007). Age differences in identifying words in synthetic speech. *Human Factors, 49,* 25–31.

Salthouse, T. A. (1996). The processing-speed theory of adult age differences in cognition. *Psychological Review, 103,* 403–428.

Sharit, J., Czaja, S. J., Nair, S., & Lee, C. C. (2003). Effects of age, speech rate, and environmental support in using telephone voice menu systems. *Human Factors, 45,* 234–251.

Steenbekkers, L. P. A., & van Beijsterveldt, C. E. M. (Eds.). (1998). *Design-relevant characteristics of ageing users.* Delft, The Netherlands: Delft University Press.

Steverink, N., & Lindenberg, S. (2006). Which social needs are important for subjective well-being? What happens to them with aging? *Psychology and Aging, 21,* 281–290.

Sturman, M. C. (2004). Searching for the inverted u-shaped relationship between time and performance: Meta-analyses of the experience/performance, tenure/performance, and age/performance relationships. *Journal of Management, 29,* 609–640

United Nations, Statistic Division. (2007). Demographic and social statistics: Human functioning and disability [Data file]. Retrieved September 24, 2007, from http://unstats.un.org/unsd/demographic/sconcerns/disability/disab2.asp

U.S. Censu s Bureau, American Factfinder. (2005). 2005 American Community Survey. Retrieved October 18, 2006, from http://factfinder.census.gov/servlet/DTTable?_bm=y&-state=dt&-ds_name=ACS_2005_EST_G00_&-_geoSkip=0&-mt_name=ACS_2005_EST_G2000_B18002&-redoLog=false&-_skip=0&-geo_id=01000US&-_showChild=Y&-format=&-_lang=en&-_toggle=ACS_2005_EST_G2000_B18002

Waldman, D. A., & Avolio, B. J. (1986). A meta-analysis of age differences in job performance. *Journal of Applied Psychology, 71,* 33–38.

Welford, A. T. (1958). *Ageing and human skill.* London: Oxford University Press.

Welford, A. T. (1977). Motor performance. In J. E. Birren & K. W. Schaie (Eds.), *Handbook of the psychology of aging* (pp. 450–496). New York: Van Nostrand Reinhold.

Welford, A. T. (1985). Changes of performance with age: An overview. In N. Charness (Ed.), *Aging and human performance* (pp. 333–369). Chichester, UK: John Wiley & Sons.

Enhancing Mutual Awareness, Productivity, and Feeling: Cognitive Science Approach to Design of Groupware Systems

Petra Kohler, Sebastian Pannasch, and Boris M. Velichkovsky

Abstract We address two classic problems in the design of groupware systems. The first problem is that of spatial orientation and coordination of attention. Unless members of a distributed work group can follow shifts in each other's attentional focus, they are unable to understand who is talking about what with whom. A mixed-reality system, cAR/PE!, which was specifically designed to support distributed team work in an industrial (automotive) setting, is introduced. The second problem we address is related to the inevitable heterogeneity of most communication networks. In general, only some links will be mediated by high-speed broadband connections. This means that at least some participants have to be represented in conversational space by their anthropomorphic models, or avatars. What are the emotional consequences of replacing a human being with a virtual character? Will a normal affective attitude towards the person still be possible? New cognitive studies are presented to demonstrate that the solution to both problems is feasible and can result in improved mutual awareness, productivity, and emotional involvement of persons involved in computer-mediated interaction and work.

1 Introduction

Computer-mediated communication and distributed work environments are becoming increasingly important in the global economy. In particular, large enterprises maintain widespread operations and large numbers of employees working on the same project, although they are geographically separated. In the car industry, for example, widely distributed suppliers, with their specific roles in designing car components, must maintain continuous contact with their corresponding departments. Consequently, employees in different geographical locations work collaboratively in project groups. Although such project groups can use videoconferencing systems or other groupware systems, project members

P. Kohler (✉)
Daimler AG, Division of Data and Process Management, Ulm, Germany
e-mail: petra.p.kohler@daimler.com

P. Saariluoma, H. Isomäki (eds.), *Future Interaction Design II*,
DOI 10.1007/978-1-84800-385-9_2, © Springer-Verlag London Limited 2009

prefer face-to-face meetings in the majority of cases (Lorenz, 1995; Morgan, 2004). In other words, despite the fact that groupware systems have been designed to save travelling costs and time, project groups are not using them.

The primary deficit is perceived as missing information on who is talking about what with whom. This constitutes a deficit in *situation awareness*, a state "in which external and internal stimuli are perceived and can be intentionally acted on" (Ortinski & Meador, 2004, p. 1017). To minimize this lack of situation awareness in groupware systems, episodes of *joint attention* should be supported as well as possible (Colburn, Cohen, & Drucker, 2000). When experiencing joint attention, individuals are aware of the same objects at the same time, which is a prerequisite of social coordination and personal relationships (Tomasello & Carpenter, 2007; Vygotsky, 1934/1962).

Previous studies verified the importance of explicit online representation of attention state while two people cooperate in solving construction tasks (Velichkovsky, 1995). In a subsequent investigation, Vertegaal, Velichkovsky, and van der Veer (1997) presented the GAZE Groupware System, a simple prototype virtual workspace sensitive to the gaze direction of participants. Work group members were represented by static 2D images within the visual field of every member. The virtual workspace could be rotated to face another group member on-screen, according to the user's dominant gaze direction. The system was based on transferring a minimal amount of voice and gaze coordinate information (images of participants were stored at endpoints of the network). Nevertheless, GAZE demonstrated the possibility of improving joint attention states by supporting improved task and conversational awareness in videoconferencing systems. These early studies represent the theoretical basis for the present study.

2 Theoretical and Methodological Considerations

There are exciting new approaches to improving mutual awareness and personal cohesiveness in distributed group work. They are illustrated here with two recent example investigations. Despite substantial differences in explicit goals, methodology, and practical implications, both examples deal with subsets of virtual reality tools that are beginning to be actively used to influence the cognitive and affective states of users of computer-supported communicative interactions.

Mixed reality (Milgram & Kishino, 1994) offers one such approach to distributed group work. Using their own computers, distributed team members are able to work together in a simulated common virtual meeting room. The hypothesis is that the media richness (Barua, Chellappa, & Whinston, 1997) of mixed reality supports the intuitive use of the system and enhances the mutual awareness of the team members, which leads to better group performance. For this reason, the cAR/PE! project (collaborative Augmented Reality for Presentation and Engineering) was initiated in 2003 with Daimler AG

(Regenbrecht et al., 2003). The goal was to develop a tool for distributed group work based on mixed, reality technology. In this chapter, we present the results of two empirical studies evaluating cAR/PE! with product development teams. In addition, we present results of recent experiments with virtual characters. This new paradigm tests the possibility of replacing video images of some participants with dynamic digital models.

The analysis of distributed group work is, necessarily, all encompassing. It is important to use a theoretical framework for designing groupware systems and structuring factors according to their importance for a successful practical interaction (for similar arguments, see Cañas, Salmeron, & Fajardo 2004; Saariluoma, 2004). Therefore, before presenting results, the underlying theoretical framework is described.

Verbal and nonverbal behavior is important in building a common understanding in face-to-face interaction. Earlier studies conducted by Fish, Kraut, and Chalfonte (1990) indicate that the number of interactions in face-to-face meetings is higher than in videoconferences. A major problem is the deficit of awareness regarding who is talking about what with whom (Gutwin & Greenberg, 1996). This decreases the efficacy of multimedia communication and the acceptance of groupware systems. In order to address this deficit, joint attention should be supported as far as possible (Colburn et al., 2000; Vertegaal et al., 1997). When experiencing joint attention, individuals perceive the same objects at the same time, which is a fundamental precondition for social coordination. Studies conducted by Velichkovsky (1995) verify the importance of explicating locus of attention when two users collaborate to solve construction tasks (puzzle) remotely.

Vertegaal et al. (1997) developed a framework for describing these aspects of awareness. The framework describes macrolevel and microlevel awareness in groupware and videoconference systems. "Macro-level awareness includes all forms of awareness, which convey background information about the activities of others prior to or outside of a meeting" (Vertegaal et al., 1997, p. 87). Microlevel awareness describes "... online information about the activities of others during the meeting itself. ... It consists of two categories: *Conversational awareness* and *Workspace awareness*. Conversational awareness contains information about who is communicating with whom; workspace awareness contains information about who is working on what" (Vertegaal et al. 1997, p. 88).

Conversational awareness requires the transfer of visual information, such as gaze direction and gesture. Vertegaal et al. (1997) divided elements of conversational awareness into temporal and spatial locations of attention. Their model is hierarchically organized. It distinguishes the syntax level with the locus of attention (spatial aspects) and attention span (temporal aspects) from the semantic level, which they divide into entity and action. "Entity identifies which objects or persons users are attending to at a given time. Action describes how this relationship varies over time" (Vertegaal et al., 1997, p. 89) The pragmatic level describes "expectations about the spatial and temporal behavior of others based on their history of attending to actions, objects and people" (p. 89). This level is divided into attention range (expectations in the spatial domain) and future attention (expectations in the temporal domain).

Gutwin and Greenberg (1996, p. 2) define workspace awareness as "the collection of up-to-the minute [*sic*] knowledge a person uses to capture another's interaction with the workspace.... Workspace awareness aids coordinating tasks and resources, and assists transitions between individual and shared activities." The elements of workspace awareness are presence, location, activity level, actions, intentions, changes, objects, extents, abilities, sphere of influence, and expectations. The basic mechanisms that maintain workspace awareness are direct communication, indirect productions ("utterances, expressions, or actions that are not explicitly directed at others, but that are intentionally public"), consequential communication (visible or audible signs of interaction), feed through ("the observable effects of someone's actions on the workspace's artifacts") and environmental feedback (p. 4).

The quality of awareness strongly depends on external factors such as the design of the virtual meeting room, interaction between participants, and presentation of the task. The model developed by Vertegaal et al. (1997) provides a framework for evaluating groupware systems. However, different approaches to the design of groupware systems should also be objectively compared in order to provide a sound basis for evaluation. The essential elements of group work are the group and the task. A group has to solve a task with available tools and materials in order to create a product. In a conventional meeting, all group members are located together in a common room where each group member is aware of the meeting environment, participants, and the aim of the conversation. The room presents a structure for relating these elements. In other words, each group member can determine with a quick glance where all elements (people, materials for the task, walls, etc.) are located. Behavior is mainly direct and therefore flexible and fast. Tools and materials are easily accessible in a common environment.

A typical groupware system does not provide a genuinely shared environment. Group members are present indirectly, via information transmitted by cameras and headphones. The tools and materials cannot be used in the same way as in a conventional meeting. Grudin (2005) comes to the conclusion that although additional digital support can increase efficiency, a common working environment seems to be very important. Therefore, the group, the task, and the environment are regarded as important elements for group work. Tools and materials support the interaction between group members and become increasingly more important when using groupware systems. Many actions of a conventional meeting have to be transferred into interaction with a space mouse or, for example, data gloves. The kinetic interactions (touching, turning, tasting, etc.) should not be underrated in their importance because they lay down the foundation of learning processes (Piaget, 2000).

Figure 1 shows the model for the elements of distributed group work, with the most important components to be considered when developing a groupware system. This model provides a basis for comparing different approaches, and

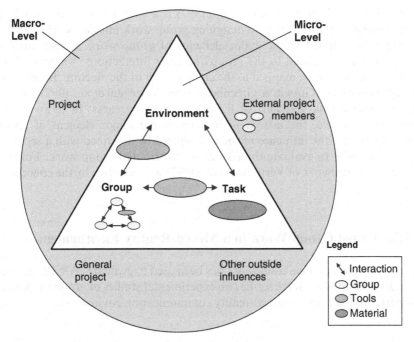

Fig. 1 A model showing the different levels, the elements and their relations for distributed group work

evaluating their differences with the framework described by Vertegaal et al. (1997).

This model has two levels of organization. The macrolevel provides background information, for example, the time schedules and goals of the project, knowledge about people, related projects and/or different departments of the company (Vertegaal et al., 1997). The elements of the microlevel, on the other hand, are the group, the environment of the meeting, the task, the materials, the interaction processes, and the tools. The group is one unit consisting of individuals who interact with each other, with the environment, and with the task. The common environment structures the relationship between individuals as well as their relationship to the task. The task can be represented by materials and/or mental activity, and tools can support participants' interaction.

In summary, the following characteristics are important for group work: macrolevel (premeeting information) and the microlevel consisting of the group, task, and environment. Also important are the (a) interaction between group and task, (b) interaction between task and environment, and (c) interaction between group and environment. Furthermore, there are direct and indirect interactions between group members on the microlevel. Instruments and materials are also important for interaction and information transfer. All these elements have to be considered when developing any tool for distributed group work.

The framework of Vertegaal et al. (1997) is a sound basis from which to evaluate different approaches to designing group work interfaces. This framework can be mapped to the major elements of group work. Conversational awareness can be related to the group and their interactions, whereas workspace awareness can be mapped to the environment of the meeting. In previous conceptualizations (Gutwin & Greenberg, 1996; Vertegaal et al., 1997), knowledge about the task was part of the workspace awareness. In terms of the explanations above, the task is to be seen as the major element of group work. Therefore, the influence of the task should be described with a separate concept in order to evaluate the efficacy of distributed group work. For this reason, the framework of Vertegaal et al. (1997) was enriched by the concept of *task awareness*.

3 Distributed Group Work in a Mixed-Reality Environment

The enhanced theoretical framework has been used to evaluate cAR/PE! groupware. In what follows, we describe two experimental studies of group work with this particular version of mixed-reality communication environment.

3.1 Studies with cAR/PE!

When using cAR/PE!, group members were able to work together in a common albeit virtual meeting room. They could see each other via cameras on their PC and communicate in real time via headsets (Fig. 2). Participants were

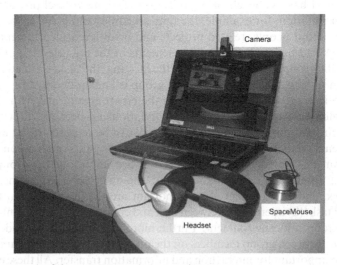

Fig. 2 Photograph of the cAR/PE! workplace equipment

Fig. 3 cAR/PE! virtual conference room with two participants represented by their video avatars

represented by video avatars arranged around a virtual table (Fig. 3). With the space mouse, participants could move their video avatar within the virtual environment. They could also use a pointer on a 2D virtual presentation screen in the virtual meeting room. The pointer had the same color as the frame of the participants' video avatar. Photographs of a real automotive side door were projected on the 2D display in the cAR/PE! room. One member of the group operated as a presenter and could change the photographs using his/her keyboard.

Eleven structured interviews were conducted with employees from different departments working in distributed work groups prior to the studies. Additionally, five meetings in the departments of development and planning were analyzed. In this exploratory phase, information about product development teams was collated. Two types of tasks in the product development teams were identified: less demanding tasks of cost optimizing and more complex tasks of design. Both tasks related to the same sedan side door. We assumed that the task complexity has an influence on the applicability of cAR/PE!. In the first study, cAR/PE! was compared with a conventional meeting condition. The model for the elements of distributed group work provided an objective basis from which to compare conventional meetings with cAR/PE!. The differences were observed and evaluated using the enhanced framework derived from the work of Vertegaal et al. (1997). Based on this framework, the following hypotheses were formulated and tested.

1. *Shared environment and own environment.* In a conventional meeting the group members were in the same environment. In cAR/PE! group members were located together in the virtual meeting room. Additionally, each group member had a second environment in cAR/PE!, which could have had a disturbing influence on group members' attention. Consequently, workspace

awareness was expected to be higher in a conventional meeting than in cAR/PE!.

2. *Interaction person and environment.* In a conventional meeting, interaction with the environment could be enhanced by the direct use of multiple senses, whereas in cAR/PE!, interaction was indirect and slower than in a conventional meeting. Therefore, in a conventional meeting the means of interaction could better support workspace awareness than in cAR/PE!.

3. *Group and interaction in the group.* In a conventional meeting, all group members were physically in the same room; their interaction was direct and multifarious. In cAR/PE!, all group members were visible in a virtual meeting room; interaction between group members was indirect and could be disturbed by low-quality audio or video signals. A higher level of conversational awareness could be expected in a conventional meeting.

4. *Interaction person and task.* In a conventional meeting, material for solving a task was physically available, whereas in cAR/PE!, photographs alone could be used as external representation of objects. Higher task awareness should be found in conventional conditions. However, as stated above, the task awareness depends in the first line on the task itself.

5. *Interaction task and room.* A room structures the relationship between group members and the task. This structure could support memory since encoding and retrieval of information crucially depends on the task and the spatial-temporal context (Birbaumer & Schmidt, 1996). In the conventional meeting, a real room is the common context, whereas in cAR/PE!, the virtual room provides the encoding context for the group members.

Considering these predictions, the best workspace, task, and conversational awareness should be observed under the condition of a conventional meeting. The level of conversational and workspace awareness strongly depends on the task, which determines all components of group work, such as the arrangement of group members, tools, materials, aim of group work, and group process. The importance of the task when evaluating any work system is repeatedly stressed in the literature on work psychology. The following hypothesis was formulated with respect to the influence of task: Group performance will be equal for the cost-optimizing task in cAR/PE! and in the conventional meeting, whereas for the design task, group performance will yield differences in favor of the conventional meeting. In order to test this hypothesis, we analyzed mental models, interaction with the construction element, group results, and the problem-solving process.

A controlled field study with a 2×2 factor, between-subjects and within-subjects combination design was employed to test the effects of different task complexities and meeting conditions on the dependent variables ($N = 30$, all men, average age 42.3 years). Both factors were combined, resulting in four experimental conditions. Since participation in the experiment was voluntary and took place during the regular working hours, each group was subjected to two sessions in order to minimize the required number of participants. This meant a combination of a within-group and a between-group design. Whereas the between-group measurements were an objective of the study, the within-group design was useful in controlling an error variance. Groups and order of experimental conditions were randomly distributed to avoid sequence effects. Prior knowledge of tasks can affect performance and the development of mental models (Birbaumer & Schmidt, 1996). Therefore, mental models for each participant were elicited before discussing it within the group, as well as after.

The general hypothesis that group performance would be equivalent for the cost-optimizing task under both meeting conditions, but higher in the conventional meeting when solving the design task, was supported when considering all the dependent variables. The statistical analysis also confirmed that the evolved mental models of the participants in the design task were more elaborate under the conventional meeting than with cAR/PE!. However, groups had almost identical mental models when solving the simpler cost-optimizing task under both conditions. A higher number of interactions with task elements (the sedan door, in this case) were expected in the conventional meeting (Fish et al., 1990). The difference of the mean values for the number of interactions with the sedan door was marginally significant ($p \leq .06$). The descriptive analysis showed that the difference between the mean values was in favor of cAR/PE! and *not* in favor of the conventional meeting.

This result can be explained when considering observations reported by the coders. It should be said, first of all, that group work was coded in terms of several episodes (Table 1). Techniques of event history modeling were applied to the data (Blossfeld & Rohwer, 2002).

Although participants more frequently interacted with the sedan door in cAR/PE!, this interaction was different to that of the conventional meeting. Under conventional conditions, participants mainly explored the sedan door visually. This underlines the importance of mutual eye movements for collaborative problem solving (Velichkovsky, 1995). The conclusion can be supported by the descriptive results, as cAR/PE! groups searched longer and more frequently for information than conventional meeting groups. Transition rates from Episode 2 to Episode 3 were three times higher in the cAR/PE meeting condition. Obviously, the different presentations and interaction options with the sedan door had the expected influence on task awareness, especially when solving the design task. While the conventional meeting groups solved the

Table 1 According to Irle (1971), a category system for the problem-solving process

1	Definition of the problem	6	Suggestion
2	Search for information	7	Break
3	Generation of alternatives	8	Joke
4	Evaluation of alternatives	9	Poor sound
5	Decision	0	Miscellaneous

design task better than the cAR/PE! groups, it was not clear if this was due to the complexity of the task or the possibility of touching objects. Indeed, the interaction possibilities were different: pointing at and touching the sedan door versus only pointing at its photograph.

A 2×2 factorial analysis of variance was conducted to examine group performance between the four experimental conditions. Overall, performance was better for the conventional meeting, independent of the task ($p < .05$). Examining the data on a descriptive level, it becomes clear that in the cost-optimizing task, groups were quite similar in both meeting conditions. However, for the design task, group performance was significantly better in the conventional meeting condition. This was confirmed by a t test for independent samples ($p \leq .05$). The problem-solving process of the cost-optimizing task was different in some ways, when comparing both meeting conditions. For example, in this task (but not the design task) the backward episode transition rates from 3 to 2 were higher in conventional meeting groups. Episode 2 was more frequent and took longer for groups in the conventional meeting condition, but, for cAR/PE! Groups, Episodes 1 and 4 were found more frequently and with longer durations. Moreover, indicators for a good group performance could be identified. Successful groups were found to have higher scores for shared mental models with a high co-occurrence of Episodes 2, 3, and 5. Except for one group, no differences were found for the less demanding cost-optimizing task in both meeting conditions. Therefore, no further hypotheses were set up.

On the other hand, the problem-solving processes of groups solving the design task in both meeting conditions have to be treated differently since the problem-solving process was systematically different. In particular, a higher frequency and longer duration of Episode 5 was salient for conventional meeting groups. These groups also demonstrated a higher transition rate from Episode 3 to 5 than for cAR/PE! groups. The backward transition rate from 5 to 3 was not tested due to the small sample size for the cAR/PE! condition. However, conventional meeting groups changed about four times more often in this direction than cAR/PE! groups. This central role of decision (Episode 5) demonstrates that conventional meeting groups were more results-oriented, whereas cAR/PE! groups repeatedly searched for more information (Episode 2). These results confirm the loss of information due to the limited transfer suffered in the communication process when using computer-supported systems (Gutwin & Greenberg, 1996).

Working on the design task in the cAR/PE! environment, in particular, participants typically looked at the photographs of the sedan door on the presentation board instead of addressing their partners, which negatively influenced the conversational awareness. Furthermore, group members interacted significantly more often with the sedan door under these conditions. Based on the coders' observations, it can be assumed that group interaction was different in conventional meetings, in that participants explored the sedan door more visually. Therefore, the task awareness was different in both communication conditions. A possible reason might be the slowed interaction due to the devices used in cAR/PE!. Participants had to move the space mouse in order to change the focus of attention, which is much slower than movements of the eyes or the head. Many participants also complained about the poor audio quality in cAR/PE!. Insufficient interaction possibilities had an impact on all kinds of awareness in the relatively complex design task, as information could only be gathered slowly and with substantial voluntary efforts and conscious control.

When solving the less demanding cost-optimizing task in cAR/PE!, participants generally talked about the variables of the task. The photographs on the presentation board were not as important as in the design task. Even though any technical problems associated with the cAR/PE! environment were also present in this task, there was no need for frequent changes in the focus of attention. Participants' conversational and workspace awareness were on a higher level when sitting around the virtual table, thinking aloud, and looking at each other. Consequently, their task awareness was sufficient to guarantee a solution corresponding to that of the groups working in face-to-face conditions.

3.2 Studies with cAR/PE!2

In this previous study, we showed that cAR/PE! was appropriate for tasks of low complexity but that performance in complex design tasks was better in conventional conditions. However, as mentioned above, it remains unclear if the latter result was due to the task complexity or the presence of tangible objects. Hence, in a second study, the solution of design tasks was investigated in greater detail, with two meeting conditions. Secondly, the previous study did not examine the importance of a highly articulated virtual workspace, the main factor of presence experience. It is often assumed that such a context is important for the efficient operation of distributed group work (Grudin, 2005; Gutwin & Greenberg, 1996). The importance of having a common workspace for the problem-solving process has also been analyzed in the following study.

A further aim of our second study was to improve the technical parameters of cAR/PE!, as well as the experimental design. These changes were applied according to practical considerations: CAD models are often used in design meetings, whereas less complex design tasks with real elements rarely have to be solved in engineering groups. Due to this practical relevance and in order to allow for precise conclusions, the following changes were made: In the first part of the second study, a CAD car model was used, virtually represented in cAR/PE!2. It was compared with the same CAD car model that replaced the physical design element of the first study's conventional meeting.

In the second part of the second study, the importance of a common workspace and high workspace awareness was examined, due to the importance of these factors reported in the literature (Gutwin & Greenberg, 1996). Investigations of learning in context in cognitive science support this assumption (Birbaumer & Schmidt, 1996). However, there are few empirical studies of the influence of a common workspace on group work in real-world situations, although without this, we can not discover what is involved in developing working solutions, or even whether or not proposed solutions are workable (Grudin, 2005).

cAR/PE!2 differed from cAR/PE! in a number of ways. Firstly, modifications were made to the cAR/PE! room. An icon bar was added alongside the space mouse so that, by double-clicking an icon, participants could quickly jump to different positions in the virtual meeting room. With two further icons, the mode of the space mouse could be changed. One icon allowed the user to roam through the virtual meeting room, while with the other the virtual car could be moved and examined from all sides, independent of other participants. An obvious advantage was that participants could work independently but still be visible to others. The cAR/PE!2 software used car models in VRML file format exported from the CAD software CATIA. These models could be moved in all directions and pointed at by the space mouse. The mouse could be also used as a pointing device on the virtual presentation board. The color of the pointer was the same as the frame of the user's video avatar. The new sound software-codec (GSM-6 k for speech and H.263-CIF/QCIF for video) used less bandwidth and had a lower latency. Additionally, the quality of the video became better. The screen of another laptop next to the cAR/PE!2 laptop could be used for application sharing by the presenter and the participants. This additional information on the presentation board was expected to facilitate the decision phase during the solution of the task.

In the cAR/PE!2 no room condition in the second part of the second study, the participants had the same technical facilities, that is, icon bar, space mouse, and so on. The only difference was that the group members had no common working room. Instead of an articulated visual environment, they were located in front of a monochrome background. Figure 4 shows screenshots of both conditions used.

On a theoretical level, the study was designed to analyze different forms of awareness while working in the modified groupware system. Conversational

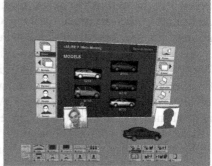

Fig. 4 Screenshots of cAR/PE!2 with two participants with the virtual conference room (*left*) and the no room condition (*right*)

awareness was kept constant at a high level because the importance of this concept has been sufficiently proven in literature (Velichkovsky & Hansen, 1996; Vertegaal et al., 1997). In the first part of the second study, groups had to solve a design task in conventional meeting2 and in cAR/PE!2 to verify the appropriateness of this software for solving complex design tasks. Groups had to redesign a body shell of the new Mercedes SLK into an amphibious car, which was presented as a virtual object (CAD model) in both meeting conditions. In the second part, the workspace awareness was varied in two different meeting conditions to examine the importance of a common visual workspace. The participant had to solve the same task, that is, task awareness was again kept constant under both conditions. There was a number of differences to the previous conditions:

1. *Shared environment and person's own environment.* As in the first study, one of the primary differences was the shared environment. In the conventional meeting2, all group members were together in the same physical room. In cAR/PE!2, participants were together in a virtual meeting room. In cAR/PE!2 no room, there was no structuring element; group members worked together in the same session but only in front of a monochromatic background. In both cAR/PE!2 conditions, interaction was indirect as compared to the conventional meeting2, where direct interaction was still superior. Additionally, in both cAR/PE! (2 and no room) conditions, each group member had his/her own environment that may have had a disturbing influence. Concerning the environment, the highest workspace awareness and conversational awareness were still found in the conventional meeting2; the lowest in cAR/PE!2 no room.
2. *Group and interaction in the group.* In cAR/PE!2, group interaction was indirect but group members could see each other and the task simultaneously. Therefore, conversational awareness and task awareness were comparable with the conventional meeting2. Because of the missing environment, conversational awareness in cAR/PE!2 no room was lower than in cAR/PE!2.
3. *Task and interaction with the task.* The virtual design object was the same for all conditions: It was untouchable. Each participant had his own view of the virtual object and could point to it with a pointer. In both distributed conditions (cAR/PE!2 and no room), each group member could move the virtual object. In the conventional meeting2, only one person could move the virtual object. Task awareness was presumably the same under all meeting conditions because of the virtually presented object.

Considering these differences, the conventional meeting2 was still expected to lead to a higher workspace awareness and conversational awareness. In cAR/PE!2, workspace awareness was higher than in cAR/PE!2 no room but lower than in the conventional meeting2. Notwithstanding the workspace awareness and the conversational awareness and presuming a good functioning of the new software, the task awareness had to be constant in all three meeting conditions.

Because of the low workspace awareness and, hence, lower conversational awareness using cAR/PE!2 no room compared with cAR/PE!2, a difference was expected here in favor of cAR/PE!2. It was assumed that a minimum of workspace awareness was necessary to solve the task. Workspace awareness and conversational awareness were higher in the conventional meeting2 compared with cAR/PE!2, but because group members could see each other and the task simultaneously, conversational awareness could possibly be higher in cAR/PE!2. Finally, the common virtual meeting room should support workspace awareness at a high level in cAR/PE!2. The difference in performance between cAR/PE!2 and the conventional meeting2 was expected to be minimal. Comparing cAR/PE!2 with cAR/PE!2 no room, a pronounced difference in group performance and, consequently, conversational awareness, was expected because of the assumed importance of a minimal workspace.

A field study with Daimler AG product developers ($N = 45$, all men, average age 43.7 years) was conducted to test the outlined hypotheses. The meeting condition was the independent variable. The participants' mental models about the task, the problem-solving process, and the group results represented the dependent variables. The task was kept constant: The participants had to convert the body shell of the new Mercedes SLK into an amphibious car. The factor *meeting* was different and evaluated through the conditions of a meeting with cAR/PE!2 versus the conventional meeting2 in the first part of the study, whereas in the second part cAR/PE!2 was compared with cAR/PE!2 no room. Techniques of event history modeling were again applied to the data with a system of episode coding slightly diverging from the first study.

One should note that statistical analyses resulted in no significant differences in shared mental models of the participants between meeting conditions in the first and in the second part of the study. At least in part, this could be attributed to a low discriminative power of the methods of knowledge elicitation (see Bergholz, Kohler, Lum, & Velichkovsky, 2007).

In contrast to the expectations, there was still a nearly significant difference ($p \leq .09$) between group performance in favor of the face-to-face condition when comparing conventional meeting2 with cAR/PE!2. We explain this by the many disturbances caused by the software. Event transition analysis showed that cAR/PE!2 groups were less frequently in Episodes 2 (identification of part structures), 3 (development of solution principles) and 4 (evaluation of solution principles). At the same time, they more often reflected on the group process (Episode 9). Furthermore, the protocol written on the presentation board supported the decision episode (evaluation of solution principles). However, when analyzing the data in more detail, it became evident that cAR/PE!2 and conventional meeting2 groups reflected on the group process approximately to the same extent: The higher frequency of Episode 9 was caused by the disturbances in communication. After these disturbances, the groups reflected seven times on the group process in the process of coming back into the group discussion. These disturbances negatively influenced the workspace and conversational awareness because the participants spent time talking about software, for example, how to use the space mouse or what else they experienced in the cAR/PE!2 environment.

In the second part of the second study, there was no assumed difference when comparing performance in the conditions cAR/PE!2 and cAR/PE!2 no room. The problem-solving processes were slightly different however. In particular, this resulted in different episode transition rates, as the cAR/PE!2 groups seemed to be more sensitive to disturbances in the quality of information (poor sound). For instance, Episode 9 (reflection on the group process) occurred 17 times under both meeting conditions, but cAR/PE!2 groups reflected more often after every single disturbance in the process whereas cAR/PE!2 no room groups reflected on the process after only two interruptions in a row.

To sum up the results in the context of our theoretical background, the concepts of workspace, task, and conversational awareness have to be better differentiated. Although a common virtual meeting room for distributed group work supports the orientation of group members and therefore the awareness of who is talking about what with whom (Vertegaal et al., 1997), many features are unnecessary and rather distracting for the discussion and solving of the task. The strategy aimed at gaining as much context information as possible may lead to information overflow and should be avoided. In other words, the spatial information has to be presented in a relatively abstract form. Groups should have only the information necessary to solve the task and to support the conversation awareness in the group like the virtual meeting rooms of cAR/PE! and cAR/PE!2.

4 An Emotional Engagement While Meeting a Virtual Other

Due to a general heterogeneity of communication networks today and in the future, a common situation in distributed group work will be when at least one of the partners has to be replaced by his/her virtual simulation. The implications of this are explored further here.

4.1 Motivation of the Studies with Virtual Characters and Preliminary Results

The cognitive and emotional consequences of the replacement of a group member with a virtual character are not completely clear. In the literature on emerging android science, one finds notions as "uncanny valley" showing that anthropomorphic characters may provoke aversive emotional effects in human observers (Mori, 1970). The uncanny valley describes the paradoxical effect where increasing familiarity of virtual characters with human likeness is accompanied with a higher level of acceptance until a point is reached at which subtle deviations from human appearance and behavior lead to negative emotional response towards robots (Ishiguro, 2006; MacDorman & Ishiguro, 2006). Thus, moderate-to-low similarity might be more appropriate for the communicative application. Therefore, we investigated visual attention, arousal, facial expression, and subjective experience of human observers in simulated interactions with virtual characters of such a moderate degree of similarity in two further experiments.

Some features of a character's behavior are of particular interest. In previous fMRI studies, the special importance of a feature that could be called *social gaze* has been established (Schilbach et al., 2005). Even beyond an adequate communicative gesture, eye-to-eye contact with a human observer leading to the experience of being personally addressed plays a decisive role in the activation of the medial prefrontal structures of cortex (MPFC), known to be involved in the higher-order, self-referential encoding of information (Craik et al., 1999; Velichkovsky, Pomplun, & Rieser, 1996). In contrast, the same characters looking at a place near to observers (30° to the right or to the left; see Fig. 5) were perceived at a substantially lower level of processing than was evident from the predominantly posterior parietal activation. This latter is related to spatial orienting of attention (Posner, Rueda, & Kanske, 2007).

The following study aimed at supplementing this research by examining the effect of self-involvement on attention, arousal, and facial expression during social interaction. To this end, eye movements, pupil size, and facial electromyographic (EMG) activity were recorded while participants watched the video sequences developed by Schilbach et al. (2005). The results again showed that attention allocation was specifically related to self-involvement (i.e., direct gaze contact), regardless of the social meaning being conveyed. Arousal, as measured by pupil size, was primarily related to perceiving the virtual character's

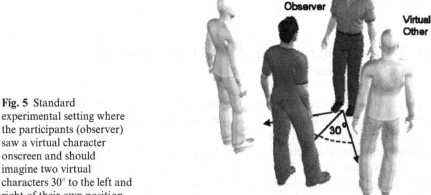

Fig. 5 Standard experimental setting where the participants (observer) saw a virtual character onscreen and should imagine two virtual characters 30° to the left and right of their own position

gender. In contrast, facial EMG activity was determined by the perception of socially relevant facial expressions irrespective of whom these were directed towards. We trust that these results not only provide important clues to the functions implemented in distinct regions of the MPFC but also suggest directions for future technological solutions.

4.2 Emotional Effects on Human Observers Are Gaze Contingent

In our final experiment reported in this chapter, participants watched animated virtual characters, which varied in terms of gender, gaze direction (direct, averted), and facial emotional expression (anger, neutral, happiness). The dependent variables were facial EMG (as registered at the standard corrugator and zygomatic sites), fixation duration, pupil size, and subjective emotional experience. A sample of virtual characters from this study is presented in Fig. 6.

Virtual characters (6 male, 6 female) were presented in front of a gray background. In the video clips (see Fig. 7 for the different segments), only their heads and shoulders were visible. Illumination and camera settings of the scene were kept constant. To give the characters a more natural appearance, all of them displayed the same pattern of small jerky horizontal eye movements, which simulated saccades. The characters' hair color (light or dark) and direction of their entrance (from the left or from the right) were systematically varied and counterbalanced. In one fifth of the randomly selected films, the agents made a blink between 4700 and 4900 ms. The video clips were created using the

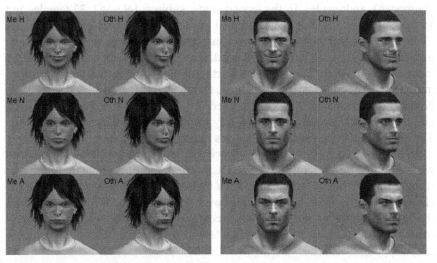

Fig. 6 Female and male virtual characters in the direct gaze condition (Me) and averted gaze condition (Oth), showing a happy face (H), a neutral face (N) or an angry face (A)

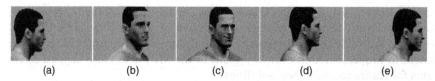

Fig. 7 Snapshots from different segments of an interaction episode: (**a**) Walk in (0–1500 ms); (**b**) Turn (1500–2500 ms); (**c**) Emotion (2500–5500 ms); (**d**) Turn (5500–6500 ms); and (**e**) Walk out (6500–7500 ms)

software package Poser 6.[1] The different facial expressions were obtained by manipulating polygon groups on a 3D mesh that makes up the character's facial structure. Animation of facial and body motion was realized by interpolating images between different facial configurations and body positions. The single pictures of a scene were rendered with Poser 6 and subsequently conflated to films with MATLAB[2] using the INDEO 5.1 Codec.

Prior to the main experiment, two pilot studies were conducted to control for socially relevant attributes of the virtual characters and to validate the emotional facial expressions. In the first pilot study ($N = 62$, 36 females and 26 males, all recruited at the Dresden University of Technology, average age 23.2 years), participants were exposed to different views of 24 virtual characters, which had to be rated in terms of their dominance, sociability, naturalness, attractiveness, sympathy, and gender on 7-point bipolar rating scales, as well as in terms of their age and ethnic origin (European, Asian, African). For the subsequent experiment, we selected only those characters that were evaluated as having medium levels of attractiveness and sympathy together with a high level of naturalness, and that were matched to the participant group's age category (25–35 years), ethnic origin (European), and gender. In the second study, subjects ($N = 52$, 37 females and 15 males, all recruited at the Dresden University of Technology, average age 23.7 years) watched video clips of the characters displaying happiness and anger toward the observer. They rated the valence, naturalness, and intensity of the expressions on 7-point bipolar scales. Furthermore, they classified the expressions into the six basic emotions anger, sadness, fear, happiness, disgust, and surprise on 5-point unipolar scales. Valence ratings corresponded to the expressions' valence and the expressions were unambiguously identified in the basic emotion rating. The intensity of happiness and anger was rated on the same level.

In addition to this evaluation, the characters' dynamic facial expressions were validated by a recently developed real-time computer system for automatic recognition of human facial expressions (Sebe et al., 2007). When tracking the changing features of a character's face over time of interaction, the happy and the angry expressions were correctly recognized by the computer system in all cases.

---

[1] Curious Lab, Santa Cruz, California

[2] MathWorks, Natick, Massachusetts

Forty-four volunteers (22 females and 22 males, all recruited at the Dresden University of Technology, average age 23.1 years) participated in the final experiment. They gave informed consent to participate in the experiment and were kept naïve in terms of the study's purpose. We investigated the role of four independent variables: the character's gender (female vs. male), gaze direction (direct vs. averted), and facial expression (anger vs. happiness vs. neutral) as within subjects' factors and the human participant's gender as between subjects' factor resulting in a $2 \times 2 \times 3 \times 2$ mixed factorial design. The participants' task was to rate their emotional experience during the perception of the virtual characters on the Self-Assessment Manikin (SAM; Lang, 1980), a nonverbal self-report measure.

Fixation duration and pupil size were recorded with a head-mounted Eye-Link Eyetracking System[3] with online detection of saccades and fixations. Gaze direction was calculated using bright pupil detection. The system has a sample rate of 250 Hz with a spatial resolution of 0.5°. Pupil size was measured in arbitrary integer units referring to pupil diameter. Facial EMG was measured bipolarly over the regions of the *M. zygomaticus major* and the *M. corrugator supercilii* on the right side of the face according to the guidelines of Fridlund and Cacioppo (1986). Additionally, a reference electrode was attached to the right earlobe and a ground electrode was attached to the left earlobe. We used Ag-AgCl miniature surface electrodes filled with electrode paste. Before attaching them, skin was cleaned with electrode paste and alcohol. EMG activity was recorded using a BrainAmp[4] amplifier, digitized at 1000 Hz and stored on a laboratory computer.

The most interesting result of the study was that facial EMG and subjective experience ratings of human observers reflected the virtual character's expression, especially in the direct gaze condition. For instance, as can be seen in Fig. 8, zygomatic activity increased with time, differentiating the facial expressions more clearly if virtual characters looked directly at the observers. To examine this interaction, simple effect analyses were conducted. Results revealed a significant effect only of facial expression, if the character was oriented towards the observer, that is, in the emotion segment for the direct gaze condition, $F(2, 35) = 5.675, p = .01$. Zygomatic activity was significantly higher for happiness than for anger ($p = .02$), and significantly higher for the happy than for the neutral face ($p = .01$).

For the corrugator muscle (see Fig. 8), there was also a significant three-way interaction between the time segment, gaze direction, and facial expression, $F(4, 144) = 4.526, p = .02$. Simple effect analyses revealed significant effects of facial expression for direct gaze during turn segment, $F(2, 35) = 12.325, p < .01$. Bonferroni-adjusted pairwise comparisons showed that corrugator activity was higher for the neutral expression than for anger ($p = .03$) and happiness

---

[3] SR Research Ltd., Toronto, Canada

[4] Brainproducts GmbH, Munich, Germany

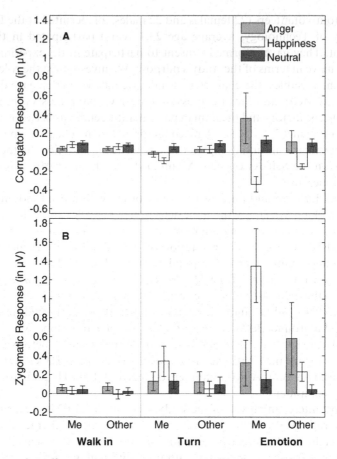

Fig. 8 Interaction effect between time segment, gaze direction, and facial expression on activity of *corrugator* (**A**) and *zygomatic* (**B**) muscles

($p < .01$). Furthermore, there were significant effects of facial expression during the emotion phase for direct gaze, $F(2, 35) = 12.009$, $p < .01$, as well as for averted gaze, $F(2, 35) = 11.344$, $p < .01$. If observers were looked at directly, corrugator activity was significantly higher for the angry ($p = .040$) and the neutral face ($p < .01$), compared to the happy face. For averted gaze, only the difference between the neutral expression and happiness was significant ($p < .01$).

A rather similar pattern could be seen in the subjective ratings. Physiological parameters, such as pupil size and fixation duration, were influenced by the character's gaze direction, facial expression, and gender. All in all, these data testify to an elementary form of social interaction. Although the interactions used in the current experiment only consisted of initiating eye contact and displaying a facial expression, the results demonstrate that virtual characters are capable of inducing significant physiological and subjective reactions in human observers. Virtual agents are perceived as potential interaction partners, not as inanimate objects. In particular, observers' reactions to facial features, which are powerful means for communication, reflect processes that contribute to forms of higher social cognition such as joint attention (Tomasello & Carpenter, 2007; Velichkovsky, 1995). Visual attention, as measured by fixation duration, was attracted by socially relevant information, especially by those facial configurations that indicated different emotional attitudes. As suggested by recent research on integrative effects in the time course of human emotional experience (Klucharev & Sams, 2004), coordination of the observer's facial motility, gaze direction, and feeling may have been based on different stages of information processing. This hypothesis of an initial separation and later integration of the several processing streams can be tested in further neurocognitive and neuroergonomic investigations.

5 Conclusions and an Outlook

In the current theoretical context, the results of our studies confirm the importance of the presentation of a complex task design for group work and, therefore, the enhancement of the Vertegaal et al. (1997) framework with the concept of task awareness. Whether groups can work in the cAR/PE! environment as efficiently as in conventional meetings depends largely on the task at hand. The model for the elements of distributed group work was efficient in systematically finding differences between the conditions. Differences in task solution processes can be structurally explored and objectively compared. The enhanced framework provided a sound basis from which to evaluate the apparent differences and to conduct hypotheses testing.

From a practical point of view, the possibility of improving mutual awareness and ipso facto group performance in a distributed work setting is of importance. As demonstrated, even minimal technical modifications improved group performance, to the extent that computer-supported and face-to-face interaction produced almost identical results. The disturbances and breaks observed in cAR/PE!2 meetings are also an indicator that these groups still had lower workspace and conversational awareness than when working in conventional conditions. It can be assumed that when working for a longer time with the updated software, participants would gain more expertise using cAR/PE!2 and consequently demonstrate at least the same performance as in conventional face-to-face meetings. Overall, we are rather optimistic about the development of hypercommunication systems that could considerably improve our natural facilities in their application to distributed group work.

As we progress towards such systems, many questions should be answered in detail. We demonstrated, for example, that virtual environments and their possible inhabitants can, and perhaps should be, represented on a rather abstract level, avoiding the necessity of using all the power of available computer graphics tools. New research paradigms can offer new insights towards this end. Social neuroscience has recently shed light on the underpinnings of understanding others' minds, while cognitive and affective neuroergonomics leads us in the search for practical solutions that will enhance our mutual awareness, submersion, and work productivity.

Acknowledgment Thanks are due to Wencke Bergholz, Sven-Thomas Graupner, Tim Lum, Andreas Mojzisch, and Franziska Schrammel for their support and coauthorship in some of the described investigations. Fiona Mulvey made valuable comments on the manuscript. Finally, we appreciate grant support from Daimler AG and the European Commission (Projects COGAIN, PERCEPT, and MINET, the two latter under NEST-Pathfinder initiative).

References

Barua, A., Chellappa, R., & Whinston, A. B. (1997). Social computing: Computer supported cooperative work and groupware. In G. Salvendy (Ed.), *Handbook of human factors and ergonomics* (2nd ed., pp. 1760–1782). New York: John Wiley & Sons.

Bergholz, W., Kohler, P., Lum, T., & Velichkovsky, B. M. (2007). *Shared mental models in face-to-face and groupware work: Increasingly similar but the task complexity matters.* Manuscript submitted for publication.

Birbaumer, N., & Schmidt, R. F. (1996). *Biological psychology* (3rd ed.). Berlin, Germany: Springer.

Blossfeld, H.-P., & Rohwer, G. (2002). *Techniques of event history modelling: New approaches to causal analysis* (2nd ed.). Mahwah, NJ: Lawrence Erlbaum Associates.

Cañas, J. J., Salmeron, L., & Fajardo, I. (2004). Toward the analysis of the interaction in the joint cognitive system. In A. Pirhonen, H. Isomäki, C. Roast, & P. Saariluoma (Eds.), *Future interaction design* (pp. 85–104). London: Springer-Verlag.

Colburn, R. A., Cohen, M. F., & Drucker, S. M. (2000, July). *The role of eye gaze in avatar mediated conversational interfaces* (Microsoft Research Tech. Rep. No. MSR-TR-2000-81). Retrieved December 12, 2007, from research.microsoft.com/research/pubs/view.aspx?tr_id = 391

Craik, F. I. M., Moroz, T.M., Moscovitch, M., Stuss, D. T., Winocur, G., Tulving, E., et al. (1999). In search of the Self: A positron emission tomography study. *Psychological Science, 10*, 27–35.

Fish, R. S., Kraut, R. E., & Chalfonte, B. L. (1990). The video window system in informal communication. In *Proceedings of the Conference on Computer-Supported Cooperative Work* (CSCW '90; pp. 1–11). New York: ACM.

Fridlund, A. J., & Cacioppo, J. T. (1986). Guidelines for human electromyographic research. *Psychophysiology, 23*, 567–589.

Grudin, J. (2005). Communication and collaboration support in an age of information scarcity. In K. Okada, T. Hoshi, & T. Inoue (Eds.), *Communication and collaboration support systems* (pp. 7–17). Ohmsha: IOS Press.

Gutwin, C., & Greenberg, S. (1996). Workspace awareness for groupware. In *Companion of ACM CHI'96 conference on human factors in computing systems* (pp. 208–209). Vancouver, British Columbia, Canada: ACM.

Irle, M. (1971). *Macht und Entscheidungen in Organisationen: Studie gegen das Linie-Stab Prinzip* [Power and decisions in organizations: Study against the line-staff principle]. Frankfurt am Main: Akademische Verlagsgesellschaft.

Ishiguro, H. (2006). Android science: Conscious and subconscious recognition. *Connection Science, 18*, 319–332.

Klucharev, V., & Sams, M. (2004). Interaction of gaze direction and facial expressions processing: ERP study. *Neuroreport, 15,* 621–625.

Lang, P. J. (1980). Behavioral treatment and bio-behavioral assessment: Computer applications. In J. B. Sidowski, J. H. Johnson, & T. A. Williams (Eds.), *Technology in mental health care delivery systems* (pp. 119–137). Norwood, NJ: Ablex.

Lorenz, C. (1995, November 10). In two minds: Real versus "virtual" co-location. *Financial Times,* p. 5.

MacDorman, K. F., & Ishiguro, H. (2006). The uncanny advantage of using androids in social and cognitive science research. *Interaction Studies, 7*(3), 297–337.

Milgram, P., & Kishino, F. (1994). A taxonomy of mixed reality visual display. *IEICE Transactions on Information Systems, 2,* 1321–1329.

Mori, M. (1970). Bukimi no tani [The uncanny valley]. *Energy, 7,* 33–35.

Morgan, K. (2004). The exaggerated death of geography: Learning, proximity and territorial innovation systems. *Journal of Economic Geography, 4,* 3–21.

Ortinski, P., & Meador, K. (2004). Neuronal mechanisms of conscious awareness. *Archives of Neurology, 61,* 1017–1020.

Piaget, J. (2000). Commentary on Vygotsky. *New Ideas in Psychology, 18,* 241–259.

Posner, M. I., Rueda, M. R., & Kanske, P. (2007). Probing the mechanisms of attention. In J. T. Cacioppo, L. G. Tassinary, & G. G. Berntson (Eds.), *Handbook of psychophysiology* (3rd ed., pp. 410–432). New York: Cambridge University Press.

Regenbrecht, H., Ott, C., Wagner, M. H., Lum, T., Kohler, P., Wilke, W., et al. (2003). An augmented virtuality approach to 3D videoconferencing. *The Second IEEE and ACM International Symposium on Mixed and Augmented Reality,* Tokyo, Japan, p. 290.

Saariluoma, P. (2004). Explanatory frameworks for interaction design. In A. Pirhonen, H. Isomäki, C. Roast, & P. Saariluoma (Eds.), *Future interaction design* (pp. 67–83). London: Springer-Verlag.

Schilbach, L., Helmert, J. R., Mojzisch, A., Pannasch, S., Velichkovsky, B. M., & Vogeley, K. (2005, July). *Neural correlates, visual attention and facial expression during social interaction with virtual others.* Paper presented at the Toward Social Mechanisms of Android Science: A CogSci Workshop, Stresa, Italy.

Sebe, N., Lew, M. S., Sun, Y., Cohen, I., Gevers, T., & Huang, T. S. (2007). Authentic facial expression analysis. *Image and Vision Computing, 25,* 1856–1863.

Tomasello, M., & Carpenter, M. (2007). Shared intentionality. *Developmental Science, 10*(1), 121–125.

Velichkovsky, B. M. (1995). Communicating attention: Gaze position transfer in cooperative problem solving. *Pragmatics and Cognition, 3*(2), 199–224.

Velichkovsky, B. M., & Hansen, J. P. (1996). New technological windows into mind: There is more in eyes and brains for human-computer interaction. In *Proceedings of the Conference on Human Factors in Computing Systems* (CHI '96; pp. 496–503) New York: ACM Press.

Velichkovsky, B. M., Pomplun, M., & Rieser, H. (1996). Attention and communication: Eye-movement-based research paradigms. In W. H. Zangemeister, S. Stiel, & C. Freksa (Eds.), *Visual attention and cognition* (pp. 125–154). Amsterdam: Elsevier.

Vertegaal, R., Velichkovsky, B. M., & van der Veer, G. (1997). Catching the eye: Management of joint attention in cooperative work. *SIGCHI Bulletin, 29*(4), 87–99.

Vygotsky, L. S. (1962). *Thought and language.* Cambridge, MA: The MIT Press. (Original work published in 1934).

The Future of Interaction Research: Interaction Is the Result of Top–Down and Bottom–Up Processes

José J. Cañas

Abstract Interaction research has two goals: a theoretical one and a practical one. The theoretical goal is to discover which factors determine the effectiveness of interaction with technology. The applied goal is to provide designers of technology with recommendations on how they must design them. In order to reach both goals, academic and industrial practitioners traditionally have used methodologies that assume the interface and the user can be studied separately as the only means to discover the rules that relate them. However, empirical evidence shows that interaction is the result of the joint work of human cognitive functions (top–down processes) and system characteristics (bottom–up processes). This joint work implies that the human and the technology depend on each other and cannot be studied separately. Therefore, a methodology is needed that takes into account this mutual dependency of human cognitive functions and system characteristics. Finding such methodology is a task for current and future interaction research.

1 The Problem that Interaction Design Research Is Facing

The term *human–machine interaction* refers to the design of the interface where a person and a machine interact during the execution of a task. The goals of a professional who works in the analysis of the interaction depend largely on the context in which such analysis operates. These goals can be classified into two broad categories. On one hand are the theoretical goals set to explain the interaction behavior. On the other hand are the practical goals set to improve system design, user's performance, user's satisfaction, and so on.

Interface designers work either in academic or industrial environments. Those who work in academia are mainly interested in explaining interaction behavior and only suffer the pressures to publish research papers. Those who work in industrial contexts need to find specific design solutions, usually within

J.J. Cañas (✉)
Department of Experimental Psychology, University of Granada, Granada, Spain
e-mail: delagado@ugr.es

P. Saariluoma, H. Isomäki (eds.), *Future Interaction Design II*,
DOI 10.1007/978-1-84800-385-9_3, © Springer-Verlag London Limited 2009

the pressures to reduce costs and obtain benefits in short-term projects. In either case, as noted by Zacks and Tversky (2003), they have traditionally used two methods to design interfaces so that users interact with the interfaces in an efficient manner. One method consists of using an approach in which designers apply general knowledge obtained through investigations conducted within cognitive psychology to the specific design problems (e.g., Norman, 1988; Shneiderman, 1998). The other method consists of analyzing a particular task and a particular interface to determine the optimal characteristics (e.g., Nielsen, 1993).

These two methods identified by Zacks and Tversky (2003) are mechanistic. In a mechanistic view of a system, one assumes that the whole is equal to the sum of its parts. Therefore, both of these methods assume the human being and the device can be studied separately first, and then one would study the rules that relate them. These rules would be those that would determine the effectiveness of the interaction.

However, for many years, psychologists and cognitive neuropsychologists have known that the human cognitive system carries out its tasks by combining processes, operating within both goal-driven (top–down) and perceptually driven (dependent on stimuli of the task; bottom–up) processes. For example, changes in the focus of attention are guided by the knowledge a person has about where sought-after information will appear (top–down processes) and the inherent characteristics of the stimuli (bottom–up processes). There is ample neuropsychological evidence which shows that these two types of processes have different brain substrates. The top–down processes have frontal locations and bottom–up processes have parietal locations (Buschman & Miller, 2007).

Therefore, if interaction could be the result of the joint work of both top–down and bottom–up processes, the study of the interaction should change from a mechanistic to an organic view of a system. In an organic paradigm, the whole is more than the sum of its parts. The difference between these two views of a system is that, in an organic paradigm, a system cannot be explained by explaining its parts. If interaction is seen from the viewpoint of organic paradigm, it is something that cannot be explained only by the properties of the parties and the rules that relate them (Simon, 1969). Therefore, the starting assumption should be that interaction is the sum of the characteristics of the human being plus the characteristics of the interface plus the rules that relate them.

In this approach to analysis, there is an important aspect that could have clear consequences for the future of interaction design: When the system changes (e.g., the artifact is redesigned or the human being learns to perform the task better), so does information processing, possibly changing the roles of the top–down and bottom–up processes. The practical consequence of this proposal could be predicted from a design principle called the principle of mutual dependency (Cañas, Salmerón, & Fajardo, 2005). This principle states that the human cognitive functions involved in the task will depend on the functions that are present in the interface. Furthermore, the functions of the

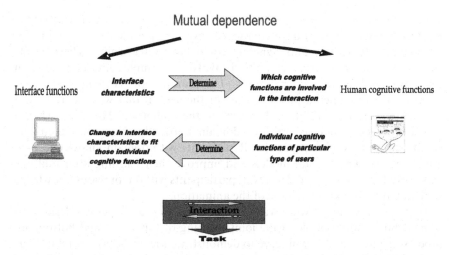

Fig. 1 The mutual dependency principle: (a) Interface characteristics determine which cognitive functions are involved in the interaction; (b) Individual cognitive functions of particular types of users determine changes in interface characteristics to fit those individual cognitive functions

interface that help in performing a task will be those that are more appropriate to the human cognitive functions that are involved in the task (see Fig. 1). For example, the appropriate interface functions of a particular artifact will be those that correspond to the structure and function of the human working memory involved in the interaction with that artifact.

Therefore, according to this principle of mutual dependency, designers should consider that any modification, substitution, or introduction of a new function into the interface will imply a change in, and for, the human cognitive functions that intervene in the task. In addition, anything that is particular or constraining in the characteristics of the human cognitive functions that are present, in some or in all users of that interface, will imply a limitation in the possible functions that are included in the interface. For example, users that have some limitations on their working memory functions would require interface functions that overlook these limitations.

Therefore, according to this principal, the two mechanicist methods identified by Zacks and Tversky (2003) would be inappropriate when applied independently. It would be impossible to find design guidelines that will be efficient for all users and in all contexts. In the same way, it is impossible to predict how a user will interact with a system without considering all possible design characteristics.

The importance of this interactive effect of top–down and bottom–up processes has already been proved in the field of interaction design. The results of many research studies done on the effectiveness of new design characteristics have shown that it is impossible to evaluate the interface characteristics without considering some human cognitive characteristic at the same time. For example, Kriz and Hegarty (2007) have conducted several experiments to examine the effect that interactivity and signaling could have on learning. Their results showed that learning from animation involves a complex interplay between top–down and bottom–up processes. The majority of participants in their experiments developed a mental model of the system that was incorrect and inconsistent with information displayed in the animation. However, when a top–down factor such as previous domain knowledge was considered, the results showed a different pattern. Participants with domain knowledge were able to revise their mental models and improve their learning after multiple exposures to the animation. However, participants without previous knowledge were not able to take advantage of the animation.

In the next section, I will review a topic—research on hypertext design—in some detail as an example of the joint working of top–down and bottom–up processes. This example will serve to demonstrate the advantage of taking this methodological perspective.

2 Case Example: Research on Hypertext Design

The human cognitive system is characterized by its capacity to acquire, to store, and to retrieve information. Throughout their evolution, human beings have acquired information from the environment directly or through systems (devices) where that information has been previously stored by other human beings (i.e., books). Nowadays, hypermedia systems have become one of the more important sources from which human beings acquire information. A hypermedia system is one in which the information is contained in a set of pieces connected by links that represent the relations among them. The information can be presented in any format (text, images, etc.). In the special case in which it contains only textual information, it is known as a hypertext system instead of hypermedia system. The most familiar example of a hypermedia system is the Internet.

The activity that a person performs to acquire information contained in hypermedia system is navigation. In order to navigate, a person begins on a unit of information (page) and continues through the links to other units of information. Navigation can have two objectives. First, a person might want to find a particular unit of information, known as a searching task. But also very frequently, a person navigates with the goal of understanding the information found and acquiring knowledge, and thus these are known as learning or understanding tasks. For example, in the case of hypermedia systems used in an educative environment, navigation has the goal of understanding and learning.

Hypermedia navigation faces two problems that limit its utility and that have interested many researchers: (a) When the goal is to look for information, people undergo a phenomenon called *disorientation,* during which the person does not remember the visited information and loses the sense and the objective of the search; and (b) When the goal is to learn and to understand, conclusive experimental evidence does not exist regarding what is learned and whether people learn more from a hypermedia system than from linear systems (the traditional book). Conclusive experimental results have not demonstrated that hypermedia systems are superior to the linear systems in any learning criteria that have been considered (Chen & Rada, 1996; Dillon & Gabbard, 1998; Shapiro & Neiderhauser, 2004). These two problems are related. For example, some empirical evidence shows that disorientation results in poor learning (Ahuja & Webster, 2001). For that reason, solutions (e.g., the use of content maps) are being considered that would decrease or eliminate disorientation.

In any case, to avoid the problems associated with navigation and to design the hypermedia systems in such a way that they are really an alternative that improves searching, understanding, and learning, it is necessary to conduct research into how the human cognitive system interacts with these systems to search for and find information. Also needed are theoretical models that could allow predictions on the effectiveness of the tasks of searching and learning. This research has already been under way for almost a decade in several locations around the world, and it has been demonstrated that a critical variable in explaining the navigational behavior of learners is the navigation strategies used by them. For example, Pirolli and Card (1999) have proposed a model, based on the ecological theories of biology, where users of hypermedia systems are conceived as "animals" that develop strategies for searching out information (food) in their surroundings (hypermedia systems). In this line, the results of current research have demonstrated that the strategies for reading in hypertext systems affect the understanding of the content, as well as the adoption of activities of active processing. More concretely, the selection of a strategy for effective reading is very important for users with no previous knowledge of the topic because an inadequate reading strategy can make them follow a pattern of incoherent navigation, which in turn leads to a poor understanding of the content (Salmerón, Kintsch, & Cañas, 2006).

In the present state of the investigation into this topic, it is now considered necessary to investigate the factors that determine the strategy that a person adopts for navigation. In this sense, researchers who work in this area think that the adoption of a particular strategy depends on several factors that concern both the structure of the system and the characteristics of the human cognitive system. Nevertheless, the complexity and the number of these determining factors of the strategies can make the investigation difficult and could lead researchers to confusing results or to erroneous conclusions. Therefore, Madrid and Cañas (2007) have proposed a scheme, based on the ideas of top–down and bottom–up processes and the mutual dependency principal, that can allow researchers to identify the appropriate factors and their interactions (see Fig. 2). Empirical research by Madrid and Cañas is exploring the interactive effects of two sets of factors. One set of factors depends on the interface: what it

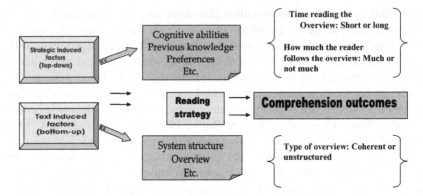

Fig. 2 Framework proposed by Madrid and Cañas (2007) to explain how top–down and bottom–up processes and the mutual dependency principal would allow researchers to identify the appropriate factors and their interactions that would affect reading strategies and, then, comprehension and learning

contains and what the designer has designed. From a cognitive scientist's point of view, these factors will affect bottom–up processing. The second set of factors is related to the reader's cognitive characteristics, interest, motivation, and so forth. This is the top–down processing. In this theoretical scheme, the adoption of a particular strategy for navigation must be explained based on the characteristics of the human cognitive system (top–down processes) and the characteristics of the hypermedia system (bottom–up processes).

Correspondingly, in a study on the factors that depend on the structure of the system, Salmerón, Baccino, Cañas, Madrid, and Fajardo (2008) have found that when readers have a semantic map (an overview) of the structure of the hypertext, an interaction takes place between the reading strategy, previous knowledge, and coherence of the text during the time dedicated to processing the map and the text itself. This interaction affects the result of the understanding. The time of processing is greater for the map and the text when the reading strategy is not coherent with the structure shown in the map or the text is unfamiliar.

As far as the characteristics of the human cognitive system, Juvina and van Oostendorp (2004) have already conducted an experiment to determine the cognitive predictors of navigation behavior in hypertext systems. The results showed that spatial abilities, the capacity of working memory, and episodic memory are related to navigation behavior. Concretely, a low working memory capacity is a good predicting factor of disorientation problems, whereas the spatial abilities are predictors of the level of task performance. In the same line, Madrid, Salmerón, Cañas, and Fajardo (2005) have examined the role of nine cognitive factors in the determination of navigation strategy. The results showed that spatial abilities are related to the amount of information read, and that the level at which the reader follows the structure shown on a map is affected by the capacity of working memory. The authors interpreted these results from the perspective of cognitive load. Navigation is a task that exceeds a user's cognitive resources, fundamentally because the reader must perform two simultaneous tasks: She must decide what to understand when she is reading and what she wants to read next.

From the point of view of the characteristics of the human cognitive system, navigation in hypertext requires many cognitive resources to plan the search, to determine if the found information is what one looked for, to understand the content, and to integrate this content with the knowledge stored in one's long-term memory (as shown by the results on the differences due to previous knowledge; see Salmerón et al., 2006). In a recent revision of the literature on this topic, DeStefano and LeFevre (2007) have indicated that, due to its characteristics, hypermedia systems require a greater number of working memory, decision-making, and understanding resources. In addition, this excessive demand for resources cannot easily be palliated by some of the characteristics that have been introduced by the designers to improve navigation. For example, the inclusion of semantic maps, which supposedly facilitate navigation, increases the demand of cognitive spatial resources, and that negatively affects understanding.

All these data indicate the necessity of introducing the concept of cognitive load in the explanatory model of the election of navigation strategies. This concept can integrate the joint influences of the dependent factors of the structures of hypermedia system and of the human cognitive system, as Sweller, van Merriënboer, and Paas (1998) indicated some years ago. However, these authors studied the effect that cognitive load had in the execution of navigation tasks with the assumption that this effect is direct, without considering that this effect might be indirect . It is possible that cognitive load is also a consequence of the interaction between the characteristics of the structure of hypermedia system and the characteristics of human cognitive system, and its effect takes place throughthe determination of navigation strategies, as can be seen in Fig. 2. If this is true, a hypothesis can be derived from this perspective. For example, it could be that the strategy chosen by a person during navigation would, in addition to the particular interests that one has, serve to reduce the person's cognitive load, and thus maintain performance at a suitable level. Therefore, cognitive load can be included as an important explaining construct in the scheme, but it leads again to the interactive effect of top–down and bottom–up processes. A situation could occur in which a certain interface characteristic requires more cognitive load, but the user adapts her reading strategy to address this increment on cognitive load, thereby reducing the negative effect of this interface characteristic.

As can be seen in this example, therefore, it is not possible to conduct an investigation on the effects of the introduction of a feature of the interface without considering that this feature will affect the joint work processes of top–down and bottom–up processes. The example demonstrates that it is not possible to use the methods identified by Zacks and Tversky (2003) separately.

It is necessary to use a methodology that takes into account the principle of mutual dependence. However, some work should be done to develop such methodology, which is addressed in the next section.

3 Methodological Proposal for Designing Top–Down and Bottom–Up Processes

To develop a methodology that takes into account the joint work of top–down and bottom–up processes simultaneously, two issues must be addressed up front:

1. Which features of the interface that are the most appropriate for each type of user, in a particular context, a particular situation, and so on, must be determined. The research on hypertext systems fits into this task. It is not sufficient to say that there is a relationship between prior knowledge and structure of the Web. It should be able to be said, for example, "for students with little knowledge on this topic, the best structure is such-and-such one."

    An important aspect of this task is to study the cognitive factors tied to specific characteristics of system users. It will be necessary to consider, for example cognitive functioning as it relates to cognitive deficiencies and aging. Fajardo, Cañas, Salmerón, and Abascal (2006) continue to study how the characteristics of people with auditory deficiencies affect their searching task performance on the Internet. With respect to aging, cognitive deterioration has an effect on the use of the new technologies of telecare (Ojel-Jaramillo & Cañas, 2006). *Telecare* is a set of technologies that provide help to dependent, especially elderly, people by providing access to teams of professionals who can attend to the client's needs 24 hours a day, 365 days a year via a telephonic network. These technologies should be designed with consideration to the differences and deterioration elderly people exhibit as they age.

    But this research alone does not lead directly to a proposal of design guidelines. It is necessary to do the following task simultaneously.

2. Knowledge about the user who is interacting with the interface and the conditions in which she is interacting are needed. For example, any design solution proposed to hypertext designers must address one important issue: Once the activity, human characteristics, and interests of a particular reader are known, this information must be used to make decisions about interface characteristics. Yet the interface has to act online, adapting to that particular reader at that particular time. For example, readers with low previous knowledge about the topic benefit from having a very coherent hypertext structure that leads or directs them to what to read next (Salmerón et al., 2006). Readers with high previous knowledge, meanwhile, learn more when they read within a complex structure where they are free to navigate. Certainly designers do not want to have to design several hypertext structures;

they want specific guidelines to design just one structure. Therefore, researchers must guide designers in how to implement online procedures to identify and accommodate readers who have little prior knowledge.

To this aim, several solutions have been proposed, all of them based on online assessments of reader behavior. Yet, some of these solutions are impossible to implement. For example, some have proposed having some kind of test that readers have to answer prior to interacting with the system. However, a more promising line of research is to evaluate reader knowledge by using some kind of automated procedure. For example, it might be possible to analyze the reader's navigation path and compare it to some previously stored paths that have been identified as belonging to empirically and theoretically identified readers with different knowledge levels.

As it happens with previous knowledge, it is also necessary to obtain online measures of cognitive load, another top–down factor that would allow characteristics of the hypermedia system to adapt to the continuous changes in this human factor. Cognitive load has two effects. On the one hand, a hypertext system needs to be designed in a way that requires a low cognitive load. On the other hand, some readers are more willing than others to expend more cognitive resources on reading and, therefore, they will have more or less cognitive load for navigation, depending on the amount of cognitive resources expended on the reading task. While recommendations can guide designers on what to do to reduce cognitive load due to interface characteristics, designers also need to know how to determine what kind of readers will interact with their systems and what they will do.

These measures of cognitive load must be online because, by definition, cognitive load changes during the interaction. As predicted by the mutual dependency principle, if the system detects that the user has few cognitive resources available, the interface can be changed to reduce the demand, although if the user realizes this, she may decide to use the liberated resources from the main task to take on another task simultaneously. Therefore, a further need for developing some online measure of cognitive load is needed to detect this trade-off on cognitive load.

Subjective measures of cognitive load (questionnaires) are not appropriate for this goal because they are off-line and thus do not allow simultaneous measurement of the user developing her navigation strategies. In the same way, the measured calls for "double task" are unsuitable because, by themselves, they suppose a source of cognitive load that would make difficult the task of adapting the system characteristics. Therefore, one alternative could be to use psychophysiological and nonintrusive measures of cognitive load. For that reason, some authors are proposing the utilization of registries of ocular movements with nonintrusive equipment (Di Stasi, Alvarez-Valbuena, Antoli, Gea, & Cañas, 2008). The pupil diameter, blinking rate, saccades, and so on, of readers can be measured while they are interacting with the systems.

An example from the work of Kashihara, Hirashima, and Toyoda (1994) illustrates this point. These authors were faced with the problem of how to estimate the cognitive load supported by the students while comprehending a text. In their work, they suggested that one way to improve the comprehension was to increase the load during reading. They assumed, based on the results of psychological research (Carroll, Mack, Lewis, Grischkowsky, & Robertson, 1985; Charney & Reder, 1986), that learning can be facilitated by imposing more effort on the novice. Therefore, they set their research to find a way of controlling cognitive load by means of instructions during learning. To this aim, they proposed an explanation effect model to estimate a student's load and then tailor an explanation for the student. The model assumes that the load estimate would depend on the student's understanding capability because the same explanation imposes a different load according to this student's characteristics. Therefore the authors proposed that any system that provides explanations must have a "student model" that represents the understanding capability. This student model could be represented through several parameters. The system sets these parameters by monitoring a student's understanding process, modeling her capability of understanding. In addition, the system gradually updates the parameters by testing the student's understanding of a number of explanations and refining the load estimate. These functions enable the system to control the cognitive load through explanation

Based on this model, the system computes an explicit representation of a student's learning load. This load representation depends on how a student's learning process is modeled. The instructions enable the automated tutor to apply a load. Since a student may become overloaded, it is important to adjust problems or explanations to be neither too simple nor too complicated. This requires an estimate of how much load the instructions will impose on the student. This estimate should be done according to the student's learning capacity because the same instruction imposes a different load, depending on her capacity. Therefore, the tutor needs to control the amount of content or instructional information within the load estimate. When, for example, a student is expected to face an easy task with a low load, the tutor should provide less instructional information in order to impose a heavier load on her. Conversely, when an overload is applied, the tutor needs to provide more instructional or more easily comprehensible information. As a result, the authors were able to design a system that adjusted to the load of the student who tried to understand explanations describing a topic, based on the estimation of the student's current load and the learning goals. This is an example of how to combine top–down and bottom–up factors in an instructional setting.

Another example of this approach can be found in the work of Jameson, Schäfer, Weis, Berthold, and Weyrath (1999) on adaptive interfaces. These authors' work identified a significant design problem: Knowledge resources (time and working memory) depend on the context of use of an interface. They used an example of a situation where two users of the same interface at an airport consulted the train schedules on a PDA. One of the users runs through the airport because she knows that a train is possibly departing in a few minutes. Another user sits comfortably in a room without any hurry because she suspects that her train will not come until much later, although she will have to concentrate as well because unrelated information given over the airport loudspeakers can distract her. The authors explored several approaches to this problem that could affect design decisions: (a) assume minimal user resources when designing the interface; (b) allow users to specify appropriate system behavior; or (c) have users characterize their own resource limitations. They conducted empirical research to conclude that it is necessary to design systems so that the system can recognize and/or adapt to users' changing resource limitations. Moreover, they concluded, there are reasons to base the design on an explicit model of the causes and consequences of such resource limitations.

4 Conclusions: Future of Interaction Research

One of the fundamental problems facing the design of future interaction is finding a methodology to help designers in their goal to create the best interface for users in any context and any condition of interaction. This methodology should enable better design of user interfaces in the traditional sense of ease of use, reduced problems of interaction, and the time needed to learn the device. Equally important nowadays, however, new devices and interfaces need new methodologies that take into account the reality that interaction is the result of the intersection of top–down (human cognitive functions) and bottom–up (interface characteristics) factors. To meet the challenges required for the design of intelligent systems for ubiquitous computing, for example, a methodology must allow designers to foresee universal users working in unknown contexts and in any kind of interaction conditions. Certainly a key objective in the design of ubiquitous computing devices is to determine what type of interface would be the most appropriate for each situation in which a user might be located. Therefore, it is necessary to implement usability methodologies that may be used to evaluate the user experience interacting with the prototypes as it develops while, secondly and more importantly, also anticipating any conditions of interaction in future scenarios. This second aspect is essential if intelligent systems are to be truly innovative. In the traditional design of computer systems, the type of user and usage scenario is defined from the earliest stages of predesign. However, in developing intelligent systems for ubiquitous computing, scenarios and users will need to be considered universal in many cases (Akoumianakis & Stephanidis, 2003).

A possible alternative could be to develop a design methodology based on the principle of mutual dependency (Cañas et al., 2005). This principle presents several key guidelines:

1. The optimal functions that should be incorporated in the interface are those that are better suited to the human cognitive functions. To that end, there are

several approaches, such as starting with a consideration of the worst possible situations from the point of view of human cognitive functions (e.g., deterioration of such functions) and building adaptations for where these situations improve, or having an online evaluation of the cognitive functions that are involved in each particular situation, as well as storing a map within the system that relates each cognitive function with every feature of the interface in order to adapt the features, as needed, to each cognitive function.

2. Human cognitive functions that are involved in a task depend on the built-in functions of the interface. Procedures can be designed into the system to induce the human cognitive functions through a particular feature of the interface. For example, a procedure in the system could change the characteristics of the interface to induce a state of low or high cognitive load.

3. The modification, replacement, or introduction of a function at the interface involves the adaptation of human cognitive functions to it. The ability to detect any changes in the interface in process is important, since changes in the interface could modify the human cognitive functions and in what direction.

4. Finally, the development (e.g., through learning) or limitations (e.g., due to a disability) in some human cognitive function implies a limitation on the possible functions of the interface that could be implemented. The individual characteristics of each user and how the features of the interface would have to change to suit these characteristics must be understood.

This paper demonstrates the methodological work facing future research on interaction. Research in this area is inevitable and required because effective designs cannot be achieved without methodologies that take into account that the interaction is the result of the joint work of top–down and bottom–up processes. This methodological work should be based on a sound theoretical foundation of exactly how the combination of the results and contents of the top–down and bottom–up processes occurs. One promising line of research in this issue is the work on apperception conducted by Saariluoma (2003). Apperception refers to the process by which the content of information obtained from sensory processes are combined with the contents stored in memory to form a mental representation that guides human behavior. Therefore, in order to understand how the characteristics of the interface obtained through bottom–up processes are combined with the contents retrieved by top–down processes, it is necessary to understand how apperception works.

References

Ahuja, J. S., & Webster, J. (2001). Perceived disorientation: An examination of a new measure to assess Web design effectiveness. *Interacting with Computers, 14*, 15–29.

Akoumianakis, D., & Stephanidis, C. (2003). Blending scenarios of use and informal argumentation to facilitate universal access: Experience with the Universal Access Assessment Workshop method. *Behavioural and Information Technology, 22*, 227–244.

Buschman, T. J., & Miller, E. K. (2007). Top-down versus bottom-control of attention in the prefrontal and posterior parietal corties. *Science, 315*, 1860–1862.

Cañas, J. J., Salmerón, L., & Fajardo, I. (2005). Toward the analysis of the interaction in the joint cognitive system. In A. Pirhonen, H. Isomäki, C. Roast, & P. Saariluoma (Eds.), *Future Interaction Design* (pp. 85–104). London: Springer-Verlag.

Carroll, J. M., Mack, C., Lewis, N., Grischkowsky, N. L., & Robertson, S. (1985). Exploring a word processor. *Human-Computer Interaction, 1*, 283–307.

Charney, D. H., & Reder, L. M. (1986). Designing interactive tutorials for computer users. *Human-Computer Interaction, 2*, 297–317.

Chen, C., & Rada, R. (1996). Interacting with hypertext: A meta-analysis of experimental studies. *Human-Computer Interaction, 11*, 125–156.

DeStefano D., & LeFevre, J. A. (2007). Cognitive load in hypertext reading: A review. *Computer in Human Behavior, 23*, 1616–641.

Di Stasi, L., Alvarez-Valbuena, V., Antoli, A., Gea, M., & Cañas, J. J. (2008). *Saccadic peak velocity as an index of cognitive load when interacting with the Web.* Manuscript in preparation.

Dillon, A., & Gabbard, R. (1998). Hypermedia as an educational technology: A review of the quantitative research literature on learner comprehension, control, and style. *Review of Educational Research, 68*, 322–349.

Fajardo, I., Cañas, J. J., Salmerón, L., & Abascal, J. (2006). Improving deaf users' accessibility in hypertext information retrieval: Are graphical interfaces useful for them? *Behaviour and Information Technology, 25*, 455–467.

Jameson, A., Schäfer, R., Weis, T., Berthold, A., & Weyrath, T. (1999). Making systems sensitive to the user's changing resource limitations. *Knowledge-Based Systems, 12*, 413–425.

Juvina, I., & van Oostendorp, H. (2004). Individual differences and behavioural aspects involved in modelling web navigation. In C. Stary & C. Stephanidis (Eds.), *User-centered interaction paradigms for universal access in the information society* (pp. 77–95). New York: Springer-Verlag.

Kashihara, A., Hirashima, T., & Toyoda, J. (1994). A cognitive load application in tutoring. *User modeling and user-adapted interaction, 4*, 279–303.

Kriz, S., & Hegarty, S. (2007). Top-down and bottom-up influences on learning from animations. *International Journal of Human-Computer Studies, 65*, 911–930.

Madrid, R. I., & Cañas, J. J. (2007). How reading strategies affect the comprehension of texts in hypermedia systems. In D. A. Alamargot, P. Terrier, & J. M. Cellier (Eds.), *Studies in writing: Written documents in the workplace* (pp. 205–216). Oxford, UK: Elsevier.

Madrid, R. I., Salmerón, L., Cañas, J. J., & Fajardo, I. (2005). Cognitive factors related to text comprehension with hypertext overviews. In G. Chiazzese, M. Allegra, A. Chifari, & S. Ottaviano (Eds.), Methods and technologies for learning (pp. 597–598). Southampton, UK: WIT Press.

Nielsen, J. (1993). *Usability engineering.* Boston: Academic Press.

Norman, D. A. (1988). *The psychology of everyday things.* New York: Basic Books.

Ojel-Jaramillo, J. M., & J. J. Cañas. (2006). Enhancing the usability of telecare devices. *Human Technology, 2*, 103–118.

Pirolli, P., & Card, S. (1999). Information foraging. *Psychological Review, 106*, 643–675.

Saariluoma, P. (2003). Apperception, content-based psychology and design. In U. Lindemann (Ed.), *Human behaviours in design* (pp. 72–78). Berlin, Germany: Springer.

Salmerón, L., Baccino, T., Cañas, J. J., Madrid, R. I., & Fajardo, I. (2008). *Processing of graphical overviews: Evidence from eye movements.* Manuscript submitted for publication.

Salmerón, L., Kintsch, W., & Cañas, J. J. (2006). Reading strategies and prior knowledge in learning from hypertext. *Memory and Cognition, 34*, 1157–1171.

Shapiro, A., & Niederhauser, D. (2004). Learning from hypertext: Research issues and findings. In D. H. Jonassen (Ed.), *Handbook of research on educational communications and technology* (2nd ed., pp. 605–620). Mahwah, NJ: Erlbaum.

Shneiderman, B. (1998). *Designing the user interface: Strategies for effective human–computer interaction* (3rd ed.). Reading, MA: Addison-Wesley.

Simon, H. (1969). *The science of the artificial.* Cambridge, MA: MIT Press.

Sweller, J., van Merriënboer, J., & Paas, F. (1998). Cognitive architecture and instructional design. *Educational Psychology Review, 10,* 251–296.

Zacks, J. M., & Tversky, B. (2003). Structuring information interfaces for procedural learning. *Journal of Experimental Psychology: Applied, 9,* 88–100.

User Psychology in Interaction Design: The Role of Design Ontologies

Pertti Saariluoma, Hanna Parkkola, Anne Honkaranta, Mauri Leppänen, and Juha Lamminen

Abstract In the various forms of interaction design, it is essential to analyze, understand, and predict human behavior. This is equally true with devices such as information systems that are meant to interact with people. The importance of these problems has inspired scientists to develop numerous approaches to investigate and explicate human actions. However, they have mainly been characterized by intuitive and folk psychological approaches to the human mentality in interaction. To improve the scientific foundations of design, we present here a psychology-based approach to collecting user knowledge, as well as a related design practice. The former can be called user psychology and the latter the action-oriented design. User psychology is an approach that applies psychological knowledge and methods to analyzing and solving interaction design problems. It works to develop explanatory design practices so that it is possible to say on which psychological grounds one design alternative is better than another or why a solution is ineffective. One step toward improving explanatory design practices is to develop effective design ontologies to manage the design processes. Here, we discuss the nature of user psychological knowledge and analyze the process of developing respective ontological solutions.

1 Introduction

Understanding human–technology interaction (HTI) has become an important scientific and practical problem for several reasons. Firstly, the continuing development of information and communication technology (ICT) has opened new possibilities for human living, but the development makes interaction problems more complex. Secondly, it has been noticed that it is essential to make interactions easier with devices such as information systems if one wishes people to fully adopt new ICT products. Finally, emerging technologies, such as

P. Saariluoma (✉)
Department of Computer Science and Information Systems, University of Jyväskylä, Jyväskylä, Finland
e-mail: ps@jyu.fi

P. Saariluoma, H. Isomäki (eds.), *Future Interaction Design II*,
DOI 10.1007/978-1-84800-385-9_4, © Springer-Verlag London Limited 2009

agents, ubiquitous, pervasive, and embedded systems, shall be very challenging for people to use because the direct keyboard and WYSIWYG-type interaction mode is often replaced by much less concrete forms of interaction. Improvement in human technology interaction is thus one important factor regulating the development of the rising ICT society.

If interactions are not well organized, people simply reject the new possibilities. The comparison between short message service (SMS) and wireless application protocol (WAP) demonstrates a typical example of the difficulties and provides interaction researchers with lessons for future. While SMS has become one of the biggest successes in mobile services, WAP, despite its sound basic idea as a mobile parallel to the Internet, did not work. It presupposed more complex interaction patterns than SMS does, and manufacturers failed to teach people the required skills (Parkkola, 2003).

New technologies make it possible to produce a multitude of new ICT services, but people know very little about them and are not necessarily interested in learning what is needed to adopt them (Kämäräinen & Saariluoma, 2007). This means that the vital cycle between invention and innovation may become unnecessarily slow, which slows down the development of information society, as well as substantially increases the development costs. The business logic is very simple here: Companies will have more money for development if more users adopt a new service quickly.

Designers of the future must abandon outdated thought models and think in new ways. One of the major challenges shall be finding a new way of interaction thinking. The immediate interaction with devices through traditional HCI forms is no longer the only vision (Carroll, 1997; Helander, Landauer, & Prabhu, 1997; Olson & Olson, 2003; Rosson & Carroll, 2002). Such thinking is, in many cases, too narrow because it does not cover the whole spectrum of human action and mentality. Devices and information systems are not central to human life and actions; they are tools for people. Moreover, it is not necessary to focus on finding uses for existing technologies, but rather to define and design the actions of people, and then find technical solutions to support these. This is why it is essential to build design practices on wider analyses of human nature, activities, and mentality. How such a holistic analysis can be realized is one of the major challenges for modern interaction-oriented cognitive and information systems science.

2 Development of Interaction Research

When designers begin to design a new product, they should have a solid idea about the users and their actions. For example, to improve family communication in the near future, they have to consider this problem area from several different human points of view, instead of limiting themselves to immediate device interaction or usability problems (Parkkola, 2006a; Parkkola, Saariluoma, & Berki, in press). This applies to all of the modern services. The development of the product must be based on people's actions. The change in interaction design practice from the immediate interaction to a wider understanding of the human mentality makes it necessary to know if and how the traditional interaction analysis really can solve such problems.

The first attempts to understand users, such as the early psychology of programming or the early analysis of human roles, human action, and mentality, were recognized as problems, even though no scientific psychology was applied (cf. Royce, 1987). Experienced system designers considered how their own minds would react in these interaction situations and generalized from their own experiences to form conceptions of human thinking and reacting. One cannot claim these approaches had not been successful. Classic programming inventions, such as the early 3G programming languages (e.g., Fortran and BASIC) and programming paradigms (e.g., structured programming), had psychological motives as the foundations for learnability and memorability of code (Dahl, Dijkstra, & Hoare, 1972; Nielsen, 1993). Nevertheless, these early programming innovations did not necessarily lead to improved user understanding. Progress was based on standard intuitive folk psychology.

The second approach to answering the challenges of interaction, which also is a form of folk psychology, was to adopt usability experiments and iterative testing (e.g., prototyping models by Floyd, 1984; the spiral model by Boehm, 1988; or the analyses by Nielsen, 1993). Typically, these ideas led to systematic testing that no longer focused only on technical issues but also called attention to human performance (e.g., Knittle, Ruth, & Patton Gardner, 1986; Nielsen, 1993). However, the tests were not intended to systematically improve a psychological understanding of users' mental processes. The goal was simply to make improvements to the technologies under development at that particular moment. Of course, this approach has greatly improved the knowledge regarding various use problems.

The next method for obtaining information about users' actions were deployed via contextual task analysis (Beyer & Holtzblatt, 1998; Mayhew, 1999) and related traditions such as scenario-based analysis (Jarke, 1999; Tollmar & Persson, 2002; Torgny, 1998; Whiteside, Bennett, & Holtzblatt, 1988). In contextual task analysis, designers systematically observe what people do in organizations and base the systems design on this collected information. However, no psychological or social scientific knowledge is required or applied in analyzing the human dimension. This means that only rather practical questions can be asked and solved because any scientific elaboration of the problems would be difficult in the absence of psychological understanding of human behavior.

Though it would be unjust to claim that folk psychological approaches have not been useful, it would be equally incorrect to avoid pointing out the difficulties. Folk psychological thinking has its inherent problems (Stich, 1983). Its progress is relatively slow in absence of systematic theory testing and development. In interaction research, progress has taken place mostly in technical systems, but not in understanding the human mentality. Therefore, interaction problems are addressed one at a time, often repeating the same process, and rarely advancing the field.

Folk psychology causes problems in developing design practices because the level of conceptualization is very low. While systems should have good learnability and memorability, these are no more than norms (Nielsen, 1993). Extensive analysis of the phenomena of learning and memory, however, would make it possible to say how learnability and memorability can be systematically improved (see Baddeley, 1997, for an introduction to the psychological tradition in these issues).

Good testing practices in ICT interaction analyses should be founded on psychologically reliable processes. This means that a sufficient number of experimental subjects are used and the experiments are controlled in a proper way. "Quick and dirty" methods may be practical in some situations, but one cannot reliably build usability testing on them. This is why it is important to take seriously the principles of modern experimental and empirical psychology in interaction testing, instead of relying on folk psychological intuitions.

Intuitive and unsystematic design thinking also causes difficulties in finding roles for different types of expertise. For example, the software tester's role and the usability specialist's role can be seen differently, depending on the ICT design models used. In the early ICT design models (e.g., the waterfall model by Royce, 1987) the software tester's responsibility area was both technical testing and usability testing. The technical testing was based strictly on scientific principles while usability testing was fully intuitive, based on folk psychology without knowledge of scientific psychology.

Over the decades, the ICT design models have advanced, but the role of human specialists is still quite vague within these models. In modern ICT design models, the software tester's main responsibility area can be, for example, to localize technical problems by using modern testing tools and documenting the problems for the developers and designers. The usability specialist's responsibility area is larger and includes, for example, the usability requirements, usability design, usability tests, and usability development in general. Additionally, the usability specialist may have a technical background without any understanding of scientific psychology, in which case the usability knowledge might be fully grounded in folk psychology.

The critical question today is how far we can rely on folk psychological approaches when thinking about the properties of the human mind. These practices are based on the personal and private experiences of the researchers. While this type of psychological investigation prevailed for thousands of years, it was totally dismantled by the growth of scientific psychology between 1872 and 1912. Thus, folk psychology was rendered notoriously unreliable because, for example, several conditions of the human psyche, such as subconscious phenomena, could be investigated (Boring, 1950). Indeed, these problems remain equally unsolvable in folk psychological interaction design.

This critique is not meant to imply that everything done in folk psychological paradigms is incorrect. An analysis of human work contexts, for example, is a necessity. The point made here is different and important: Folk psychology is not the most reliable, productive, or accurate way of conceptualizing and operationalizing the human mind and/or the elements of human activity within interaction research. The development of new possibilities in the ICT world creates parallel demands on the quality of human action analysis, and demands as well more scientifically rigorous procedures. The concepts, methods, and theoretical approaches of modern psychological thinking in design, as well as in testing, are needed to replace folk psychology.

3 Modern User Psychology

Certainly scientific psychological analysis had begun to develop even in the early stages of interaction research. Shneiderman (1976) applied basic experimental analysis to understand skills when analyzing programming and illustrated that human working memory is an essential theoretical construct when considering the behavior of programmers. Around the same time, a number of important psychological papers were published on the psychology of computer programming, which essentially improved understanding of user psychology (Adelson, 1981; Anderson, Farrell, & Sauers, 1984; Anderson & Jeffries, 1985; Carroll, Thomas, & Malhotra 1980; McKeithen, Reitman, Rueter, & Hirtle, 1981; Pennington, 1987). These papers among others helped introduce the paradigm of scientific psychological analysis of computer use. Much of the theoretical psychological knowledge of users' behavior and mentality has been developed under this paradigm.

The first extensive theoretical synthesis was made by Card, Moran, & Newell (1983) in the form of the GOMS (goals, operations, methods and selection rules) architecture to describe computer users in practical contexts, such as text editing. Later, this cognitive modeling paradigm was greatly extended and became fundamental in the scientific consideration of human mentality in use contexts (Anderson, Matessa, & Lebiere, 1997; Hoves & Young, 1997; Kieras & Meyer, 1997).

These early developments have led to technologically oriented and motivated research. The key challenges have been finding new uses for existing technologies, and testing iteratively existing solutions and prototypes of new systems (Rosson & Carroll 2002). The dependency of developers on the advancement of new technologies makes the usability research too slow to be of real use in designing technical interaction solutions. User analysis should direct the development of technologies. Consequently, one should begin with users as the point of departure for interaction analyses, rather than beginning with existing technologies.

User psychology research begins with the user and users' psychological properties. Moran (1981) suggested this term, and the construction of cognitive models is user psychology in practice (Card et al., 1983). This means the psychologist begins by analyzing what users are before any actual application development and design work is begun. Certainly the concept of user psychology is every bit as valid as commonly used practices such as traffic psychology or industrial psychology.

The user psychological approach has always been overshadowed by the difficulties in communicating with industry (Carroll, 1997). Industrial people often view themselves from a practical point of view, and thus they at times may perceive the psychological user approach as too theoretical and distant from the actual design work. Indeed, this makes sense because relatively little energy has so far been invested in developing user psychological design methods.

The task of usability research is to develop uses for existing and emerging technologies and to test these to assure that they work (Rosson & Carroll, 2002). This work can have either scientific psychological or folk psychological foundations (Nielsen, 1993; Olson & Olson, 2003; Rosson & Carroll, 2002). Nevertheless, this kind of work is always bound by or related to a number of tacit user requirements that are built into the technology long before the aspects or facets of the actual user have been considered.

User psychology, however, has somewhat different goals. It investigates the psychological preconditions for use (Oulasvirta & Saariluoma, 2004, 2006; Saariluoma, 2004, 2005a,b). This means that user psychology must be able to explicate usability problems within psychological concepts and investigate them with psychological methods. The main goal is to replace the traditional intuitive interaction design with scientifically justifiable and reliable methods.

As a result, user psychology provides an approach for interaction designers. It allows them to elaborate the analysis of human behavior in several ways. Research outcomes are more reliable because the psychological methods have been well tested through practice. In addition user psychology allows designers to rely on diverse psychological knowledge bases in searching for usability solutions. While traditional usability engineering employs concepts such as memorability and learnability as criteria for smoothness of interaction, that is still quite different from using specific psychological knowledge about the human memory to improve these two aspects of interaction (e.g., Baddeley, 1997). Learnability and memorability are external measures, not the internal principles that would be applied to improve interaction (for the criteria, see Nielsen, 1993). More extensive application of user psychological knowledge makes it possible to base the design concepts on psychological findings and theories.

4 Towards Explanatory Design

When considering how to use user psychological knowledge in design, it is important to make distinctions between folk psychology and scientific psychology, and between science and intuition. The crucial difference can be found in explanatory ability. Science is capable of explaining its solutions, providing a scientific answer—not an educated guess—to the "Why?" question (Hempel, 1965; Saariluoma, 1997). Modern user psychology, as we see it, must be explanatory and not intuitive or merely modeling. It answers questions with known and tested scientific laws, principles, or facts.

Take, for example, the question regarding why pop-ups are so disturbing to Internet users. Plausible explanatory answers could be because pop-ups cause an orientation reaction or because they interrupt the main task (Oulasvirta, 2006, for interruption; Posner, 1980, for orientation). Thus, an orientation reaction is a simple explanation, but it also provides the solid empirical understanding, analysis, and testing for what happens to users when they encounter pop-ups.

That user psychological design should be explanatory (Saariluoma, 2005a,b) is not a dramatic demand because design, in modern engineering practice, is always explanatory. Engineering design science begins quite straightforwardly with the idea that engineering must be based on the natural sciences and experimental knowledge (Pahl, Beitz, Feldhusen, & Groete, 2005, p. 1).

When an engineer designs a machine, he or she must take into account a number of natural laws. It is necessary, for example, to factor in the strength of the materials and the reliability of the construction (Pahl et al., 2005). Such rules of thumb as "if the designer is uncertain, let's put twice the amount of steel to make the construction secure" do not belong to the today's engineering. Nevertheless, such explanatory design practices in interaction design are seldom apparent. The argumentation is mostly folk psychological and excludes any deeper understanding of the human mentality. An exception is computational modeling, which seeks to apply basic cognitive properties in design processes (Card et al., 1983).

However, modeling and cognitive psychology offer only a partial solution to the problems of explanatory design. The demands of user understanding have gone beyond the limits of cognitive concepts: Cognitive concepts and theories cannot provide complete answers to all type of interaction problems. It is necessary to develop explanatory practices or frameworks from what is known about other dimensions of human mentality. Therefore, human dynamic and sociocultural properties are becoming increasingly more important (Saariluoma, 2005a,b).

The only way to bring user psychological design to the level of normal engineering design is to move to explanatory design practices and put aside folk psychological design paradigms. This does not necessarily mean that all intuitive elements should be rejected in interaction design: They have not been eliminated from engineering design practices either. There is always room for creative thinking; but even within creativity, interaction designers should be capable of explaining their key solutions based on scientific grounds and their standard design solutions should rest upon scientific grounds.

The development of modern technology sets new demands for the psychological analysis of users. For example, with the numerous variety of technologies and services available in the market, prospective users must be introduced to and then learn to like the technology or service. In the Web service world, or perhaps the area of home electronics, the dynamic dimensions of the human mind shall undoubtedly play a bigger role. It is not sufficient that people understand how to use a new device or service, but they also have to like it and be motivated to use it (Parkkola, 2006b).

The versatility of user psychological problems requires that the variety of problems be resolved through an array of concepts, theories, and methods. Within scientific psychology, the main areas provide different perspectives on interaction. There is no unified psychological point of view on interaction; one may investigate it through either cognitive or socioemotional terms. The "right" way of looking at a problem depends on the nature of the problem.

Very few psychologically relevant issues would be unimportant in modern user psychological analyses (Saariluoma, 2004). On par with the traditional cognitive analyses of attention, memory, learning, and thinking are emotions and motives (Norman, 2004; Saariluoma, 2004, 2005a,b). Even apparently unrelated areas, such as culture (Calhoun, Teng, & Cheon, 2002), personality (Caprara, Barbaranelli, & Guido, 2001), or family communication (Latvala, 2006; Parkkola, 2006a; Parkkola et al., in press; Pulkkinen, 2000), should not be overlooked.

Today, the most advanced user understanding has been reached in the field of cognitive processes. Perception, attention, memory, as well as motor process, have been extensively studied for the last 25 years (e.g., Baddeley, 1997; Styles, 2005). That is why this knowledge can be extensively applied in interaction research (see e.g., Helander et al., 1997). However, we still know relatively little about some very important cognitive structures in use contexts, such as models and thinking (see, however, Payne, 2003).

Cognitive psychology has been under intensive research, but many other fields are largely neglected. Emotions, for instance, are the internal system that defines the importance of a matter to a person and plays a vital role in issues such as the pleasantness of use, acceptance, and purchasing decisions (Norman, 2004; Power & Dalgleish, 1997). Paradoxically, while it is very common to speak about user needs in folk psychology, what is actually presented often has little to do with human needs in a psychological sense. It would be more accurate, then, to analyze user motives when investigating, for example, why some people use a specific technology and others do not. This knowledge would elaborate important questions such as how people attach themselves to brands and products, and how to segment user groups.

The concept of group is also important in user psychological thinking. Designers may address how to make mobile social software and other group tools efficiently, based on what is known about group processes or how various cultures differ in adopting ICT. A typical example of a group-based field would be family communication services, which are under development and design (e.g., Latvala, 2006; Parkkola, 2006a; Pulkkinen, 2000).

User psychology can thus be organized around different "language games," depending on the nature of the design problem. Problems are bound to

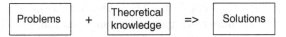

Fig. 1 The explanatory framework has three major components: the usability problem, relevant theoretical knowledge, and the derived interaction solutions

respective fields of psychology. The combination of a problem, a respective psychological theory basis, and a solution model can be called the *explanatory framework* (Fig. 1). One of the leading ideas in user psychology is explanatory design, and this is based on explanatory frameworks (Saariluoma, 2004).

User psychology has its specific perspective on human–technology interaction. It focuses on users, and on the psychological preconditions of their behaviors and actions. This means that user psychology may question the role of some psychological construct in interaction, rather than studying the uses of the devices. Typical examples of user psychology are the analysis of the role of long-term working memory during interruptions (Oulasvirta & Saariluoma, 2004, 2006) or the investigation of visual information chunking in spreadsheet interaction (Saariluoma & Sajaniemi 1989, 1991, 1994). In these examples, the focus is not on any specific device but on the possible roles of psychological mechanisms in the person's interaction with a device.

5 Ontology as a Tool

Though explanatory frameworks provide a rational basis for solving user psychological problems in design, an important gap in linking it with technological development still exists. This reflects the difficulty in mediating psychological knowledge to technical designers. Psychologists seldom are specialists in information systems and designers are normally not deeply involved with the theories of modern psychology and the empirical evidence backing them. The differences between technical and human research traditions have commonly made it difficult to mediate knowledge from one group to another (Snow, 1959). This serious gap in the shared knowledge, concepts systems, and vocabulary of psychologists and designers, and the difficulty in finding common ground for communication, may explain why the application of psychological analysis has been so rare in practical design (cf. Carroll, 1997).

One way of solving the communication difficulties could be the effective use of ontologies in design. Ontologies traditionally have been used to communicate between organizational groups. Design ontologies are information systems referring to objects, actions, and events that are relevant in guiding and controlling the design process. Ontologies can be defined many ways, but the above definition seems to capture much of the essence of these constructs (Borst, Akkermans, & Top, 1997). The main property of ontologies is that they describe the contents of their references (Chandrasekaran, Josephson, &

Bejamins, 1999; see also Leppänen, 2005). Ontologies provide a means for systematizing and transferring organizational information, as well as the tools for collaborative design and the use of everyday knowledge in organizations (Grueninger, Atefi, & Fox, 2000; Leppänen, 2005). This suggests that ontologies might provide a practical tool for mediating knowledge between human-driven and technical design processes.

In order to enable the effective use of ontologies for mediating knowledge from user psychological work to practical design, it is essential to find out what determines the most essential attributes of such ontologies. There are numerous alternatives available with varying conceptual grounds. Chandrasekaran et al. (1999), for example, present four variant ontologies that are based on the notion of *thing*. Two elementary concepts, living and nonliving, can be used. Sowa (1984) speaks of concrete, process, object, and abstract. Borst et al. (1997) present an analysis of mechanism, in which they first give three major attributes: connectivity, effort, and domain. Subsequently, they give different values to these attributes.

The presented variants are only examples (see Leppänen, 2005, for an extensive overview of existing solutions). The crucial problem is to find effective ground concepts. Chandrasekaran et al. (1999) provide, for example, a good ontology for engineering purposes but, in interaction situations, human dimensions are more important than in engineering design. Therefore, it is necessary to look for a basic concept that is essentially human. Because people use technology to support their actions, action would be a logical basic concept for technology design.

6 Action-Oriented Thinking in Design

In order to understand what designing for human actions means, it is necessary to have a general idea about the structure of human action. This means defining the ontology of action and the attributes in that ontology. In practical design, such a structural analysis of action helps in designing the requirements for the technology under development. A general action ontology may help in defining both what is similar in actions and what is different between them. This is essential for distinguishing between separate actions and in guiding the technological design. There are numerous ways of building ontologies for action. This particular one has been inspired by Parsons (1949), but does not follow his thinking in detail. The main ontological attributes used here are: intention, interest, object, instrument, actor, context, and subaction (Fig. 2).

All actions have goals, or, when mentally represented, the goal is expressed as *intention* and *interest* (Brentano, 1874/1973). Actions are always carried out for some reason. We sing to achieve personal satisfaction, we go to the shop to buy food, we call our parents for support or information, and we fish for fun or as a profession. In any case, what we do is defined by the future expectations

Fig. 2 Action ontology.
This ontology expresses the
main attributes of action.
They may be all or partly
used in analyzing the highest
level of actions

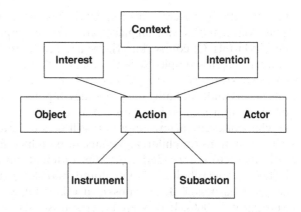

underlying our action. A category akin to intention is interest, which defines emotional and motivational aspects of intention. In the end, intentions and interest define why people do what they do.

The analysis of these two ontological attributes of action must be psychologically reliable. Psychological reliability means that it is not sufficient to define only the cognitive goal, but the needs and motives associated with intentions must be described as well (Heckhausen, 1991). A psychological analysis of what the intentions and interest are in a particular case and an explanation why people have the intentions and interest they have must be provided.

Intention thus defines the rational goal of people. Without knowledge about users' goals, researchers are unable to define what users do. However, human actions also have emotional dimensions. Emotions are not necessarily as articulable as the cognitive aspects of human behavior but they are more influential with respect to the lines of action actually chosen. We direct ourselves to pleasurable goals. Of course, these goals may be distant and the path toward them may be full of difficulties, but emotional aspects of the goals remain highly important when explaining what people do (Abele-Brehm & Gendolla, 2000; Lazarus & Lazarus, 1994; Power & Dalgleish, 1997). Understanding the emotional nature of an action is essential for describing the motivation behind the intention. Therefore, interests must be analyzed, and not only the intentions.

Actions are targeted at some *object*. It may be a piece of knowledge (e.g., the time when mother comes home) or something more concrete, such as a product or service (e.g., feeding the baby or having clean clothes). In analyzing an action, it is essential to understand the object of that action because the object is crucially important in forming intentions and interests, as well as in understanding the ways people attempt to reach it. Furthermore, mental or spiritual objects are often pursued in a different manner than physical objects. In any case, analyzing the object of an action is a necessary condition for fully understanding an action.

As mentioned earlier, people use technologies as an *instrument* to support their actions and achieve their goals. Technologies are among the physical instruments. However, an instrument can also be some mental means to reach a goal. Mathematics and language are good examples of mental rather than physical tools. Of course, knowledge and information systems are very important instruments people use in completing their actions.

The next step is to clearly define the actual *actors* or agents. In user contexts, this means understanding the properties of potential users. Thus, in the action-oriented approach, this means defining who the actors are and what their psychological characteristics are. It will be a different task to design communication actions for children, parents, or grandparents.

If the actors are elderly, or from different cultures, the defining should include geropsychological or cultural knowledge in the description of the actors (Charness & Jastrzembski, in this volume; Craik & Salthouse, 2000: Matsumoto, 2000). If they are experts, it is essential to use the knowledge of the psychological characteristics of expertise to describe these actors (Ericsson, 2006; Ericsson & Lehman, 1996). People of different ages also have varying cognitive and physical capabilities, and that must be defined in an action ontology.

Actions always take place in some *context,* with psychological, social, and physical contexts the most significant. The social context involves other people and the way they are organized within the particular action. The social context may be formed by one's friends and family but it also may be some formal organization with precisely defined norms and rules of acting. A valid description of action presupposes an accurate description of the social context. In the family context, for example, it is necessary to consider who the actors of the family are, what kinds of relationship they have, and what other people or institutions influence daily family life.

The physical environment is equally important. Many of the physical contexts may be random, such as the place a mobile phone call is made, while others may be task specific, like the place for laundering. It is important to make models of the technical environment. In practice, these models are often prototypical technologies or interaction models. However, if an action is being designed that is not yet bound to a technology, technical attributes are not needed in the description of the environment. It may be that we are interested in designing a communication service for parents and 6-year-old children who move about in the neighborhood. We then need to have an understanding of the needs of both the parents and the children regarding possible weather conditions or activities in the playground area, but any idea about the technical capabilities of the services are not yet required.

The next attribute of human action that must be included in a cognitive scientifically and psychologically reliable description of action is a description of the *subactions* or action units (Pink & Stone, 2004). To call her child, a mother needs to define to whom she wants to be connected, open the connection, relate the message, and close the connection. This rather simple interaction requires considerable user knowledge of the subactions before attaining a sufficient understanding of the action as a whole. For example, it is necessary to consider how people designate various recipients of an action and how many potential recipients there might be. The analysis of the subactions is often difficult because many subactions have subconscious elements. None of us knows, for example, how many action recipients there might be in our life and how to differentiate between them if they have the same kind of identifiers used during connections.

The essential aspect of the current approach is that the attributes are explicated in scientific psychological terms. Instead of folk psychologically formulating overall action scenarios, it is essential to explicate and analyze each component of action as scientific psychological concepts and investigate them with psychological methods. This feature separates scientific analysis of actions from traditional intuitive and modern psychological design.

7 From Psychological Analysis to Action-Oriented Design Process

User modeling cannot be an art for the sake of art: It is done to improve design practices. In action-oriented design, an analysis of action is used to design new technologies or redesign actions. Therefore, a designer must define, in a new way, the attributes of the action under design. The list of action attributes posited in Fig. 2 provides a guide for this kind of design activity. However, many additional action attributes have not been discussed here.

Action-oriented design is a constructive activity that is, in some sense, comparable to machine design, and thus the designer is actually a constructor. An action-oriented designer may spend time eliminating unnecessary features in actions, thereby simplifying them. However, the most obvious difference between action design and traditional machine design is in their scientific bases. While machine design relies on the laws of nature, action-oriented design must rely on areas of human research such as cognitive science, psychology or sociology.

When thinking carefully about traditional simulative psychology and its models of the human mind, it is obvious the authors had some engineering ideals in their minds. Card et al. (1983) developed a number of important cognitive concepts that described users' minds in mathematical terms. This was an important kernel of interest. It may indeed be possible to reach stricter design practices to facilitate some elementary means of predicting human behavior in interaction situations. Models provide a strong sign of the reachability of this goal. The main challenge is undoubtedly that the cognitive language of psychology does not have expressive power sufficient for many of the vital issues of humans, such as emotions, personality, and group behaviors.

Saariluoma (2005a,b) called interaction design that relies on the laws and principles of psychology, or any other problem-relevant science, explanatory or argumentative design. This means that design solutions are based on scientific knowledge instead of the intuitive experiences of designers. To obtain such knowledge for designing actions, one needs to rely on user psychological knowledge and research. The crucial difference between intuitive design and explanatory design is easy to understand: It is hidden in the way design decisions are made. No scientific knowledge or arguments are used in intuitive design.

Today, we are far from the ideal in scientific design through which we could predict how people carry out actions. This is why we must often rely only on testing. Such a predictive and explanatory way of designing, which is the practice in machine engineering, cannot be found currently in designing actions, even though there is no logical obstacle to this. The development of new design practice depends on the level of user psychological understanding within ICT-action environments, and the efficiency of the design activity is dependent on the way user psychological knowledge can be associated with the action analysis and construction.

In the movement toward action-oriented design, it should be no surprise that some level of intuition remains, since highly sophisticated design environments such as machine engineering have their intuitive residuals. Nevertheless, no significant obstacle prevents researchers from using design science effectively.

A brief practical example from the academic world might clarify here. Some years ago, one of the authors had to design a multidisciplinary e-learning network, named Connet, which involved seven universities. Of course, several action design problems exist in such a network. One of the most challenging was to organize teaching in such a way so that students with quite distinct academic backgrounds, from philosophy to engineering and programming, could equally participate in the network. At this stage, the major problem concerned how to organize teaching, not which technology should be used. The solution was generated through problem-based learning because each of the students could, in this manner, contribute to the common discussion about products and other relevant things. Since problem-based learning has a solid theoretical grounding, one might think that the design decision was explanatory. However, the technology for keeping contact and communicating between and among the universities and groups, located geographically several hundred kilometers from each another, was solved later, long after the needs of the people and the groups' issues were explored. This example illustrates in a simple form what action-oriented design means. It means recognizing the actions and their attributes prior to designing the tools (e.g., ICTs) for the environment. Action-oriented design can be an activity completely independent of the technical design; it is not necessary to involve any technology in designing actions.

The actual design process is also organized around the action models. This means that the designers first define the attributes of action needed for describing it. At the same time, they should look for psychological knowledge that can provide a scientific backbone for the designed action, thus making it scientifically grounded and explanatorily argued. In the end, this practice associated with intensive user psychological research should lead to less intuitive action design in ICT interaction design. Such processes are necessary, considering the increasing speed at which potential new technologies are created.

The next step in using the concept of ontologies in technology design should be the comparison of different theories of ontologies and testing their suitability for technology design. In addition, more practical instructions for the use of ontologies in design are needed.

References

Abele-Brehm, A. E., & Gendolla, G. H. E. (2000). Motivation and emotion. In J. H. Otto, H. A. Euler, & H. Mandl (Eds.), *Emotionspsychologie* (pp. 297–305). Weinheim, Switzerland: Beltz.

Adelson, B. (1981). Problem-solving and the development of abstract categories in programming languages. *Memory and Cognition, 9*, 422–433.

Anderson, J. R., Farrell, R., & Sauers, R. (1984). Learning to program LISP. *Cognitive Science, 8*, 87–129.

Anderson, J. R., & Jeffries, R. (1985). Novice LISP errors: Undetected losses of information from working memory. *Human-Computer Interaction, 1*, 107–131.

Anderson, J. R., Matessa, M., & Lebiere, C. (1997). ACT-R: A theory of higher level cognition and its relation to visual attention. *Human-Computer Interaction, 12*, 439–462.

Baddeley, A. D. (1997). *Human memory.* Hove, UK: Psychology Press.

Beyer, H., & Holtzblatt, K. (1998). Contextual design: A customer-centered approach to system design. San Diego, CA: Academic Press.

Boehm, B. (1988). A spiral model of software development and enhancement. *IEEE Computer, 21*, 61–72.

Boring, E. (1950). *A history of experimental psychology.* New York: Appleton-Century-Crofts.

Borst, P., Akkermans, H., & Top, J. (1997). Engineering ontologies. *International Journal of Human-Computer Studies, 46*, 365–406.

Brentano, F. (1973). *Psychologie vom empirischen Standpunkt* [Psychology from an empirical point of view]. Hamburg, Germany: Felix Meiner. (Original work published in 1874)

Calhoun, K. J., Teng, J. T., & Cheon, M. (2002). Impact of national culture on information technology usage behaviour: An exploratory study of decision making in Korea and the USA. *Behaviour & Information Technology, 21*, 293–302.

Caprara, G. V., Barbaranelli, C., & Guido, G. (2001). Brand personality: How to make the metaphor fit? *Journal of Economic Psychology, 3*, 377–395.

Card, S., Moran, T., & Newell, A. (1983). *The psychology of human computer interaction.* Hillsdale, NJ: Erlbaum.

Carroll, J. (1997). Human computer interaction: Psychology as science of design. *Annual Review of Psychology, 48*, 61–83.

Carroll, J. M., Thomas, J. C., & Malhotra, A. (1980). Presentation and representation in design problem solving. *British Journal of Psychology, 71*, 143–153.

Chandrasekaran, B., Josephson, J., & Bejamins, V. R. (1999). What are ontologies, and why do we need them? *IEEE Intelligent Systems, 14*, 20–26

Craick, F., & Salthouse, T. (2000). *The handbook of aging and cognition.* London: Erlbaum.

Dahl, O. J., Dijkstra, E. W., & Hoare, C. A. (1972). *Structured programming.* New York: Academic Press.

Ericsson, K. A. (2006). *The Cambridge handbook of expertise and expert performance.* Cambridge, UK: University Press.

Ericsson, K. A., & Lehman, A. (1996). Experts' performance. *Annual Review of Psychology, 47*, 273–305.

Floyd, C. (1984). A systematic look at prototyping. In R. Budde, L. Kuhlenkam, L. Mathiassen, & H. Zullighoven (Eds.), *Approaches to prototyping* (pp. 1–18). Berlin, Germany: Springer-Verlag.

Grueninger, M., Atefi K., & Fox, M. S. (2000). Ontologies to support process integration in enterprise engineering. *Computational and Mathematical Organization Theory*, 6(4), 381–394.

Heckhausen, H. (1991). *Motivation and action*. Berlin, Germany: Springer.

Helander, M., Landauer, T., & Prabhu, P. (Eds.). (1997). *Handbook of human-computer interaction*. Amsterdam: North-Holland.

Hempel, C. G. (1965). *Aspects of scientific explanation and other essays in the philosophy of science*. New York: Free Press.

Hoves, A., & Young, R. (1997). The role of cognitive architecture in modelling the user: Soar's learning mechanisms. *Human-Computer Interaction*, 4, 311–343.

Jarke, M. (1999). Scenarios for modeling. *Communications of the ACM*, 42, 47–48.

Kämäräinen, A., & Saariluoma, P. (2007). Under-use of mobile services: How advertising space is used. In V. Evers, C. Sturm, M. A. Moreno Rocha, E. C. Martínez, & T. Mandl (Eds.), *Designing for Global Markets 8* [Proceedings of the Eighth International Workshop on Internationalization of Products and Systems; pp. 19–29]. Rochester, NY: Product & Systems Internationalization, Inc.

Kieras, D., & Meyer, D. (1997). An overview of the EPIC architecture for cognition and performance with application to human-computer interaction. *Human-Computer Interaction, 12*, 391–438.

Knittle, D., Ruth, S., & Patton Gardner, E. (1986). Establishing user-centered criteria for information systems: A software ergonomics perspective. *Information & Management, 11*, 163–172.

Latvala, J.-M. (2006). *Digitaalisen kommunikaatiosovelluksen kehittäminen kodin ja koulun vuorovaikutuksen edistämiseksi* [Development of a digital communication system to facilitate interaction between home and school]. Doctoral dissertation [Jyväskylä Studies in Education, Psychology and Social Research, No. 292]. Jyväskylä, Finland: University of Jyväskylä.

Lazarus, R. S., & Lazarus, B. N. (1994). *Passion & reason: Making sense of our emotions*. Oxford, UK: Oxford University Press.

Leppänen, M. (2005). *An ontological framework and a methodical skeleton for method engineering: A contextual approach*. Jyväskylä, Finland: University of Jyväskylä Press.

Matsumoto, D. (2000). *Cultural psychology*. Stanford, CA: Wadsworth.

Mayhew, D. (1999). *The usability engineering lifecycle: A practitioner's handbook for user interface design*. San Francisco: Morgan Kaufmann Publishers.

McKeithen, K. B., Reitman, J. S., Reuter, H. H., & Hirtle, S. (1981). Knowledge organization and skill differences in computer programmers. *Cognitive Psychology, 13*, 307–325.

Moran, T. (1981). An applied psychology of the user. *Computing Surveys, 13*, 1–11.

Nielsen, J. (1993). *Usability engineering*. Boston: Academic Press.

Norman, D. (2004). *Emotional design: Why we love (or hate) everyday things*. New York: Basic Books.

Olson, G. M., & Olson, J. S. (2003). Human-computer interaction: Psychological aspects of the human use of computing. *Annual Review of Psychology, 54*, 491–516.

Oulasvirta, A. (2006). *Studies of working memory in interrupted human-computer interaction*. Doctoral dissertation (Department of Psychology Rep. No. 38). University of Helsinki, Finland.

Oulasvirta, A., & Saariluoma, P. (2004). Long-term working memory and interrupting messages in human–computer interaction. *Behaviour & Information Technology, 23*, 53–64.

Oulasvirta, A., & Saariluoma, P. (2006). Surviving task interruptions: Investigating the implications of long term working memory theory. *International Journal of Human Computer Studies, 64*, 53–64.

Pahl, G., Beitz, W., Feldhusen, J., & Groete, K. (2005). *Konstruktionslehre* [Engineering design]. Berlin, Germany: Springer.

Parkkola, H. (2003, November). *Observations about the use of technologies in family communication*. Paper presented at the Social and Cultural Dimensions of Technological Development Symposium, Jyväskylä, Finland. Available at http://www.cc.jyu.fi/~hanpark/ publications/Obsuse.pdf

Parkkola, H. (2006a). *Designing ICT for mothers*. Unpublished doctoral dissertation, University of Jyväskylä, Finland.

Parkkola, H. (2006b). What do mothers demand from information and communication technologies? In J. Multisilta & H. Haaparanta (Eds.), *Proceedings of the Workshop on Human Centered Technology* (Porin Yksikkö, Julkaisu 6, pp. 143–151). Pori, Finland: Tampereen teknillinen yliopisto.

Parkkola, H., Saariluoma, P., & Berki, E. (in press). Action oriented classification of families' information and communication actions: Exploring mothers' viewpoints. *Behaviour & Information Technology*.

Parsons, T. (1949). *The structure of social action*. New York: Free Press.

Payne, S. (2003). Mental models: The very ideas. In J. Carroll (Ed.), *Models, theories and frameworks* (pp. 135–154). San Francisco: Morgan Kaufman.

Pennington, N. (1987). Stimulus structures and mental representations in expert comprehension of computer programs. *Cognitive Psychology, 19*, 295–341.

Pink, T., & Stone, M. (2004). *The will and human action*. London: Routledge.

Posner, M. (1980). Orienting of attention. *Quarterly Journal of Psychology, 32*, 3–25.

Power, M., & Dalgleish, T. (1997). *Cognition and emotion: From order to disorder*. Hove, UK: Psychology Press.

Pulkkinen, L. (2000, May). *Life-span perspective on human-centered technology*. Presentation made at the Thematic Seminar and Demonstration on Human Centered Technology organized by the Jyväskylä Region, Finland, Brussels, Belgium.

Rosson, M. B., & Carroll, J. M. (2002). *Usability engineering: Scenario-based development of human-computer interaction*. San Francisco: Morgan-Kaufmann.

Royce, W. W. (1987). Managing the development of large software systems: Concepts and techniques. In *Proceedings of the 9th International Conference on Software Engineering* (pp. 328–338). Los Alamitos, CA: IEEE Computer Society Press.

Saariluoma, P. (1997). *Foundational analysis: Presuppositions in experimental psychology*. London: Routledge.

Saariluoma, P. (2004). *Käyttäjäpsykologia* [User psychology]. Porvoo, Finland: WSOY.

Saariluoma P. (2005a). Explanatory frameworks for interaction design. In A. Pirhonen, H. Isomäki, C. Roast, & P. Saariluoma (Eds.), *Future interaction design* (pp. 67–82). London, UK: Springer-Verlag.

Saariluoma, P. (2005b). Mitä on käyttäjäpsykologia? [What is user psychology?]. *Psykologia, 40*, 181–186.

Saariluoma, P., & Sajaniemi, J. (1989). Visual information chunking in spreadsheet calculation. *International Journal of Man-Machine Studies, 30*(5), 475–488.

Saariluoma, P., & Sajaniemi, J. (1991). Extracting implicit tree structures in spreadsheet calculation. *Ergonomics, 34*, 1027–1046.

Saariluoma, P., & Sajaniemi, J. (1994). Transforming verbal descriptions into mathematical formulas in spreadsheet calculation. *International Journal of Human-Computer Studies, 41*, 915–948.

Shneiderman, B. (1976). Exploratory experiments in programmer behavior. *International Journal of Computer and Information Sciences, 5*, 123–143.

Snow, C. P. (1959). *Two cultures and the scientific revolution*. Cambridge, UK: Cambridge University Press.

Sowa, J. (1984). *Conceptual structures*. Boston: Addison-Wesley.

Stich, S. (1983). *From folk psychology to cognitive science: A case against belief*. Cambridge, MA: MIT Press.

Styles, E. (2005). *Attention, perception and memory*. Hove, UK: Psychology Press.

Tollmar, K., & Persson, J. (2002). Understanding remote presence. In *Proceedings of the Second Nordic Conference on Human-Computer Interaction* (pp. 41–50). New York: ACM Press.

Torgny, O. (1998). Future home environments and media forms. Centre for User Oriented IT Design, Royal Institute of Technology (Report TRITA-NA-D9808, CID-35). Stockholm, Sweden: CID. Retrieved October 12, 2006, from http://cid.nada.kth.se/pdf/cid_35.pdf

Whiteside, J., Bennett, J., & Holtzblatt, K. (1988). Usability engineering: Our experience and evolution. In M. Helander (Ed.), *Handbook of human computer interaction* (pp. 791–817). Amsterdam: Elsevier.

Field Experiments in HCI: Promises and Challenges

Antti Oulasvirta

Abstract Experimental methods have been under criticism since the advent of mobile and ubiquitous technologies, due to clear limitations in their suitability for studies in the field. However, the laboratory paradigm cannot be directly transferred to field conditions because of its strict notions of experimentation. This chapter examines the theory of *quasi-experimentation* as an alternative conceptualization of causality, control, and validity. Several threats to experimental validity in field experiments in HCI are discussed. These concerns must be addressed at all levels of experimentation, from the design and execution of a field experiment to analysis of data. Noteworthy also are new technical solutions that have enabled high-fidelity data collection and that generally support endeavors in ensuring validity. If field experimentation is to become the de facto standard of research in human–computer interaction, the methodological core and technical tools must be developed in concert.

1 Introduction

> *Reason must approach nature in order to be taught by it. It must not, however, do so in the character of a pupil who listens to everything that the teacher chooses to say, but of an appointed judge who compels the witness to answer questions which he has himself formulated.*
>
> Immanuel Kant, 1781/1999, *Critique of Pure Reason* (p. xiii)

According to Hacking (1983) and Shadish, Cook, and Campbell (2002), experimental procedures have been invented multiple times in the history of science. They note that Leonardo da Vinci's experiments in the 16th century and Galileo's 1612 treatise on floating bodies are considered landmarks in the natural sciences. In medicine, experimental procedures were employed to evaluate smallpox inoculation in 1721, and in Captain James Lind's studies onboard his ship to discover a

A. Oulasvirta (✉)
Helsinki Institute for Information Technology [HIIT], Helsinki University of Technology and University of Helsinki, Helsinki, Finland
e-mail: antti.oulasvirta@hiit.fi

P. Saariluoma, H. Isomäki (eds.), *Future Interaction Design II*,
DOI 10.1007/978-1-84800-385-9_5, © Springer-Verlag London Limited 2009

cure for scurvy in 1747, as well as in Semmelweiss's 1847 trials to reduce hospital infections. In 1879, Charles Sanders Peirce utilized randomization to investigate the psychophysical question of "just noticeable differences" in weights, and Hermann Ebbinghaus published a set of rigorously controlled experiments on his own memory a few years later in 1885. Statistician Ronald Fisher carried out the first randomized trials in agriculture, publishing the first coherent account of the methodology in 1923. During the 20th century, experimentation consolidated its position as the sine qua non scientific method in many if not most empirical disciplines.

Human–computer interaction is no exception. The early students of human-computer interaction (HCI) were strongly influenced by experimental methods in psychology. Paul M. Fitts (1954), based in Ohio, experimented on target acquisition performance by varying selection conditions, later synthesizing the results in an information-theoretical framework that was dubbed the Fitts' law. Douglas Engelbart's team at Stanford (Engelbart & English, 1988), working in the 1960s, arrived at the conclusion, through a set of experiments, that the computer mouse, which they invented, is an optimal input device for an office information system in comparison to the lightpen and the tablet. The work at Palo Alto Research Center by Stuart Card and colleagues that led to the cognitive model GOMS (Goals, Operators, Methods, and Selection rules) was based on a combination of experimental work and computational modeling (Card, Moran, & Newell, 1983). Finally, the 1990s saw a shift toward experimentation also in evaluation when Jakob Nielsen's (1993, 1995) usability engineering methods gained ground among HCI practitioners.

The argument for experimental methods in HCI has been the same as in experimental research in general—increased power in disentangling causal relationships from mere incidental occurrences. Experiments help illuminate complex chains of causal links, help distinguish between the validity of competing explanatory theories, and reveal descriptive causal relationship between conditions. By the same token, experimental methods have been viewed as central in endeavors other than hypothesis-testing, particularly in evaluation of constructed artifacts.

Even a cursory reading of HCI literature reveals that the paradigm of experimentation has been and still is confined to the laboratory. Recently however, arguments have been put forward that advocate experimenting in the field. Consider the prototypical abstraction of HCI: a user trying to accomplish a task in a command–feedback loop that includes the computer interface. The quintessential analytical constituents of interaction have been (a) the user, (b) the task, and (c) the interactive system. For a researcher perceiving interaction in this manner, there is no real need for conducting field experiments. Compare that framework to use situations of some prototypical ubiquitous and mobile applications: tourists searching for sights in a city with a location-aware map, a group of rally spectators discussing and sharing videos in a group media space, schoolmates messaging via mobile devices and PCs, commuters reading comics and watching TV on their mobile devices, information workers checking e-mail in the backseats of taxis, or joggers sharing music during exercise. Our intuitions tell us that there may be causalities in these situations that cannot be staged or reproduced in the laboratory, such as the geographical plan of the city, the rally event, users' own homes and schools, the train, the taxi trip, or the activity of jogging. To the extent that those have a causal role in interaction, the tripartite model of HCI is imperfect and incomplete, as is the laboratory as a setting for experimenting.

This is by no means a new message for students of HCI. The field of Computer-Supported Cooperative Work grew out of similar frustration when it was realized how prominently people and organizational dispositions feature as causal factors in the use of information systems. Analogous arguments can be found in papers dealing with activity theory (Kuutti, 1996), distributed cognition (Hutchins, 1995), and theory of situated action (Suchman, 1987). The divorce of these areas from HCI was so heated that the methodological premises of "the old" HCI were rejected along with the theoretical one. Controlled experiments still seem rare in these areas.

There are two sufficient conditions for preferring a field study: first, an interest toward a causal agent that operates *external* to the human–computer loop and/or a suspicion thereof, and second, a belief that the causal chain wherein that agent operates cannot be properly reproduced or staged in the laboratory. In other words, field experiments are required when phenomena do not fit in the laboratory or cannot be simply staged there in a convincing manner. It would be nonsensical to conduct a study of typing performance on a mobile device in the field, unless one was interested in the effects of, say, real-world multitasking or lighting conditions. By contrast, valid evaluations of mobile maps can only be carried out in the field.

Against the backdrop of the success of the laboratory paradigm in HCI, and given its fundamental limitations in the context of newer technologies, it is surprising to note how rare field experiments are in present-day HCI. A metare-view of mobile HCI research methods by Kjeldskov and Graham in 2003 summarized six concerns of researchers related to field studies:

a. Time and/or personnel resources
b. Skills and/or technological competence
c. Control of experimental variables
d. Expensive data collection
e. The presence of researcher changing the phenomenon of interest
f. Observations that do not generalize.

Kjeldskov and Graham conclude that the bias towards building systems limits the development of cumulative knowledge on mobile HCI. Six years later, the situation has not improved significantly. Some systematic field experiments have been built around the experience sampling method (ESM), but this way of data collection has been of limited applicability.

Now one can ask whether this state of affairs is due to insurmountable problems in the foundations of experimental methodology or due to our inability to discover solutions to the specific theoretical and practical barriers that field experimentation faces. History has shown that for a method to be widely adopted, sufficient levels of both theoretical and pragmatic maturity must be attained. The breakthrough of usability engineering practice, for example, was largely due to Nielsen's (1995) work in combining a theory of errors, a method for predicting the sufficient number of users, examples of experimental design, templates for measurements, and guidance for research instrumentation, such as "the usability lab" presented in Fig. 1. The predictive modeling approach suggested in the bold manifesto of Card et al. (1983) never reached comparable popularity, despite the fact that their cognitive user

Fig. 1 Two setups for experimentation in HCI. On the *top*, Jakob Nielsen's (1995) laboratory setup at Sun Microsystems that worked as a model and baseline for many laboratories built around the world in the 1990s. On the *bottom*, one of the first published "mobile usability labs," developed in joint effort between Nokia Research Center and HIIT (Roto et al., 2004)

modeling methodology was advanced, solved many pertinent problems, and it was theoretically coherent. As Hacking (1983) puts it, scientific breakthroughs are often based on a union of speculation and articulation, calculation, and experimentation.

The road leading to a sound basis for field experiments in HCI is undoubtedly rife with pitfalls. The present paper examines the theory of quasi-experimentation by Shadish et al. (2002) as an alternative to the prevailing laboratory experimentation paradigm. Only a very selective examination of their theory is possible here. The selection of the particular issues is based on this author's experiences from close to 20 field studies. The aims are (a) to rethink what experimentation means, (b) to identify threats that are unique in field experiments in HCI, (c) to gather requirements for good experimental practice, and (d) to assess various tools that are available for researchers interested in embarking on field experimenting.

2 Rethinking Experiments as Quasi-Experiments

An Experiment, like every other event that takes place, is natural phenomenon; but in a Scientific Experiment the circumstances are so arranged that the relations between particular set of phenomena may be studied to the best advantage. In designing an Experiment the agents and phenomena to be studied are marked off from all others and regarded as the Field of Investigation.

James Maxwell in 1876 (as cited in Galison, 1987, p. 24)

A causal relationship can be argued to exist if the cause preceded the effect, the cause was related to the effect, and we have no other plausible explanation for the effect other than the cause (Shadish et al., 2002). The "canon of discovery" proposes four general bases for inferring a causality from observations: (a) if observed phenomena have only one factor in common, (b) if observed phenomena are common except for one factor, (c) if a phenomenon changes systematically whenever a certain event takes place, or (d) if a phenomenon is partially produced by known factors and there is only one factor that can produce the remaining part (Nagel, 1979). Consequently, the goal of experimentation is to create conditions, or "mark off a phenomenon," so that a single factor can be attributed as the cause of an observed similarity, difference, change, or amount. If that can be achieved, there are statistical methods for distinguishing differences representing probable "true differences" from mere accidents.

Running an experiment in real-life conditions outside the laboratory, however, almost by definition undercuts experimental control and summons numerous threats to validity of scientific inference. It becomes increasingly difficult, at times even impossible, to eliminate alternative explanations for the treatment. The theory of *quasi-experiments* (Cook & Campbell, 1979) was founded upon the acceptance of the imperfection of field experiments as experiments—the degree of control is limited and should be treated as such.

Having said this, it must be noted that some of these perturbations over which we have limited control can actually be of interest and should be treated not only as confounding factors. Experimentation should not be viewed as driven exclusively by hypothesis-testing. Two other motives for going into the field are (a) to learn about which real-world circumstances actually affect the phenomena at hand, and (b) to assess the robustness of that phenomena in those circumstances. The former goal calls for the ability of the experimenter to gather knowledge about those events and the latter for enough repetitions to be able to sift systematic interactive events from accidental ones. In both cases, the identification and mitigation of confounds is a central task of the experimenter.

The reward of experimenting in the field, improved realism, is achieved only by sacrificing ability to fully control events. The dual dimensions of experimentation—control versus realism—allow us to place types of experiments into an order of increasing realism and decreasing level of experimental control:

1. **Laboratory experiments**.
2. **Analogue experiments** are laboratory experiments that deploy simulations and emulations of real-world conditions to increase the generalizability of results. For example, the 1990s trend of decorating usability laboratories like living rooms can be conceived as an attempt to reproduce aspects of real use situations.
3. **Quasi-experiments** are experiments where an experimental intervention is carried out even while full control over potential causal events cannot be exerted. There can be systematic differences between experimental conditions that hamper the inference of causality to a single cause. For example, one can compare two notification mechanisms in PDAs in terms of perceived load and acceptance (Ho & Intille, 2005).
4. **Natural experiments** are "after the fact" quasi-experiments, where the variation of a causal agent has taken place naturally. An example is an experiment comparing two naturally formed, causally independent user groups in terms of some variable that differ between them—say, comparing adolescents to adults in terms of adoption, appropriation, and perception a mobile messaging service.

Common to all four types of experiments is that they rely on "variation in the treatment, posttreatment measures of outcomes, at least one unit on which observation is made, and a mechanism for inferring what the outcome would have been without treatment—the so-called counterfactual inference against which we infer that the treatment produced an effect that otherwise would not have occurred" (Shadish et al., 2002, p. xvii). An effect is thus the difference between what *did happen* and what *would have happened*. What makes the inference of that difference counterfactual is that the two outcomes cannot take place simultaneously. To mention an example, an intervention experiment calculates the experimental effect by comparing dependent variables in two periods of time—for instance, Period A, use without the system, to Period B, use with the system. The experimenter then compares A and B to find out the impact of the system (for an example in mobile awareness research, see Oulas-virta, Petit, Raento, & Tiitta, 2007). The presumption is that nothing else than the treatment itself distinguishes the two outcomes.

2.1 Control and Validity

The goal for a quasi-experimental scientist is to create approximations for the physically impossible counterfactuals. All experiments are limited and thus all results are limited. The central goal of a quasi-experimenter is to be aware of these limitations and address them properly in the design and analysis of experiments.

These approximations are created by implementing various forms of experimental control. The options for a field experimenter appear almost as plentiful as those of a laboratory researcher. One can consider direct intervention to change the environment, application, materials, or the task. Various forms of preselection concerning the user can be considered, as well as classic forms of inducement, such as changing instruction, feedback, or confederates' behavior. Nevertheless, not all controls can, in practice, be fully implemented in the field. In our field experiments regarding mobile Web (Oulasvirta, Tamminen, Roto, & Kuorelahti, 2005), for instance, it had been difficult to ask participants to relax and not focus on performance, particularly in hurried environments such as railway stations. In the terminology of Shadish et al., 2002, this is called interaction between setting and treatment. There are extraneous events that can produce random variation, interact with the to-be-manipulated variable systematically, and even prevent treatments from taking place.

According to the theory, there are four types of validity of concern to an experimenter (Cook & Campbell, 1979):

1. **Statistical conclusion validity**: Is there a relationship between the manipulated cause and observed effects?
2. **Internal validity**: Given that there is a relationship, is it plausibly causal from one operational variable to another?
3. **Construct validity of putative causes and effects**: Given that the relationship is plausibly causal, what are the particular cause-and-effect constructs involved in the relationship?
4. **External validity**: Given that there is probably a causal relationship from Construct A to Construct B, how generalizable is this relationship across persons, settings, and times?

A chain of logic exists in the order of these types. In order to question internal validity, one must have knowledge of statistical conclusion validity, and in order to question construct validity, one must have knowledge of internal validity and, finally, in order to question external validity, one must have knowledge of construct validity.

2.2 The Challenge for HCI

Given this general approach, it is possible to start charting threats that are particularly severe in HCI and then examine the nature of possible solutions. With a list of validity concerns from Cook and Campbell (1979), one can approach potential problems in HCI quite systematically. Table 1 lists, quite extensively, threats that have conceivable relevance in HCI. The general impression is disheartening: The quirks and foibles of our present-day experimental practices place us detached from any ideals.

Table 1 Potential threats to causal inference in field experiments in HCI. Following Cook & Campbell (1979)

Threats	Examples
1. Statistical conclusion validity	
a. Low statistical power	Random irrelevancies due to "noise" in real-world conditions
b. Violated assumptions of statistical tests	Incorrect tests, e.g., due to non-Gaussian distributions or unbalanced designs
c. Fishing and the error rate problem	Many dependent variables, statistical tests not scaled accordingly
2. Internal validity	
a. History and maturation	User getting tired or equipment accuracy decreased due to component breakage
b. Testing	Learning across trials
c. The reliability of measures	Shaky videotape recordings missing events, the moderator unable to shadow the user
d. The reliability of treatment implementation	Difficulties in properly instructing the subject when outdoors, e.g., due to noise
e. Random irrelevancies in the experimental setting	User meets familiar people when doing a task on the street
3. Construct validity	
a. Inadequate preoperational explication	Defining user experience numerically, e.g., 1–7 in Likert scale
b. Mono-operation bias	All tests run by the same experimenter, whose personality may influence behavior
c. Mono-method bias	Only one measure utilized
d. Instrumentation changes over time	Changes in equipment over trials, e.g., video cameras changing due to breakdown
e. Mortality, differential drop-out rates	Drop-out rate higher in one condition, e.g., due to one interface variation being boring
f. Interactions with selection	One user group benefiting form "a local history", e.g., knowledge of the site of trial
g. Ambiguity about the direction of causal inference	Did environment affect behavior or vice versa?
4. External validity	
a. Interaction of selection and treatment	Compared groups differ in terms of interest toward the piece of technology at hand

Table 1 (continued)

Threats	Examples
b. Interaction of setting and treatment	Results obtained in one setting do not generalize to others
c. Interaction of history and treatment	Results obtained on particular days (e.g., holidays) do not hold
d. Hypothesis guessing	Knowing that 2D map is being compared to 3D map may affect navigation behavior
e. Evaluation apprehension	Trying to do one's best in an expensive field test with nice moderators
f. Experimenter expectancies	The moderator guides users unconsciously through habitual action, e.g., by walking ahead
g. Confounding constructs and levels of constructs	Selecting too extreme age groups for comparisons to understand the effect of age
h. Interaction of different treatments	Claiming that results generalize to conditions where only one treatment is administered
i. Interaction of testing and treatment	ESM questionnaires as a data collection method may trigger more "awareness" in users
j. Restricted generalizability across constructs	One construct telling a different tale than others, e.g., user experience not matching RTs

Locality of results is perhaps the classic issue that arises when discussing external validity in HCI. The problem is that nearly all experiments are highly local but have general aspirations. This problem arises from inevitable differences between the conditions that an experiment creates and those to which the results ought to generalize. This observation takes us to an important point that can be made from the perspective of quasi-experimentation: The debate contrasting laboratory and field experiments is built upon a false question. It is an apriorism to claim that laboratory experiments are "ecologically invalid" and field studies valid only because the former take place indoors and in circumstances controlled by the experiments.

Every experiment creates *boundary conditions* for certain phenomena to occur and those boundary conditions are either common or rare in the real world, independent of the researcher. Thus, ecological validity is a question that must be assessed based on understanding the causal factors affecting the phenomenon of interest. For example, a study of target selection performance with camera phones assumes certain selection distances, target sizes, illumination conditions, and so on, that may or may not affect performance "in the wild." The influence of these factors is an empirical question in itself. However, if these factors are properly taken into account in a laboratory setting, it does indeed have ecological validity. By the same token, nothing guarantees that field experiments have ecological validity. For example, some researchers assume that walking is representative of mobile behavior and stage their field experiments so that users walk predefined routes.

To generalize, the external validity of a field experiment in HCI can be evaluated through analysis of:

- the nature of subject pool
- the nature of information and skills and social factors brought into the experiment
- the nature of using the technological application
- the nature of tasks and materials
- the nature of environment.

Even though threats to external validity often hijack debates about experimentation, there are other threats to validity that may be as important. Among the most pressing is the problem of sound statistical practices in field experiments in HCI. The questions that need solutions include how to deal with missing data, unbalanced designs, various typical confounds, non-Gaussian distributions, and so forth. These concern both statistical testing and experimental design, as the two should go hand in hand. Future work should provide tools, as well as, perhaps, templates for statistical analysis and encouraging examples in the form of successful cases.

Regarding internal validity, low fidelity of data, inadequate control, and confounds are the most arduous challenges. The example given in the next section illustrates how these can be addressed in the design of experiments. Construct validity, the representativeness of the manipulated cause, is often threatened by excess reliance on one data source in HCI, for example relying on a single questionnaire when examining users' acceptance of a system.

The final challenge discussed here is that knowledge of the effects of manipulable variables tells nothing about how and why those effects occur. The theory of quasi-experimentation is clear on the issue that experiments cater to causal descriptives but not causal explanations. As Pawson and Tilley (1997) argue, it is a mistake to treat field studies as "black boxes," to borrow terminology from software testing, that link manipulated variables to observable outcomes. A healthier approach is to construct them as "white boxes," where the researcher can "peek under the hood" to see which causalities produced the observed changes. This necessitates a shift in the mindset of an experimenter to include in the repertoire a more qualitative kind of analysis that targets the understanding of the chain of causal factors leading from the treatment to the observed outcomes.

3 Emerging Tools and Methods

HCI is not tied to any particular procedure of data collection; the field experimenter can use anything from interviews to observations to psychophysiology. One way to classify methods available to a field experimenter is to look at their temporal relationship with interaction.

Methods relying on subjective opinions collected in researcher–informant interactions, such as interviews and questionnaires and diaries, and user-produced materials in forms of photos and video clips, are perhaps the only means to gather information on the construction of meaning as it happened, and as such they are irreplaceable. On the negative side, from the perspective of studying interaction, they can only be administered after or before the moment of interaction that they are about. They rely on the user's account of what happened, and such accounts are known to be prone to biases, distortions, and omissions.

Third-person ethnographic observation methods, such as participant observation and shadowing, by contrast, allow for capturing the actual moments of interaction as they unfold. Consequently, the researcher can be better aware of the nature of data, particularly missing data. The physical presence of a researcher can, however, have some effect on the observed behavior and the nature of this effect is not well understood in HCI. Despite the positive sides, this is perhaps the most expensive way to collect data. As a human observer is collecting the data, the reliability of the measures gives rise to a "human factors" question: How long and how accurately and systematically can the observer collect data and how accurate and reliable are the categorizations?

While these methods are sufficient for most purposes, there are tools emerging that may help overcome some of the associated problems. HCI researchers are in the fortunate position that the technologies they study can be adopted also as methodological tools for collecting data. Moreover, progress in science and technology often go hand in hand. A recent example can be seen in psychology, where the celebrated "Decade of the Brain" would not have been possible without the preceding advancements in applied physics that led to the production of a non-invasive and affordable brain imaging technology, the fMRI (functional Magnetic Resonance Imaging). The fMRI enabled access to the most intimate, unconscious workings of the human brain during psychological experimentation. Similarly, mobile applications themselves have enabled new ways of collecting data.

In the subsections that follow, two such tools—background logging and video camera systems—are reviewed. These tools are similar in that they do not presume the presence of a researcher because a technical device replaces the researcher in the task of data collection. Both also enable capturing interaction as it happens, but with potentially lower costs than by human recorders.

3.1 Desirable Qualities of Data Collection Apparatuses for the Field

General desirable qualities of a data collection apparatus for field experimenting in HCI include the following:

1. **Mobility**: The device moves with the moving user, capturing interaction reliably wherever and whenever it takes place, in both indoor and outdoor contexts of use;

2. **Capture of embodied interaction**: It captures both bodily (physical) and virtual components of command and feedback, as well as environmental events—understood broadly as encompassing social interactions—that may have an influence on those nuances of interaction that are under scrutiny.

These two desired qualities stem from the nature of the interaction with technical systems other than desktop computers, such as mobile and ubiquitous technologies. The three remaining qualities do not concern the phenomena of interest but rather the logic of quasi-experimentation. They are derived from the discussion of threats to experimental validity:

3. **Unobtrusiveness**: The system does not in itself bring about direct or indirect changes to interaction, particularly to those aspects that belong to the field of investigation;
4. **Support for multimethod approach**: It does not limit the researcher to one source of data but rather overcomes "the black box problem" by gathering indices of potential causes to observed events;
5. **Quality control**: It allows the experimenter to be aware of the reliability and fidelity of data captured both during and after the experiment, assisting in answering questions such as what caused missing data, from what situations are data gathered, how reliably the data corresponds to the actual situations they come from, and so forth.

Any single apparatus can only approximate these goals. Generally speaking, it is the goal of methodology developers to push the limit between the possible and the impossible. To illustrate two vastly different kinds of apparatuses that have emerged only recently, this section concludes by examining background logging and video-based observations. Both are powerful examples of applications of wireless technologies. Background logging on a personal mobile device has several advantages: the logging device moves with the user and is able to log everything that takes place on the device itself; it does not necessitate the presence of a researcher and can thus operate on a scale of time not easily viable by other means; it can be combined with other methods such as interviews, and it allows real-time quality control. The second technology, a hybrid multivideo system, has qualities that make it, in some respects, orthogonal to background logging. It is a special system that has to be installed on and worn by a user. It can capture more extensively the aspects of physical interaction and environment, it can be flexibly combined with all sorts of data-gathering methods, and it is less prone to missing data and other threats than is background logging. The downside is that the system itself most probably has an effect on interaction and, because of this, its nature is limited to nonlongitudinal, "one-shot" experiments.

The theory of quasi-experimentation posits that there is nothing in a method or tool per se that would be ecologically invalid, unrealistic, or obtrusive. Rather, these qualities can only be evaluated in the context of an entire experiment where that method is deployed. It is in the concrete setting of an actual experiment where causal powers of the method itself manifest, setting boundary conditions for the validity of inferring causalities between the manipulated cause and the observed effects. It is these boundary conditions that create a gap between "the ought to" and "the actual." Each particular method in turn bears idiosyncratic limitations on what comes to the reliable observation of a given phenomenon. Generally speaking, these dispositions include (a) the extent and content of recordings and, importantly, their relationship to the studied phenomenon, (b) random error and variation inherent in the measurement, and (c) the reliability of executing the method in an experiment. The two tools are evaluated from these perspectives.

3.2 Background Logging in an Intervention Experiment

Smartphones are programmable mobile phones. The other main characteristics are their sensing capabilities, storage capacity, and built-in networking. Moreover, the phone's status as a communication tool should not be forgotten: People carry phones around and use them in the management of social relationships. Another promising feature is its sensing ability. Current devices allow for automatic gathering of the following behavioral data: location, other devices in physical proximity, mobile communications, user's commands and interaction with the device, calendar events, and device state (network coverage, battery level, charger status, alarm clock, silent/audible profile). Figure 2 illustrates what a log of such information looks like.

3.2.1 Example: An Intervention Experiment

To illustrate the use of a smartphone for quasi-experimentation, let us consider the studies reported in Oulasvirta, Petit et al. (2007). The starting point for that series of field experiments was the well-known fact that the success rate of mobile phone calls is relatively low.[1] Recently, the field of HCI has witnessed the emergence of "mobile awareness systems" to mediate real-time cues of other people's current context and undertakings. Importantly, these awareness cues, such as another person's current location or alarm profile, can be used to infer the presence, availability, responsiveness, or interruptibility of that other person. Some have expressed pessimism about whether such inferences would be systematically utilized by the users to reduce the number of failed or interruptive calls. Our aim was to test this idea in a field experiment.

The particular application studied was called ContextContacts (see Oulasvirta, Raento, & Tiitta, 2005, and Raento et al., 2005), which is an awareness

---

[1] In our studies, mirroring statistics gathered in Finland, only 45–75% (average by subject, 15 subjects, 3,969 total call attempts) of calls reached the intended receiver (Oulasvirta, Petit, Raento, & Tiitta, 2007).

Scenario: Sending a short message to a contact to request a call back.

10h51m48s	Open Contact application
10h51m51s	Select the contact (Mika)
10h51m52s	Open the message composer and write the message
10h52m48s	Send the message
10h53m00s	Reception of delivery report
11h30m27s	Incoming call (Mika)
11h30m33s	Answering the call (recording starts)
11h33m59s	End of call

// Interaction log

20040623T105148	To foreground
20040623T105148	Showing contacts
20040623T105151	Items: [Antti 0 0 0]//Mika, loc: Exactum (1:00) 22 11 17// Renaud 0 0 0
20040623T105151	Items: Antti 0 0 0//[Mika, loc: Exactum (1:00) 22 11 17]// Renaud 0 0 0
20040623T105152	Sending SMS to: Mika, loc: Exactum (1:00) 22 11 17
20040623T105152	To background

// Context log

20040623T103507	profile:0 General (0 7 Off)
20040623T103629	area, cell, nw: 19000, 1952, RADIOLINJA
20040623T104620	devices: 0060579a6f70 [Janne] 0002eea07729 [Antti]
20040623T105148	UserActivity: active
20040623T105148	ActiveApp: [101fbad0] contextbook
20040623T105152	ActiveApp: [100058c5] mce
20040623T105248	SMS : sent msg #1053236 to Mika:"Please call me asap!"
20040623T105352	ActiveApp: [100056cf] ScreenSaver
20040623T105552	UserActivity: idle
20040623T113027	app event: STATUS: call
20040623T113027	app event: STATUS: call status 3
20040623T113027	ActiveApp: [100058b3] Phone
20040623T113033	UserActivity: active
20040623T113033	app event: STATUS: call status 4
20040623T113033	app event: STATUS: recording call
20040623T113359	app event: STATUS: recorded

// Communication log

20040623T105248	EVENT ID: 2268 CONTACT: -1 DESCRIPTION: Short message DIRECTION: Outgoing DURATION: 0 NUMBER: +123456789 STATUS: Sent REMOTE: Mika
20040623T105300	EVENT ID: 2269 CONTACT: -1 DESCRIPTION: Short message DIRECTION: Incoming DURATION: 0 NUMBER: +123456789 STATUS: Delivered REMOTE: Mika
20040623T113033	EVENT ID: 2270 CONTACT: -1 DESCRIPTION: Voice call DIRECTION: Incoming DURATION: 207 NUMBER: +123456789 STATUS: REMOTE: Mika

Fig. 2 An illustrative example from ContextLogger's recordings (Raento, Oulasvirta, Petit, & Toivonen, 2005). The ContextLogger records a user's interactions, contexts, and communications

software integrated into the phone book of a smartphone. It presents seven real-time "awareness cues" that are automatically, without user input, transferred and presented within a user group.

An A–B intervention methodology from clinical medicine and clinical psychology was utilized where a baseline of behavior was gathered in a period of time denoted by A, after which the technology ("the treatment") was introduced for period B. In such a study, the effect or impact of the technology under study is defined as observed differences between the two periods. Because technology effects are often slow to emerge and depend on the interplay of social interaction and practice related factors, longitudinal studies are necessary. Three teenager groups participated in the study for a total period of time of 265 days. Throughout that time, ContextLogger was running in the background, recording all available information.

From the studies we gathered 370 MB of raw data, including short recordings from 667 calls, 56,000 movements, 10,000 activations of the phone, 560,000 interaction events with our applications, 29,000 records of nearby devices, and 5,000 instant messages.

Automatic logs of contextual data and interaction covered between 53% and 93% ($M = 73\%$, $SD = 14\%$) of the study period. Reasons for missing data include running out of battery, turning off the phone, as well as faults in the logger software. Yet, this data-gathering method afforded a set of sophisticated high-resolution analyses, such as how often the cues were viewed on the phone, how this access was distributed between different locations such as school and home (as interpreted from location information of ContextLogger), how long the cues were looked at just before placing a call (and after an unsuccessful call), and how these cues referred to locations in the beginnings of phone calls (as manually coded from over 600 phone call recordings).

In the analysis phase, we separated the different variables, such as location, interaction, and proximity, and loaded them into a relational database. Current values of variables could then be queried for any single point in time, allowing them to be correlated with calls, which were our main unit of analysis. The call recordings were used as focal points of interviews, and the recordings, together with interview data, were used to gain a qualitative understanding of the situations represented by the values of observed variables.

Concerning the impact of the awareness system on communication practices, the main findings of that study were as follows: One group exhibited an increase of 12 percentage points in the success rate of within-group phone calls during Period B, when the awareness application was used, and this turned out to be statistically significant. Both groups (to whom we could administer this analysis) looked at the phone book for a significantly longer time just before the phone call (the so-called pre-call delay measure, Fig. 3) during the B period than the A period. The most frequent utilization of the cues was associated with the participants being mobile. Moreover, one user group learned to systematically relate location information at the beginning of their phone calls at a higher level of granularity in Period B than Period A. Objective data like this was in accord with the subjective, postevent interviews with the participants of the study.

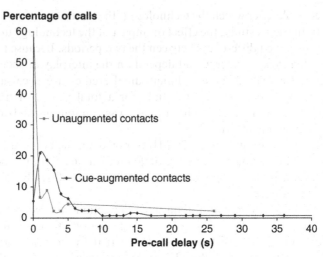

Fig. 3 Distribution of frequencies of pre-call delays in the three trials. Those contacts for whom cues were available were viewed longer just before a call was placed to them

3.2.2 Evaluation[2]

Counterfactual inference of causality in this particular study relied on comparisons between Periods A and B. Such a comparison is based on the ideal that use does not change between or during the periods. This assumption is of course problematic. For example, in one of the groups, the summer holiday took place during Period B, which lowered the frequency of use and changed the nature of communication. Furthermore, users learn and change over the period of the experiment, which should be taken into account in the intervention structure. For example, an A–B does not counter learning effects, and the A–B–A is still prone to accidental effects during Period B. Ideally, one would have several A–B pairs, but this in turn could disrupt the use itself if the period changed too often.

In addition to threats of counterfactual inference, there were other sources of threats to experimental validity stemming from the experimental procedure. One possible biasing factor was posed by the fact that we, that is, the researchers, paid the participants' phone bills, which most likely directed the group's communication to the smartphone and invited them to use the communications more regularly than they would have normally. Nevertheless, not all threats were realized to the extent we were initially afraid of. The teenagers expressed no major technical or usability problems when changing from using their ordinary phones to the smartphones for the period of the study. The studied

---

[2] This section is partly based on the manuscript Raento, M., Oulasvirta, A, & Eagle, N. (in press).

activity itself took place through the phone, so utilizing it as the data collection tool was natural. An alternative to smartphone-based logging would have been paper-based questionnaires or diaries asking the participant to mark how frequently they did something during a period of time.

More generally, smartphones can significantly reduce the costs required to record and log the mundane everyday activities of an informant and does not require an observer to be present in the activities. Improvements in ecological validity should be possible, since the automatic data collection can be done throughout the subject's everyday life and with minimal intrusion. The already available sensors can be used to infer many interesting aspects of an individual's everyday activities, such as movement at the macro level (based on GSM cell IDs), meetings and encounters with identifiable and unidentifiable people (Bluetooth presence), communications (phone calls and SMS), contents and use of contact book and calendar, and audio scenes (microphone recording). The basic sensors can be supplemented, in principle, with more sophisticated ones, such as accelometers and GPS for keeping track of movements at the micro level, physiological sensors for measuring emotions, and body-worn microphones for recording conversations. Analysis of the data can concentrate on individual events or more systematic patterns occurring over time. Depending on the population studied, the analysis can look at emergent patterns at the level of a social group, community, or geographical area. Thus, when applicable, smartphone-based data collection may augment self-report methods, offer in some cases a transition from self-report to observation, and extend the reach of experience-sampling, thus reducing the well-documented threats to validity of methods like diaries, interviews, and questionnaires.

Some of the data sources in phone-based logging are quite noisy. The Bluetooth-based detection of other subjects nearby is inherently stochastic. The absence of a signal in a Bluetooth scan cannot be used as proof that the person in question was not present. Noise per se is a threat only to statistical conclusion validity, given that the introduced noise is random. A more serious problem is caused by various inaccuracies. GSM-cell-based positioning, with city-and-district level tracking, may not give accurate enough location. It is, for example, not accurate enough to distinguish between home and the shop nearby, or an office and the lunch café. These inaccuracies can be systematic and thus should be accounted for in the analysis of data. On the positive side, foreseeable technological advances may help to overcome this problem. For example, we have explored the possibility of augmenting location tracking with Bluetooth beacons set in appropriate locations, and one can entertain combinations with GPS-based as well.

When it comes to the content of data collected and its relation to communication behavior, the subject of study, some limitations are apparent. Studying communication patterns via the mobile phone will give strong insights into a subject's relationships, especially since both the occurrence of communication as well as the content of it can be collected. However, not all communication is through the phone, not even all technologically mediated communication.

E-mail and instant messaging can be used, even, in some relationships, predominantly. If comprehensive studies of communication are to be made, the e-mail and messaging data should be collected as well. It is quite easy to gather the e-mails sent and received by a subject, but detailed knowledge of the context in which a message was read or written may not be possible.

Another threat is posed by patterns in how people carry the phones. Although the phone is carried extensively by the user, it may be left behind by choice or accident. We have shown that detecting such situations is possible when the phone is forgotten for a significant period of time, but becomes considerably harder for short periods, for example, leaving the phone in the office when going for lunch. In general, it should not be assumed in the analysis of the results that all data gathered on the device corresponds to the activities of the user.

Studies conducted with the assistance of technology are of course susceptible to failures of technology. We have experienced faulty data connections, corrupted memory cards, crashing software, and broken phones. The most fragile link is often the data connection, which may be unavailable for days at a time due to failures of the phone software or lack of network coverage. Any study should take into account the possibility that remote real-time observation is not always possible. Even if remote data collection can be unreliable, so can be local collection. Software problems and hardware failure may result in losing locally stored data. In our experience, it is more reliable to gather data remotely, because the duration of a potential failure decreases significantly. If remote collection is not possible, data should be collected from the participants quite frequently, while accounting for the possibility of data loss in the sample size and sampling strategy. The most extensive figures on the reliability of data collection come from the Reality Mining study, where overall collection coverage averaged 85.3% (Eagle & Pentland, 2006).

While mobile phone technology is increasingly familiar to people in the developed world, not all users are comfortable or familiar with smartphones. Many mobile phone subscribers only use the most basic functionality and simple phones. Switching to a more complicated phone, or switching to a different manufacturer's phone, may scare some and will most certainly influence the way they use the device. If the subjects are not familiar with the smartphone, any measurements relying on phone use (communications, self-documentation, interaction logs) from the beginning of the study should be used with care. It is hard to give specific guidance on how long a "settling-down" period should be, but it may well be 1–2 weeks. It may be worthwhile to try to gauge how familiar the users have become with the device. At any rate, individual differences in the ability to use the phone pose a threat to validity, and thus should be addressed at the outset of research.

A problem in the HCI's practice of field evaluation has been the presumption that a single administration of the treatment is enough for evaluation, while in fact it does not allow for valid inference of the counterfactual. Excess reliance on "soft" baselines, the implicit or presumed baseline about the state of affairs as they are thought to be, is undoubtedly an unhealthy practice. The example above has illustrated, if anything, that there is a possibility to perform proper comparisons, even in complex settings with emergent use phenomena. The A–B–A methodology illustrated above shows that it is possible to gather a concrete baseline on which to build the counterfactual inference.

3.3 Hybrid Video System

A few video recording systems have been presented recently for the purpose of studying mobile use of information technology. Most of these systems are based on wearable cameras placed on the users, on the mobile device, or guided by the experimenter. For example, a system by Reichl, Froehlich, Baillie, Schatz, & Dantcheva (2007) mounted a minicamera to a hat worn by the user, capturing the user's eyes, wirelessly sending data to a moderator who carried another camera and the recorder. Lyons and Starner (2001) presented a prototype where cameras and equipment were worn on the user's body, in a vest. Applied Science Laboratories (n.d.) have recently presented a commercially available mobile eye camera. Google (Schusteritsch, Wei, & LaRosa, 2007) uses a system consisting of two cameras on the mobile phone for their studies.

Our earliest attempts in applying video recording systems are described in Roto et al. (2004) and Oulasvirta, Tamminen et al. (2005). Our later version, released in 2007 (Oulasvirta, Estlander, & Nurminen, 2009), contains several improvements to operational capabilities, but also a more qualitative improvement: the ability to switch camera image in real-time between environmental cameras, for example when the user is moving in an office instrumented with cameras. Figure 4 presents the key components. Moreover, the whole setup can be carried on a belt, whereas the previous system required a backpack. Our other goals in developing this new version were (a) to extend the potential recoding time to the length of a working day, (b) to increase the level of independent usage of the system without a moderator, and (c) to make the devices more compact, robust, and versatile.

Special crafting was needed to develop further a research camera holder for a range of mobile devices. The resulting system consists of three parts:

1. Mobile/"wearable" part of the equipment that has

   - one camera holder for fixing equipment to subject's phone
   - one camera for imaging phone UI (to be connected with the holder)
   - one camera for imaging the subject's face and behavior (to be connected with the holder)
   - a "Necklace-camera" for capturing roughly the same view that the subject sees
   - a wireless 2.4 GHz video receiver
   - a video hub, the so-called video quad that gathers all of the video signals from several cameras to one recording device and provides adjustable voltage for the attached cameras.

Fig. 4 Version 2 of Fig. 1's mobile video recording system. Some characteristics: (a) All noncamera equipment except cables fit on a belt and weigh less than 2 kg in total; (b) Feed from the closest environmental camera is integrated into the four-video recording. (c) All video and audio inputs are integrated on the fly to a four-video display; (d) The cameras are flexible, can be worn or attached to the mobile device, and can operate with cables or wirelessly; (e) There is an option for remotely triggered recording events initiated via Bluetooth; (f) Operational duration is up to 4 hours without battery change or other maintenance operations

- a video HDD mpeg4 recorder
- three battery packs
- a leather belt for carrying the devices
- the necessary cables.

2. The semi-fixed part that can be either carried by the experimenter or placed to the environment consists of

- surveillance cameras (3)
- wireless 2.4 GHz video senders (3)
- 110–240 VAC to 12 VDC power adapters (3)
- video statives and fixing equipment for surveillance cameras.

3. Tools for running and preparing the tests and maintaining the set-up

- battery rechargers
- wireless receiver for setting up the environment cameras
- travel cases for the equipment.

Figure 5 presents a diagram of the overall system architecture. To illustrate the use of the system, the following subsection describes a study utilizing it.

Fig. 5 The system architecture of the system in Fig. 4. The system consists of a "core" marked with gray, including the receiver, video hub, and recorder, as well as batteries. All other parts are cameras that can utilize either wireless or cable transfer

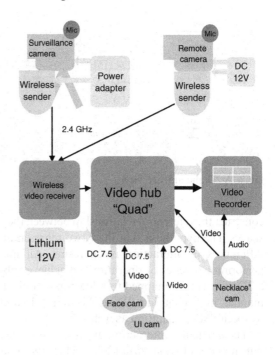

3.3.1 Example: Comparing Types of Mobile Maps[3]

To critically evaluate the system, we have conducted a field experiment following the logic of quasi-experimentation. Previous studies with the system would serve as examples as well (e.g., Oulasvirta, Tamminen et al., 2005), but the one reported here involves the most sophisticated experimental design and apparatus, and the most demanding mobile circumstances.

The starting point for this experiment was an interest in understanding how interaction with mobile maps differs between 2D and 3D representations (see Fig. 6). Using a map is a process involving both mental and physical action, wayfinding, and movement (Darken & Sibert, 1996).

In general, what makes mobile maps distinct from (typical) virtual environments (VEs)—such as virtual reality and desktop-based navigation systems—is that users are actually physically embedded in the world that the virtual model represents. When interacting with a physical environment (PE), shifting of gaze and movement of head and body are emphasized, whereas VEs are typically associated with decreased field of view and low fidelity of landmarks and non-visual cues. This difference is crucial, as it means that users have to mentally

---

[3] The study reported here has been designed and conducted with Sara Estlander and Antti Nurminen (Oulasvirta, Estlander, & Nurminen, in press).

Fig. 6 A 2D and 3D map view

construct the referential relationship between the virtual and physical information spaces. The hypothesis that these two representation types may differ stems from differences in interaction mechanisms: All movement requires maneuvering, performing a series of operations to achieve subgoals. Whereas maneuvering in a 2D view can be mapped to a few input controls in a relatively straightforward manner, movement in a 3D world cannot. In addition to 3D position, one needs to specify 3D orientation as well.

The particular interaction mechanisms of the study are described in detail in Nurminen and Oulasvirta (2008). Here the focus is on the experiment and the role of the video recording system.

To study how users of mobile maps construct the referential relationship between points in the virtual space and in the surrounding physical space, a quasi-experiment was conducted in a city environment. The subjects ($N = 16$) conducted orientation tasks and navigation tasks. Three task types were used, and in each type the target was indicated on the map. First, in the *proximate mapping task*, the target was in view from the current position, and the task was to point to the target in the real world. During preparations before moving into the field, participants were instructed to turn to face in the direction of the target and point towards it with one hand. The instructions shown on the display of the mobile device before each of these tasks was the following: "Point to the target as quickly and accurately as possible." Second, in the *remote orientation task*, the target was not in view from the current position, and the task was to point in the direction of the target in the real world. The instructions for these tasks were identical to those for the proximate mapping tasks. Third, in the *navigation tasks*, the target was not in view from the current position, and the task was to walk to the target. During preparations before moving into the field, participants were instructed to walk to the site of the target marker and stop on the pavement on the correct side of the street. The instructions shown on the display of the mobile device before each navigation task was the following: "Walk to the target as quickly and accurately as possible." Altogether 24 search tasks were performed while traversing a route of 2.4 km in the old city center of Helsinki.

Taken together, there were two main independent variables: (a) Map type: 2D (traditional street map of Helsinki) versus 3D (the three-dimensional model of Helsinki); and (b) Type of task: orientation vs. navigation. In addition, several confounds were addressed in the experimental design:

- Because the misalignment between the target and the initial direction where the user faces affects how quickly the target will be shown, the facing direction was randomized for each subject and each task.
- To minimize the possibility of learning the areas of the 2D map when using the 3D map, and vice versa, there were four loops (A, B, C and D) around at least one block, each with the starting point in the same area. Westerly and easterly loops were separated by a 300-m distance. Half of the subjects performed 2D map tasks in the westerly loops (A and B) and 3D in the easterly loops (C and D), half 2D in the easterly loops and 3D in the westerly loops. Half of the subjects did loop A before B, half B before A, and within these two groups half did C before D and half D before C.
- To eliminate order effects, half of the subjects performed 2D tasks first, and half the 3D first.
- To eliminate effects of time of day, all experiments were conducted during daylight.
- To minimize effects of learning from one task site to another, each task's starting point was at least 50 m from the previous.

The video camera system, combined with other measures, allowed for a rich description of interaction. Five kinds of measures were employed:

1. Performance measures, for example task completion times, number of restarts, number of different types of key presses, and so forth.
2. Subjective workload ratings (here, NASA-TLX).
3. Interaction logs, analyzed with a custom-made visualization and replay software. The first interaction at the beginning of a task automatically started the logging.
4. Video data on users' interaction with the device and movement in the physical environment.
5. Complete verbal protocols during the task and retrospectively after its completion.

The output data, when combined with full transcriptions of verbal protocols, is an extremely rich source for analysis of the research question (see Fig. 7). From the integrated data output, we manually coded the following:

- (User) walking: (a) User starts to walk to another position, "walking" referring to a series of more than four steps; (b) User ends the walk.
- Gaze-shifting behaviors: (a) User looks at the device; face is towards device. Supporting evidence involves fingers pressing keys in Camera 1 and changes in the playback of the interface; (b) User looks forward: face is forward or at a maximum of 45 degrees to the side relative to the body's sagittal axis and a

Fig. 7 An example of output data from the mobile observation system of Fig. 4

maximum of 30 degrees up relative to the body's axial axis; (c) User looks up; face is at least 30 degrees up relative to the body's axial axis; (d) User looks left/right; Face is at least 45 degrees to the left/right relative to the body's sagittal axis, without moving feet.

- Bodily action: (a) User turns around by moving feet; (b) User turns the device; points the mobile device in a direction other than forward, at least 30 degrees.
- Interactive performance: (a) all key-presses and divided per key; (b) total distance traveled per task, in meters (camera in 3D, center crosshairs in 2D); (c) task completion times. Figure 8 illustrates navigation logs taken from the interactive device.

These codings and data were taken to answer a host of questions of interest when comparing 2D and 3D mobile maps, such as:

- How many times per task the subject looks at the device for more than 1½ seconds
- How many times per task the subject looks at the device for less than 1½ seconds
- Percentage of time per task subject looks at the device versus the environment
- Time from the start of task to looking away from device
- Time from the start of navigation task to starting to walk towards the assumed target (walk to check the street sign does not count)
- Whether or not the subject walks at all in orientation tasks (proximate and remote)
- Whether or not the subject starts off in the wrong direction in navigation tasks
- Whether or not the subject chooses a nonoptimal route (not the shortest in terms of turning street corners) in navigation tasks
- Whether or not the subject first walks to the wrong side of the street in the navigation tasks.

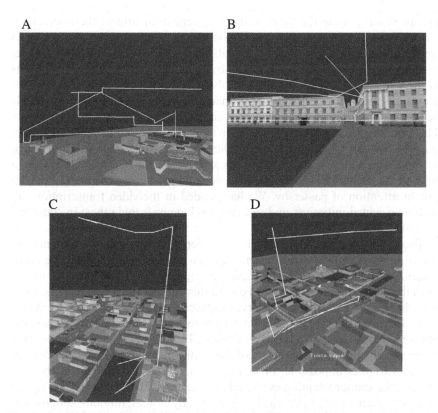

Fig. 8 Visualizations of users' actions from the interactive logs: (**A**) Learning the model by exploring it from a top-down view; (**B**) Walking around in a city square and peeking around corners; (**C**) Diving to street-level; (**D**) Scanning, diving and scanning at multiple levels, and walking around at the street level. Adopted from a previous experiment reported in Oulasvirta, Nurminen, & Nivala (2007)

3.3.2 Evaluation

A critical assessment of the experiment centers on the question of how well it has been able to exclude alternative explanations. In the case of this experiment, the critical counterfactual inference is between the use of 2D and 3D. While the researchers took pains to eliminate and minimize interfering effects from 2D to 3D use, there is no practical way in a within-subject experiment to avoid all interference. Nevertheless, because of the full coding of both physical (bodily) and interactive behavior, we can analyze, *post hoc*, whether users utilizing 2D saw areas that they revisited in 3D to see if these had an effect on the dependent variables.

In addition to the question of whether our implementations of these counter-measures were effective, we have learned about two threats that are of more general importance for all field experiments employing video cameras. First is the question of how the video camera system itself affects the interaction. Several form factors can affect interaction with the studied system: The physical weight of the system may prevent or inhibit certain behaviors and cause fatigue, and the physical form may encumber movement and cause occlusion of objects in the visual field. While our system is based on minicameras weighing a few grams, it was clear nevertheless that it had a negative effect on how the mobile device was in use. The saliency of the camera system itself is a factor, as well. The camera system marks off the user as something extraordinary to other people, and can render the subject aware of receiving attention. Our design attempted to minimize the visibility of cameras, yet the two minicameras on a pole on the mobile device and the presence of a moderator following a person caught attention of passersby. We have coded in the video transcriptions all such unexpected initiatives and can later exclude or include them in statistical analysis.

The second concerns the reliability of video recording as a measurement of subtle motor actions in field experiments. To be able to explain attained outcomes, our analysis of data was based on rigorous manual coding of events from the data, as reported above. Toward this end, we wanted to provide a full record of events leading to an observed outcome, for example, that a 2D map is better or worse than a 3D map in a certain task. In the coding, a problematic phenomenon surfaced: Certain environmental conditions and accidental events hampered the use of one or more of the minicameras, which made coding of certain variables impossible, or at least difficult. Direct sunlight in the face camera, the shutter adapting excessively to large contrasts in camera image, the necklace camera being temporarily obstructed by clothes, random compression artifacts, the experimenter-shot camera forgotten, and rain effectively preventing coding of some of the variables, particularly when the situation affected several cameras at the same times, thus disallowing the use of redundancies across the image sources. According to our analysis, these effects were primarily random and it was not likely that they impacted the experimental variables.

More worrisome were effects that were emphasized when the user was walking. The most significant effect concerns the learning of the experimenter to use the camera in a way that captures the bodily posture and gaze direction even when the user is walking. This requires walking at the same speed and at the same distance one or two steps behind the user to her left or right. When the user is standing, this task is trivial, but when the user is walking, the experimenter has to take care in walking as well, avoiding fellow pedestrians, trying to match the pace of the subject, and so on, and this requires some skill of its own. Despite several hours of practice gathered when administering the trials, some extreme walks were not adequately recorded even toward the end of the experiment.

We are not yet sure how critical this effect was on the quality and extent of missing data, or how to deal with it in the statistical analysis. Nevertheless, this problem was not as accentuated as in our previous experiment, where we could only utilize one camera that was directed by the experimenter.

4 Conclusion

According to Jonathan Grudin (personal communication, April 30, 2007), "the conundrum of HCI" is that to a person with imagination almost anything is possible, yet hard limitations exist that limit the use of technology. The discipline of HCI is therefore destined to work on two fronts: construction of the possible and empirical investigation of the impossible. Empirical work in HCI can therefore be viewed as entailing two intertwined and complementary modes of research:

1. basic studies that aim at producing understanding of phenomena and factors relevant in human–computer interaction, and
2. evaluative studies of constructed prototypes that aim at producing informative and actionable knowledge for "extra-scientific" developers and decision makers.

The common denominator underlying both modes of research has traditionally been the fact that actions and reactions between computers and humans are the focus of a scientist's analysis. In the studies of operators, programmers, managers, secretaries, students, and office workers as users, situational aspects have played a minor role. Events extraneous to the desktop have been presumed or thought to bear only incidental or unsystematic effects, and so it is unnecessary to include them in explanatory frameworks.

During the recent years, since the advent of mobile devices and ubiquitous technologies, this position has become increasingly more untenable. Consider a surgeon orchestrating the operation of a medical team, remotely, through a telepresence system; a tourist trying to locate a museum from a mobile map; a driver, turning the wheel with one hand and simultaneously calling home with the other; a group of teenagers coordinating via SMS where to meet; an information worker trying to synchronize his PDA with his laptop between two meetings; or a spectator browsing a digital pamphlet to decide which event to go and see. All of these examples have in common the fact that situational factors and events have a causal role in the course of events.

Consequently, empirical work in HCI should be able to shift to outside-the-laboratory settings. This challenge has been acknowledged and deemed particularly problematic to experimental methods. It may seem a paradox to suggest a controlled experiment in circumstances that deny full control. Therefore, one has to rethink what is meant by experimentation.

Toward this end, the possibility of utilizing the theory of quasi-experimentation as an alternative approach has been considered within this paper. It calls for marrying the design of experiments with statistical analysis so that both take into account (real) threats such as missing data, unbalanced designs, random error in measurements, difficulties in implementing treatments, and so on. Furthermore, it calls for critical practices in evaluating experiments and reviewing research papers, habitually assessing de facto threats such as low grain of measurements, systematic biases in recordings, and obtrusiveness of the experiment, among others.

On the equipment side, this paper has shown two new potentials, both associated with different threats to validity. Awareness of these problems may help not only in the task of critique but also in the task of constructing better experiments. And indeed, many tasks remain to be done. We need parallel advances in hardware design for apparatuses that enable reliable collection of data, software development for more efficient fusion and visualization of data, statistical methods to deal with typical problems, and pioneers who provide showcases illustrating the approach. While the primary aim is not to improve cost-efficiency but experimental validity, a revolution in the adoption of quasi-experimental methods can only take place if accompanied by "off-the-shelf kits" conceived, packaged, and marketed as products that appeal as worthy investments.

Despite the challenges, vistas for quasi-experimentation appear promising. In one sense, empirical research in HCI was problematized during the last decade when new personal and ubiquitous technologies appeared and demanded a radical shift in methods for empirical investigation. In retrospect, field experimentation did not secure the position it could have had in the toolbox of researchers.

The present paper has put forward a proposition that field experiments should be reconceptualized as quasi-experiments. The weaker form of the new paradigm of experimentation involves mainly more rigorous ways to address various confounds to validity. The stronger implication involves the idea that a central part of fieldwork in HCI, that concerning the evaluation of prototypes, can be rethought, formulated, and analyzed from a quasi-experimental perspective.

Acknowledgments The author wishes to express gratitude to all collaborators, particularly Mika Raento, Sara Estlander, and Tuomo Nyyssönen. Parts of the text on background logging are based on an manuscript written with Mika Raento and Nathan Eagle. This research has been funded jointly by the FP6 EU project PASION (FP6-2004-IST-4-27654) and the Academy of Finland project ContextCues. The camera system described in Fig. 5 has been developed in the PASION project.

References

Applied Science Laboratories. (n.d.). Head Mounted Optics. Retrieved July 30, 2007, from http://www.a-s-l.com/prod-head.htm

Card, S., Moran, T., & Newell, A. (1983). *The psychology of human-computer interaction.* Hillsdale, NJ: Lawrence Erlbaum Associates.

Cook, T., & Campbell, D. (1979). *Quasi-experimentation: Design & analysis issues for field settings.* New York: Houghton Mifflin.

Darken, R., & Sibert, J. (1996). Wayfinding strategies and behaviors in large virtual worlds. In *Proceedings of the SIGCHI Conference on Human Factors in Computing Systems* (CHI '96, pp. 142–149). New York: ACM Press.

Eagle, N., & Pentland, A. (2006). Reality mining: Sensing complex social systems. *Personal and Ubiquitous Computing, 10,* 255–268.

Engelbart, D. C., & English, W. K. (1988). A research center for augmenting human intellect. In I. Greif (Ed.), *Computer-supported cooperative work: A book of readings* (pp. 81–106). San Mateo, CA: Morgan Kaufmann.

Fitts, P. M. (1954). The information capacity of the human motor system in controlling the amplitude of movement. *Journal of Experimental Psychology, 47*(6), 381–391.

Galison, P. (1987). *How experiments end.* Chicago: University of Chicago Press.

Hacking, I. (1983). *Representing and intervening: Introductory topics in the philosophy of natural science.* Cambridge, UK: Cambridge University Press.

Ho, J., & Intille, S. (2005). Using context-aware computing to reduce the perceived burden of interruptions from mobile devices. In *Proceedings of the SIGCHI Conference on Human Factors in Computing Systems* (CHI '05, pp. 909–918). New York: ACM Press.

Hutchins, E. (1995). *Cognition in the wild.* Cambridge, MA: MIT Press.

Kant, I. (1999). *Critique of pure reason.* Cambridge, UK: Cambridge University Press. (Original work published in 1781).

Kjeldskov J., & Graham, C. (2003). A review of mobile HCI research methods. In *Proceedings of Mobile HCI 2003* (MobileHCI '03, pp. 317–335). London, UK: Springer-Verlag.

Kuutti, K. (1996). Activity theory as a potential framework for human-computer interaction research. In B. Nardi (Ed.), *Context and consciousness: Activity theory and human-computer interaction* (pp. 17–44). Cambridge, MA: MIT Press.

Lyons, K., & Starner, T. (2001). Mobile capture for wearable computer usability testing. In *Proceedings of IEEE International Symposium on Wearable Computing* (ISWC 2001, pp. 69–76). Los Alamitos, CA: IEEE Computer Society.

Nagel, E. (1979). *The structure of science: Problems in the logic of scientific explanation.* Indianapolis, IN: Hackett Publishing.

Nielsen, J. (1993). *Usability engineering.* London, UK: Academic Press.

Nielsen, J. (1995). *Usability inspection methods.* New York: ACM Press.

Nurminen, A., & Oulasvirta, A. (2008). Designing interactions for navigation in 3D mobile maps. In L. Meng, A. Zipf, & S. Winter (Eds.), Map-based mobile services: Design, interaction and usability. Lecture Notes in Geoinformation and Cartography, (pp. 198–224). Springer: London.

Oulasvirta, A., Estlander, S., & Nurminen, A. (2009). Embodied interaction with a 3D versus 2D mobile map. *Personal and Ubiquitous Computing, 13*(4).

Oulasvirta, A., Nurminen, A., & Nivala, A. (2007). Interacting with 3D and 2D mobile maps: An exploratory study (Tech. Rep. No. 2007-1). Helsinki, Finland: Helsinki Institute for Information Technology.

Oulasvirta, A., Petit, R., Raento, M., & Tiitta, S. (2007). Interpreting and acting on mobile awareness cues. *Human-Computer Interaction, 22,* 97–135.

Oulasvirta, A., Raento, M., & Tiitta, S. (2005). ContextContacts: Re-designing SmartPhone's contact book to support mobile awareness and collaboration. In *Proceedings of Mobile HCI 2003* (MobileHCI '03, pp. 167–174). New York: ACM Press.

Oulasvirta, A., Tamminen, S., Roto, V., & Kuorelahti, J. (2005). Interaction in 4-second bursts: The fragmented nature of attentional resources. In *Proceedings of the SIGCHI Conference on Human Factors in Computing Systems* (CHI '05, pp. 919–928). New York: ACM Press.

Pawson, R., & Tilley, N. (1997). *Realistic evaluation.* London, UK: Sage Publishing.

Raento, M., Oulasvirta, A, & Eagle, N. (in press). Smartphone: An emerging tool for social scientists. *Sociological Methods and Research.*

Raento, M., Oulasvirta, A., Petit, R., & Toivonen, H. (2005). ContextPhone: A prototyping platform for context-aware mobile applications. *IEEE Pervasive Computing, 4,* 51–59.

Reichl, P., Froehlich, P., Baillie, L., Schatz, R., & Dantcheva, A. (2007). The LiLiPUT prototype: A wearable environment for user tests of mobile telecommunication applications. In *Extended Abtracts of the SIGCHI Conference on Human Factors in Computing Systems* (CHI '07; pp. 1833–1838). New York: ACM Press.

Roto, V., Oulasvirta, A., Haikarainen, T., Kuorelahti, J., Lehmuskallio, H., & Nyyssonen, T. (2004). *Examining mobile phone use in the wild with quasi-experimentation* (Tech. Rep. No. 2004-1). Helsinki, Finland: Helsinki Institute for Information Technology.

Schusteritsch, R., Wei, C. Y., & LaRosa, M. (2007). Towards the perfect infrastructure for usability testing on mobile devices. In *Extended Abstracts of the SIGCHI Conference on Human Factors in Computing Systems* (CHI '07, pp. 1839–1844). New York: ACM Press.

Shadish, W., Cook, T., & Campbell, D. (2002). *Experimental and quasi-experimental designs.* Boston, MA: Houghton Mifflin.

Suchman, L. (1987). Plans and situated actions: The problem of human-machine communication. Cambridge, UK: Cambridge University Press.

Opportunities and Challenges of Designing the Service User eXperience (SUX) in Web 2.0

Kaisa Väänänen-Vainio-Mattila, Heli Väätäjä, and Teija Vainio

Abstract Developed countries are in a transition into service societies. In the past few years, there has been a significant rise in Internet services in people's everyday lives. With the rise of the phenomenon called Web 2.0, users of the services are starting to experience new types of dynamically evolving services. New services enable user-created content and social awareness, and they are often dynamically composed of various service "mashup" components. Even though there are numerous success stories of such services, coherent design principles of user experience of these services are only starting to emerge. One significant aspect that affects the user-centered design of Web 2.0 services is the dynamic nature of service development, with the requirement of fast and continuous iteration of the services. In this chapter, we first explore the nature of Web 2.0 services from the users' perspective. We then review the multidisciplinary nature of experience, service experience, and user experience, and summarize the essential elements of the *service user experience* (SUX). We then investigate the applicability of user-centered design principles to the service development life cycle and discuss users' new roles in service development. We present a summary of SUX design opportunities and challenges. Our main conclusions are that new, agile methods to involve users in the service development process need to be developed, and that less technically advanced users should be involved in co-creation of Web 2.0 services.

1 Introduction

Modern societies are increasingly relying on services (Dahlbom, 2003; Quinn et al., 1994). Services include both physical (health care, cleaning, renovating, security services, etc.) and electronic (media services, communication, entertainment, information services, etc.). The last 5–10 years have seen an immense

K. Väänänen-Vainio-Mattila (✉)
Human-Centered Technology (IHTE), Tampere University of Technology, Hervanta, Finland
e-mail: kaisa.vaananen-vainio-mattila@tut.fi

P. Saariluoma, H. Isomäki (eds.), *Future Interaction Design II*,
DOI 10.1007/978-1-84800-385-9_6, © Springer-Verlag London Limited 2009

rise in digital services offered via the Internet. Internet services, also referred to in this chapter as Web services or electronic services, help their users to manage their lives and to enrich it with additional information that can be both useful and entertaining. Thus, Internet services at large are becoming an inherent part of people's everyday lives.

Simultaneously, increasing attention has been paid to the usability of the interactive products and applications, that is, the efficiency, fit for purpose, and users' satisfaction with the products, applications, or services (International Organization for Standardization [ISO], 1999). In the early 2000s, the shift in product development has taken place toward user experience (e.g., Battarbee, 2004; Hassenzahl & Tractinsky, 2006; Roto, 2006). Aiming for a good user experience means designing products and systems that, in addition to being usable, invoke positive emotions (Forlizzi & Ford, 2000; Jordan, 2002; Norman, 2003), support hedonic needs (Hassenzahl, 2004) and enable flow (Csikszentmihalyi, 1990) in using the product or service. Furthermore, pleasant user experience means that the users' interactions with every contact point in the life cycle of the product are satisfying, including marketing, product purchase, or acquisition, taking it into use, customer, and other supporting services, usage of the actual product, and upgrading the product. As technologies used in the products develop, users' expectations towards interactive products are rising. Thus, exceptionally good user experiences are harder to achieve as the product markets mature.

The beginning of the brief history of Internet services, the early 1990s, was the era of static Web pages. Via such Web sites, users could find basic information on, for example, courses, companies, personal statements, and so forth. By the late 1990s, Internet applications offered a multitude of interaction possibilities, including forms, database queries, and interactive content retrieval. Even though the WAP services failed in the mobile services market in the late 1990s, the most popular Web services have since been established in the areas of gaming, information retrieval, news, and weather. In the last few years, the interaction has started to evolve towards "Web 2.0," which enables adaptive, dynamic applications, many of which contain aspects of social media and user participation in the content creation (Mayfield, 2007). The effect of these new possibilities is that the user experience of Internet services are becoming increasingly complex. Design of the service user experience is no longer in the hands of a single service provider but is developed jointly by the original service creator, other service providers and, increasingly, by the user community (Preece, 2000). Even if Web design guidelines have been offered for basic Web services (Nielsen, 2000), the new aspects of services lack traditions and thus require new design guidelines and approaches (see, e.g., Moggridge, 2006).

In Section 2, we first explore what is happening in the Internet service development field, that is, Web 2.0 services, from service users' perspectives. In Section 3, we analyze multidisciplinary viewpoints of experience, service experience, and user experience, and propose a list of service user experience (SUX) elements. In Section 4, we present how user-centered design can fit into the service development life cycle, and explore users' new roles in service development. Section 5 summarizes the SUX design opportunities and challenges. We conclude by discussing how SUX should be designed with agile methods of user involvement in the evolutionary service development life cycle.

2 Characteristics of Web 2.0 Services from Users' Perspectives

Web 2.0 is a concept that was created to describe and cover a set of new principles and development trends emerging in the Internet (O'Reilly, 2005). These trends vary from new business models to user contribution and social media. According to Tim O'Reilly, "Web 2.0 thrives on network effects: databases that get richer the more people interact with them, applications that are smarter the more people use them, marketing that is driven by user stories and experiences, and applications that interact with each other to form a broader computing platform" (Musse et al., 2006, p. 3). O'Reilly has identified several patterns related to emerging new Internet services (O'Reilly, 2005). The most relevant and meaningful phenomena for the experience of individual users and user communities are described below.

One of the key elements in many Web 2.0 services is an enabling of the active user participation, for example, in the form of social networking, reviewing, and media content production (Mayfield, 2007). Self-expression and connecting with other people are central factors in Web 2.0 services. Users add value to the service by using it and adding their own data, such as user-generated content like photos, videos, bookmarks, tags, reviews, to the user community. Services evolve and grow through users' activity within the service. Furthermore, active participation of users is evolving into co-creation of the user experience and co-production of the service.

Many of the users do not, however, contribute actively, so user data is aggregated from ordinary usage of the services. This covers not only the actions of using the service but extends to including, for example, contextual and temporal data—metadata or social metadata (Adams, Phung, & Venkatesh, 2006)—related to the usage. Each individual is implicitly contributing to the community's or other users' experiences of the service (Appan, Shevade, Sundaram, & Birchfield, 2005), for instance, in the form of providing information about their buying behavior to other users. This enriches the user experience and increases the value of the service to the individual users.

Service mashups, as hybrids of Web services, are one of the manifestations of the network effects. One example of mashup creation is when a user takes existing third-party content, data, or service and combines it with some other service or content to create a completely new service, content, or tool. Service providers typically enable the creation of mashups by providing application programming interfaces or by giving access to content and data in form of another Web service. Google Maps is a good example of a service that enables the creation of service mashups. However, it will be a challenge for the future to provide ordinary users even easier ways to create mashups (see, e.g. Murthy, Maier, & Delcambre, 2006; Wong & Hong, 2007).

Web 2.0 services are developing continuously and often this is referred to as a phenomenon of "perpetual beta," services that are endlessly under development. Such Internet technologies enable interactions that are richer than before and may utilize a multitude of user interface modalities. Services also run on multiple platforms, ranging from PCs to mobile phones and PDAs. These opportunities also set challenges for designing the user experience, not only when users themselves are developing mashup services, but also for the professional developers of services. Many of the successful services are not actually developed by professionals with user-experience-related knowledge, but amateurs or enthusiasts, who have an instinct, for example, about social-networking-related needs.

Many notable examples of Web 2.0 services are commonly accessed by users. Amazon.com provides users with the possibility to rate and submit reviews on purchased products. These can be further rated by their usefulness to other customers. The behavior of other customers is also used to inform the users, for example, regarding how many prior customers who viewed the product actually bought it or the related purchases of the customers who bought the viewed or purchased product. Users can also tag products in order to help themselves and other users find relevant products. It is helpful to see what others have done in the service, for example, as in the case of Amazon, to see what products others have recommended. This phenomenon can be understood in terms of social navigation: By making others' actions visible, users are supported in navigating the service (Claypool, Le, Wased, & Brown, 2001; Yanbe, Jatowt, Nakamura, & Tanaka, 2007). In direct social navigation, users see what other individual users have done, whereas indirect social navigation is visible through aggregate systems, such as recommendation systems (see, e.g., Dieberger, Dourish, Höök, Resnick, & Wexelblat, 2000).

Users are utilizing other users' reviews and ratings in other kinds of services as well, for example, when they are traveling and choosing accommodation for themselves, such as Booking.com. Thus, for some hotels, visitors give grades according to a hotel's suitability for solo travelers, young couples, mature couples, families with young and older children, or groups. Furthermore, grades for the staff, service, cleanliness, comfort, and value for the cost have been given in addition to overall reviews. The availability of a second opinion can inform and be comforting for many users when they are deciding where to stay while abroad.

Another widespread Web 2.0 service is Facebook.[1] On Facebook, users enjoy the browsing and navigation experience, and find something completely new (Freyne, Farzan, Brusilovsky, Smyth, & Coyle, 2007). Facebook gives

---

[1] www.facebook.com

access to a vast and increasing set of applications made by users. Instead of just sharing users' personal content, such as music pieces, photos, or video clips, users send to each other invitations to use applications or to track, for example, the actions and interests of their friends, such as the music they are listening to through last.fm (Lampe, Ellison, & Steinfield, 2006). On the other hand, it is quite obvious that, in addition to sharing "cute" applications through Facebook, users have used it in a more serious manner, for example, by creating virtual groups for something that they feel is significant in their lives, such as groups of their personal friends or for people who share the same religious or political views. Thus, a possibility to share with others something important that has value for an individual user can be vital part of using services in Web 2.0 (Lampe, Ellison, & Steinfield, 2007). Another service that fully relies on user-created content and social sharing is YouTube.[2]

3 Experience, User Experience, and Service User eXperience (SUX)

Focus on user experience has been a growing trend in the product development of consumer products in the early 2000s (e.g., Forlizzi & Battarbee, 2004; Forlizzi & Ford, 2000; Hassenzahl, 2004). User experience has become a buzzword often used as a synonym for good usability and user-centered design. In terms of product development, there is no specifically defined, common understanding of what *user experience* really means. In this section, we first review related literature for the understanding of various disciplines for the concept of experience. We then review the definitions of user experience from the human–computer interaction and product design disciplines. We also look briefly at the Internet and service research literature where the concept of service experience has been developed for electronic services as well. Based on these definitions, we describe what we believe to be the essential elements of service user experience (SUX). Figure 1 illustrates the relationships of these concepts.

Fig. 1 Relationships of experience-related concepts investigated in this chapter. Concepts of experience, user experience, and service experience contribute to the new concept of service user experience (SUX)

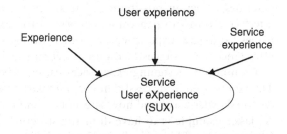

---

[2] www.youtube.com

3.1 Multidisciplinary Views to Experience

How to design experiences for people is not only a focus in the field of information systems; but such design challenges also have been discussed for centuries in the arts and humanities. Wright and McCarthy (2005) discuss the concept of the novel and "felt life," taken from literary theory, as a basis for understanding experience and suggest a dialogical analysis of the relationship between designer and user. In this section we explore briefly what specific concepts for designing experiences can be found in architecture and aesthetics.

In architecture, the concept of genius loci, which comes from Roman mythology, is about the protective spirit of a place. Genius loci usually refers to a location's distinctive atmosphere, or to a "spirit of place" rather than the protective nature of the place. Hence, it is important that we identify with a place to be able to feel the genius loci and, therefore, it is essential to acknowledge what the elements are that we try to find in a place. Norberg-Schulz (1980) argues that the features of a certain place can be classified as its history, meaning, and identity. When we are well-acquainted with a certain place, such familiar places can remind us of our childhood and, for that reason, experience is tied up with the person's own personality.

Furthermore, Norberg-Schulz (1994) argues that, when having experiences in an urban environment, instant experiences and whole experiences are key issues. Therefore, it is important that users are able to explore an urban environment in a certain order. A user's first glance of a place is significant in having an experience. When people arrive in a certain place, two views affect the kind of experience they will have in that place: The image they have derived in advance of the place mixes with their first glance of the actual space.

In addition to genius loci in urban planning theories and practices, the concept of affordance could be emphasized here in relation to design of user experience. An affordance can be defined as an action that an individual can potentially perform in a certain environment or, as Gibson (1977) has defined it, as action possibilities. The potential action can be either those that a user can recognize or all available actions, even if not recognized by an individual user. Furthermore, the concept of affordance is also a well-known term in the research field of human–computer interaction (HCI), which Norman (1988) describes as action possibilities that are perceivable by the user in the user interface. Norman furthermore connects affordances with users' goals, plans, values, and past experiences. In other words, Norman (1988) argues that affordances can "suggest" how an object may be interacted with.

Examples of designing experiences can also be found in the film industry. This can be seen in successful movies and particularly in how playwrights have designed experiences and how screenplays and manuscripts have been written. A classic example is to have dramatic structure in line with Freytag's (1863/1969) pyramid. This typically includes exposition, rising action, climax (turning point), falling action, and dénouement or unraveling. In addition, when designing an experience, translational motion and maintaining tension are essential elements.

Thus, as Vyas and van der Veer (2006) have argued, domains of art offer tools for understanding the experience phenomena because, with artistic creations, artists aim at creating experiences. In aesthetics, time seems to be a key factor in relation to the design of experience. If we focus on how people gain experiences when looking at, for example, famous paintings or sculptures, the gradual comprehension of the work of art seems to be an essential element (Moles, 1966). The time spent with the work of art affects how deeply the work of art is understood. When considering time as a central factor of having an experience, works of art can be classified into synchronic works, which have no time dimensions, and diachronic works, so-called timeart, that have separate beginning, middle, and ending parts.

Leder, Belke, Oeberst, and Augustin (2004) present a cognitive processing model of aesthetic experiences with five stages: perceptual analyses, implicit memory integration, explicit classification, cognitive mastering, and evaluation. An individual aesthetic experience is related to one's expertise of art and one's affective state in the beginning of the experience. Hekkert (2007) presents a set of aesthetic design principles for designing pleasurable products and shows that these principles mostly operate across the human senses.

Regarding the common patterns in various experiences, Dewey (1934/2005, p. 45) stated, "The outline of the common pattern is a set by the fact that every experience is the result of interaction between a live creature and some aspect of the world in which he lives." It is important to acknowledge that by examining the concepts of experiences that we have in art and architecture, such as genius loci, affordance, and gradual comprehension that already focus on exploring the interaction between the user (live creature) and an artifact, we could also enhance the design of user experiences in Internet services.

3.2 Service Experience

Hoffman and Bateson (1997, p. 6) argue that "when a consumer purchases a service, he or she purchases an experience." Hoffman and Bateson (1997) further state that the central factors that affect physical services are the inanimate environment, contact personnel/service providers, other customers, and invisible organization and systems. In marketing-related literature, the fundamental characteristics of the service experience are known as inseparability, variability, perishability, and intangibility (Kotler, 1999). However, these concepts were established for physical services, and they do not apply directly to the field of electronic services. For example, variability does not necessarily appear as such in electronic services, as the service can be copied from user to user. Also perishability is not directly relevant to electronic services. Even though the content of an Internet service may "perish" as time proceeds, the actual service normally exists over a period of time, thus allowing the user to return to it repeatedly. On the other hand, inseparability—the tight connection between the service and its customer (user)—may be a key factor in supporting a user's trust in an electronic service. Users may also become developers of the service, or at least contribute to its content and how it appears to others by generating and utilizing aggregated user data. Intangibility is still a key element in electronic services, and the user interface of the service acts as a key means to make the service feel more tangible. Edvardsson, Gustafsson, and Roos (2005) have also criticized the physical service characteristics as too narrow and outdated.

Rowley (2006, p. 342) has done an extensive literature review of electronic services and has defined electronic service experience as "the customer's experience that results from purchase through or engagement with information technology mediated service delivery." According to Rowley, key elements of an electronic service are that it is foremost an "information service" and a "self-service." Furthermore, Rowley states that, in electronic services (e-services), it is essential that users (customers) learn from the interface, as well as from more experienced friends and family. Rowley continues to describe the nature of the e-service experience as "likely to vary depending upon the activities or tasks being completed through the e-service engagement" (2006, p. 344). Moreover, users may have different roles and exhibit different competences when using an e-service.

Regarding the electronic service experience, Chen and Chang (2003) have identified three components in the online shopping experience: interactivity (connection quality, Web site design), transaction (value, convenience, assurance, entertainment, evaluation), and fulfillment (order processing, delivery, post-sales service). Constantinides (2004) identifies functionality factors (usability and interactivity), psychological factors (trust), and content factors (aesthetics and marketing mix) as Internet experience elements that influence consumer behavior. Zhang and Prybutok (2005) developed an e-service model in which Internet site service quality is one variable; the others are individual differences, e-service convenience, risk, e-satisfaction, and customer's intention. These models thus include variables relating both to users' overall abilities and perception of the service, and the basic characteristics of the service. There are, however, fewer references that detail elements for designing the service experience for the users. Furthermore, what definitions do exist do not address the special characteristics of Web 2.0 type of services.

3.3 User Experience

The concept of user experience rose to attention in the early 2000s to extend the viewpoints of HCI and usability. User experience promotes broader views of users' emotional, contextual, and dynamically evolving needs, and the impact of users' previous experiences on the new experiences. Jordan (2002) emphasizes the importance of pleasure and pride in designing products. Hassenzahl (2004) distinguishes between "pragmatic" and "hedonic" (stimulation, identification, evocation) attributes of the product in supporting good user experience. Mäkelä and Fulton Suri (2001) noted that the user experience is a result of motivated action in a certain context. The user's previous experiences and expectations influence the present experience, and the present experience leads to more experiences and modified expectations. Thus, the total user experience is a continuum that is shaped as a result of a series of smaller user experience units.

Roto (2006) investigated mobile browsing and developed a synthesis model for components affecting the user experience of mobile browsing. In Roto's model, the components affecting the user are needs, motivation, experiences, expectations, mood, and resources. In a model presented by Forlizzi and Ford (2000), user-related factors are emotions and prior experiences, and product-related factors are components such as features, usefulness, and aesthetic quality. The user–product interaction is affected by the context of use as well as social and cultural factors. Battarbee (2004) argues for the concept of co-experience, by which the user experiences are formed in social interaction. Such interactions should be studied in context, using early prototypes of the developed technology.

A recent approach to developing products with high-quality user experience is value-based design or worth-based design, introduced by Cockton (2004). In this approach, Cockton's main argument is that quality in use and fit to context are not enough, but HCI should be broadened to include the concept of value as an ultimate goal of design. Thus, users' in-depth needs and values need to be taken into account in the system design.

Hassenzahl and Tractinsky (2006) presented a research agenda for user experience. According to their model, user experience is a consequence of three categories of factors: factors related to a user's internal state, the characteristics of the designed system, and the context in which the interaction occurs. These together form a complex field of design and experience opportunities.

Figure 2 summarizes the key elements of user experience. Key issues in addition to good usability are the feeling of flow in interaction, pleasurable and hedonic aspects of product usage, and multisensory interaction.

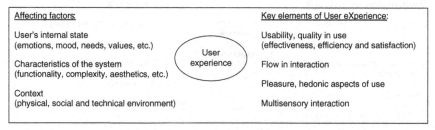

Fig. 2 The affecting factors and key elements of user experience. Affecting factors form the basis for user experience and the key elements are essential components of good user experience

3.4 Key Elements and Design Challenges of Service User eXperience

Based on the above descriptions of the characteristics of Web 2.0 services (Section 2) and experience, user experience and service experience elements (Sections 3.1–3.3), we propose in Fig. 3 the following items as key elements of SUX.

There are several new elements in SUX that become central when compared to the "traditional" user experience. In particular, these SUX elements rise from the composite and dynamic nature of the service: its contents, components, and user communities. The affecting factors that are specifically important in SUX and their corresponding SUX elements are described briefly in Table 1.

The experience-related concepts presented in Section 3.1 can aid the design of good SUX. For example, the concept of "social affordance" in social navigation could be used to help visualize the interaction elements of the social groups that are involved. When aiming at coherence in interaction, users should be able to experience the spirit of the place (genius loci), independent of the service-component creator. When considering the temporal nature of SUX, the concept of gradual comprehension of the service could describe how the experience is formed. Overall, the concepts of drama—in terms of maintaining positive tension—with exposition, rising action, climax (turning point), falling action and unraveling, could be utilized to bring excitement to SUX. This could mean, for example, providing users with unexpected content or new service components in a temporal manner.

Due to unknown service providers and anonymous social environments, the issue of trust becomes crucial (Antifakos, Kern, Schiele, & Schwaninger, 2005; Hoffman, Lawson-Jenkins, & Blum, 2006,). Kaasinen (2005) has identified the issue of trust as one of the key factors in the adoption of mobile services. Also, the reliability of the service provider to ensure that the service is available when the user needs it becomes highly important.

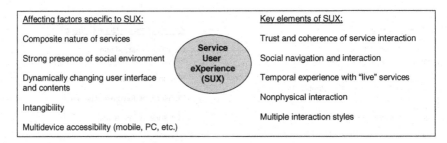

Fig. 3 Service user experience (SUX) elements. There are several specific affecting factors and key elements in SUX in addition to the basic user experience elements

Table 1 Explanations of SUX's affecting factors and key elements

Affecting factors specific to SUX	Related key elements of SUX
Composite nature of services.	*Trust and coherence of service interaction.*
Web 2.0 services are often composed of several "add-on" applications (service components), normally developed by different providers. Service mashups may create unexpected service and content combinations, which may have an effect on usability and quality of the SUX.	It is challenging to maintain a user's trust and coherence of the SUX, especially when different service providers (including user-developers) are involved. The interaction logic, visual elements, and terminology should be made coherent across service components. A service provider's reputation will affect a user's experience of trust.
Presence of social environment.	*Social navigation and interaction.*
Web 2.0 services often rely on actions from user communities, e.g., ratings by and interactions from a group of people who use the same service. Service users thus become aware of other anonymous or identified users.	In many tasks, users of Web 2.0 services rely on information they can gain from other users of the service (e.g., ratings, comments, service components). Thus there is a new element in interaction: The navigation affordances in the user interface will be enhanced with direct interaction with other users, or indirect navigation cues from other users.
Dynamically changing user interface (UI).	*Temporal nature of SUX.*
As the services are often developed iteratively over time, the service may gain extensions, both to its contents and to the UI.	Service content is often temporally bound. Also, services are developed iteratively and new components appear on an irregular basis. Users need to adapt to the dynamic, "live" nature of the services. Additionally, the ease of taking a service into use is a crucial SUX factor.
Intangibility.	*Nonphysical interaction.*
Web 2.0 services are electronic and nonphysical (as opposed to interactive systems with a physical device). The effects of interaction are intangible, and thus the user's understanding of the service source is an important factor affecting trust in the service.	SUX is created and supported by the user interface design, which needs to give enough feedback (both visual and auditive) for the user to gain a concrete "feel" of the service logic and its special characteristics.
Multidevice access.	*Multiple interaction styles.*
Services are often accessed through stationary PCs, mobile devices, or other types of information access points.	SUX should be coherent independent of the device and user interface used to access the service. Even though the visual UI will be different, the UI logic should be coherent.

4 User-Centered Design of New Services

In this section, we explore the development process of new services and discuss how user-centered design principles can and should be applied in new service development. We then present how users acquire new roles in this continuous service development process. Thus, user involvement will gain new forms in user-centered service design.

4.1 Service Development Life Cycle

Several trends can be identified related to service development. These are related to the need for fast and evolutionary development due to dynamic nature of the services (Yang & Mei, 2006), stakeholder roles, including service users' roles (Prahalad & Ramaswamy, 2004a), and the mashup nature of new services (Wong & Hong, 2007).

Service development typically starts with ideation based on preliminary (user) studies or experiences with current services. These are further developed into concepts, which are tested with the users or directly implemented. Suitable concepts are implemented and typically given to users for quick review and feedback.

The development time is decreasing due to the accelerating renewal cycle of the services (Yang & Mei, 2006). The renewal time of services is shrinking (according to one estimate, currently around 6 months), and this fast-paced development increases competition. To get to the market early and directly affects how much time can be used for conceptualizing a service, from idea to implementation (Prahalad & Ramaswamy, 2004a,b). Similar types of ideas often occur at the same time in different places and it is vital to get one's idea implemented as quickly as possible. This approach may, in a worst-case scenario, sacrifice the user experience, including basic usability, which in turn may have a drastic effect on service adoption and usage.

To get to the market quickly and to get feedback on service for further development, alpha- and beta-testing approaches are used. Services are offered for use as early, "under construction" versions, and users who take them into use are expected to give feedback. This provides a way of testing the service in real use and observing how it is adopted, but there still seems to be a lack of systematic use of this method.

In fact, services may be seen as forever beta versions. Due to the manner of provision to users, the services can be modified at any time by the service provider. Also, the users' contributions, actions, and user-developed add-ons change the service and how it appears to its users. The number of stakeholders related to service provision is growing and services are increasingly depending on other services. Mashup-like service combinations are harder to manage and this causes new challenges to service development.

4.2 User-Centered Design Principles and Processes

The key principles of user-centered design, as defined by ISO (1999), are described below.

Active involvement of users and a clear understanding of user and task requirements: Users should have a direct influence on the system design, and this implies a close interaction between the developers and actual (primary and secondary) users of the system. When the target user group is diverse (as in consumer products), appropriate user representatives should be involved in the development process. This will support the inclusion of user and task requirements in the system specification. Kujala (2003) presents a review of the benefits and challenges of user involvement.

Appropriate allocation of function between users and technology: This allocation specifies which tasks should be carried out by the system and which by the human users (Jokela, Iivari, Matero, & Karukka, 2003). The decision depends on the strengths and limitations of technology and users, and the resulting system should form a meaningful set of user tasks in the given context of use. Even when a technology is capable of performing certain tasks, it may not fit with users' expectations of the technology, for instance, in their homes (Koskela & Väänänen-Vainio-Mattila, 2004).

Iteration of design solutions: It is essential to gain feedback from the users of the system. The aim is to meet the user and organizational requirements and this can be achieved by active user involvement (Kujala, Kauppinen, Lehtola, & Kojo, 2005). Iteration assumes that there are preliminary design solutions that can be tested by the users, and the results should be fed back to refine the design solutions. The emphasis of iteration should be on early phases of the design, and low-fidelity prototypes (e.g., paper or experimental prototypes) offer a means to elicit user feedback in a cost-effective way (Spool, Scanlon, & Snyder, 1997; Virzi, Sokolov, & Karis, 1996).

Multidisciplinary design: A variety of skills and functions need to be involved in the user-centered design process, including users, managers, business specialists, programmers, marketers, technical writers, and usability specialists (Väänänen-Vainio-Mattila & Ruuska, 2000; Vredenburg, Mao, Smith, & Carey, 2002). These disciplines are needed in the design process to gain a holistic view about the requirements for the designed product, including user needs, technical features, and marketing objectives.

This same ISO standard (1999) defines the framework or overall process of user-centered design as consisting of understanding and specifying the context of use, specifying the user and organizational requirements, producing design solutions and evaluating designs against requirements until the system satisfies specified requirements. Figure 4 presents the various design actions that fulfill the process of user-centered design.

4.3 Matching User-Centered Design to Service Development Life Cycle

The principles and activities of user-centered design were initially defined for product or system design in which specific service development characteristics were not taken into account. This section investigates the user-centered design principles from the service development perspective.

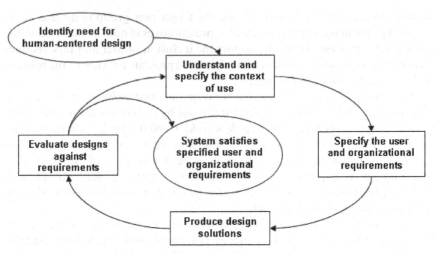

Fig. 4 The human-centered design process (activities) according to the ISO (1999)

User involvement: In the Internet service development life cycle, the users often act as the beta-testers of the service. In addition, users may be actively involved in the development of service features as well as its content. On the positive side, this may result in an increasing amount of user innovations, and a good match of the service features to the active users' tasks. However, their innovations may be useful only for a very narrow segment of the user population, and thus some potential users may be alienated from the service. Furthermore, due to the evolutionary nature of services, the task requirements may be challenging if not impossible to specify fully before the release of the service to the market.

Allocation of functions: There are no special characteristics of function allocation in service development that would differ from other types of product/system development. The service should fulfill tasks that ease users' lives, such as comparing prices and offerings from several service providers. Active user involvement can be seen as a means of ensuring appropriate task allocation. However, the views of the most active users may produce an overkill of service functionality.

Iterative design: In the Internet service development life cycle, one of the main benefits lies in the potential for quick, short-iteration cycles. In addition, as the service prototype is in actual use by the limited sample of the market, the feedback is contextually relevant and valid. On the challenge side, the iterative and "always beta" nature of the services means that there is no guarantee of a stable situation in service use. Thus, systematic user testing may be difficult to conduct. Furthermore, service content or a structure that changes over time may confuse the less adaptive end users.

Multidisciplinary design: In Internet service development, multidisciplinary design may be challenging to manage since users and other stakeholders (including developers) do not necessarily meet face-to-face, but over the Internet. In such development setups, individual users with strong viewpoints may influence the development toward their own specific interests. Thus, it would be valuable to conduct usability tests as well as expert evaluations by marketing people, technical writers, and usability experts before releasing the service for a wider use.

In terms of the user-centered design process (activities), as presented in Section 4.2, the activities in the overall process are taken into account in the service development life cycle as follows:

Understand and specify the context of use: The contextual analysis should be done prior to the service design phase. However, when designing services, the development cycle is often very fast and the first service version may be pushed into the market based on the service provider's vision, and then beta-tested within the context. The risks of failure are relatively high but the success or failure—the fit for context—of the service will become evident within a relatively short time frame.

Specify the user and organizational requirements: Similarly to the specification of the context of use, user requirements may not always be fully investigated prior to the service design due to the short-time-to-market phase. If the service is intended for use in an organization (e.g., mobile business services, as described by Wigelius, Aula, & Markova, 2007), there should be a detailed analysis of user and organizational requirements, especially the fit for work processes. In consumer services, however, the risks for large losses due to unused investments are smaller.

Produce and evaluate design solutions until requirements are met: Service designs are iterated quickly, and may be tested with "quick and cheap" market tests of a beta version of the service. The benefit of this approach is that developers can gain realistic feedback quickly from users who are trying the service in real contexts of use. However, the challenge is that if the first version of the service does not match the users' expectations, the users may dismiss the service altogether. As the saying goes, there's only one chance to make a good first impression. This may severely damage the service provider's brand reputation.

In summary, the main challenges of user-centered design service development lie in an accelerated development life cycle that may not allow for full contextual analysis nor specification of users' requirements. On the other hand, the high iterativeness, if handled well, may also be an opportunity for good user involvement and evaluation against users' requirements. However, the users who are involved may not represent the main target population of the service, and this may lead to insufficient fulfillment of potential users' needs.

4.4 Users' New Roles in Usage and Development of Services

Web 2.0 services are relying on user participation and contributions in various ways and are not successful or meaningful without these features (O'Reilly

2005). Web 2.0 services offer new types of roles for users. Users are not only consumers using the provided, ready-made service as such, but they contribute to the service both actively and passively. Actively contributing users create content in different forms (Casey, Kirman, & Rowland, 2007), such as photos, tags, blogs, and reviews, and, at the extreme, they provide solutions like service add-ons or mashups for others to use (Wong & Hong, 2007). Aggregation of data from more passive "ordinary" users covers, for example, usage of the services and behavioral patterns within the service. This behavior or navigation data can then be utilized in providing added value to other users by making it collectively visible, for instance, by showing shopping-related behavior to other users.

In Web 2.0, users are adopting new roles (Prahalad & Ramaswamy, 2004b). The following roles that relate to using and participating in the development of services can be distinguished:

User: uses the service and its functionalities, with information and content provided by the service provider, her/himself, and/or other users. Data related to an individual user and his/her service usage may be aggregated for further use within the service or another service.

Producer: actively produces content, information, and data. A producer creates, for example, media content, such as by submitting photos and videos, writing a blog, contributing to online information services, actively participating in online communities, or writing product reviews.

Innovator: tries to find or create solutions for his/her unmet needs by mixing existing services, content, and/or data, or discovers new ways or contexts for using the existing ones. The innovator may provide solutions for others to use.

Developer: develops new add-ons (applications) to an existing service using provided application programming interfaces or Web services provided by service providers, or participates in development of services through, for example, open source programming.

The developer and innovator may be overlapping roles. However, the user–innovator's emphasis is in the ideation of new service features and combinations in the early phases of the process, whereas the user–developer will participate in the actual implementation of the service.

Users as producers: Many of the e-commerce sites enable users to produce reviews, such as Amazon.com for books, eBay, Booking.com for hotels, and PriceRunner for product price comparisons. Commentary on the reviews also may be enabled. eBay and similar online auction sites encourage reviews on sellers and buyers alike. On the other hand, users produce content in the form of photos and videos for social media services like YouTube and Flickr. These contributions may also be reviewed. Users benefit from what others have produced and these contributions affect user experience of the service. Without the user contributions, the service would lack the essential elements that bring value to other users. Understanding these elements and providing them for users are part of creating the opportunity space for user experience.

Users as innovators: Users are providing innovative ideas that either they themselves can put into practice (see users as developers below), or share with service providers who can then implement them into their service (Jeppesen & Frederiksen, 2006). Users can ideate new service functions for the real context of use. Letting ordinary users innovate in their own context has been proven to be an essential source of new innovations that satisfy users' needs (Magnusson, Matthing, & Kristensson, 2003). This kind of user innovation can lead to co-creation of the service experience (Prahalad & Ramaswamy, 2004b),

Users as developers: Many of the Web 2.0 service providers offer application programming interfaces or Web services to enable the creation of add-ons, extensions, and new functionalities to the existing services. For example, Nokia's Multi-User Publishing Environment,[3] Amazon.com, and Facebook provide their users the possibility to create their own applications and share them, for others to use within the service. Through these tools, users who are capable of high-level programming can participate in the Web service creation as active developers. User–developers can also form developer communities and thus gain further power in service creation (Prahalad & Ramaswamy, 2004a,b).

Types of users who become active in Web 2.0 service development: In terms of user involvement discussed in Sections 4.2 and 4.3, it is important to consider what kind of users are the producers, innovators, and developers. Von Hippel has studied user innovators and calls them lead users (von Hippel, 2005). Lead users are at the leading edge of an important market trend and may be experiencing needs that other users will experience later on. They are on the left-hand side of the technology adoption curve, that is, as early adopters or even innovators, according to Rogers' (2003) model. Such users are more driven by the newness of technology, whereas the majority of users (the "masses") are interested in the functional (or hedonic) benefits provided by technology. To attract the masses to use a service, their needs and requirements must be known in detail. Thus the user involvement should encompass not only the early adopters but also other potential target groups. Other means are needed to involve users beyond the free-willing, proactive innovation opportunities that appeal to the developer type of users. Involving ordinary users should ensure user-centered design of new services that are both innovative and also satisfy users' needs and values. Naturally, the actual service designer's role still remains important in the creation of service user experience.

5 Summary, Conclusions, and Discussion

This chapter has discussed the nature of experience, service experience, and user experience, and proposed a new concept of service user experience (SUX). SUX has key elements that are not strongly present in the more traditional product

---

[3] www.mupe.net/

user experience. Furthermore, the nature of Web 2.0 has been discussed from the users' perspectives, as well as from the development life cycle's perspective. The user-centered design approach can provide a framework for designing products and services that fit users' needs and support user experiences, but the applicability of user-centered design to service development needs to be modified due to the highly iterative and dynamic nature of service development.

Table 2 summarizes how the SUX elements described in Section 3.4 could be supported via the user-centered design approach. Both challenges and opportunities are listed.

The user-centered design approach is a good starting point for designing SUX. However, challenges in applying user-centered design still exist. We discuss these briefly here.

First, as the service development life cycle is very fast, iterative, and evolutionary, there is a need for agile user-centered design methods. The original concept of agile software development (e.g., Abrahamsson, Salo, Ronkainen, &

Table 2 Service user experience elements and related design opportunities and challenges

SUX element	User-centered design opportunities	User-centered design challenges
Trust and coherence of service interaction	Cooperation between users and trusted service providers Co-creation/coproduction of the services by users and service developers Composite services can be developed by industry guidelines for Web 2.0 user interface design	Mashup-type sources of service elements may cause incoherence in interaction Trust must be created through open communication with the user communities Accepted Web 2.0 design guidelines need to be formed
Social navigation and interaction	Users can communicate among themselves about new service requirements Improved user ideation/innovation; participatory design	May cause unpredictable user behavior Users' tasks may not be clear in the social context, thus the user interface may be difficult to design
Temporal experience	New service elements can keep users interested in the service Design patterns, guidelines, and coherent component templates may support totally new types of exciting user experiences	Dynamic and changing content and interactions may create confusion The experience is formed over time and thus there is a need for design coherence
Nonphysical interaction	Multimodal user interfaces (visual, auditive interaction) may make experience more natural and pleasing	Nonphysical services are intangible High-quality multimodal user interface design is a challenge
Multiple interaction styles	Multiplatform interaction has potential in supporting users' tasks in various service usage contexts	User interface style guides for multiplatform interaction are needed

Warsta, 2007) states the need for overall customer involvement by proposing that a customer' representative be present on the agile development team. From the user-centered design perspective, such representative user presence is not enough, and thus more detailed but still less strenuous methods for user needs gathering, user input on design drafts, user test methods, and so on, are needed. It should be considered how such methods could be included in the service development life cycle. A new, updated user-centered design framework for service development should be formed, taking into account the requirements of agility, iterative development, and interests of different stakeholders.

Second, user involvement, or even co-creation, of the services should be planned and implemented in a way that allows different types of potential service users to give ideas and feedback about the service and its SUX. Development and innovation of new services should not lie in the hands of the early adopters alone. Further, a need exists to educate the less knowledgeable users so that they can develop personalized services or mashups that suit their needs. What kind of application programming interfaces could be offered that would support less technically skilled users to participate in user innovation and coproduction? What are the alternative user feedback mechanisms that will allow the broader population to contribute to development of good services and good SUX?

A further consideration is, who controls or "owns" the SUX and thus is responsible for providing good SUX, especially in composite services? This becomes especially critical in service ecosystems where several individual services form broader service bundles (Kaasinen, 2005), for example, tourist information services. A service provider is responsible for a single-service SUX, but when other providers or user–developers build add-on services or service components on top of the existing service, the control point dissolves. As long as the service is a consumer service that is not obligatory for any users to use, this is not a severe problem, because, after all, users can choose not to use a service with bad SUX. But when the service is to be used in a user's work environment or as an obligatory public service, coherent SUX becomes much more important. To this end, Web 2.0 design guidelines should be developed that would give guidance to the interaction design of the services, both on the interaction logic and visual design levels. These guidelines could be embedded within standard user interface components that could be used as building blocks of new services.

User experience is a multifaceted issue that involves special elements beyond the fulfillment of basic user requirements user requirements. In this chapter we have presented concepts from the the arts sector that might be utilized to create a better SUX, and viewpoints regarding user-centered service design. The designers' role in creating good emotional and hedonic value in addition to clear functional value remains essential. To this end the (pro)active roles of users as innovators and developers provides an excellent opportunity to co-create services with attractive SUX and high user value.

References

Abrahamsson, P., Salo, O., Ronkainen, J., & Warsta, J. (2007). *Agile software development methods* (Pub. 478). Espoo, Finland: VTT Publications.

Adams, B., Phung, D., & Venkatesh, S. (2006). Extraction of social context and application to personal multimedia exploration. In *Proceedings of the 14th annual ACM International Conference on Multimedia* (MULTIMEDIA '06, pp. 987–996). New York: ACM.

Antifakos, S., Kern, N., Schiele, B., & Schwaninger, A. (2005). Towards improving trust in context-aware systems by displaying system confidence. In *Proceedings of the 7th International Conference on Human-Computer Interaction With Mobile Devices & Services* (MobileHCI '05, pp. 9–14). New York: ACM.

Appan, P., Shevade, B., Sundaram, H., & Birchfield, D. (2005). Interfaces for networked media exploration and collaborative annotation. In *Proceedings of the 10th International Conference on Intelligent User Interfaces* (IUI '05, pp. 106–113). New York: ACM.

Battarbee, K. (2004). *Co-experience, Understanding user experiences in social interaction.* (Doctoral dissertation; Publication A51). Helsinki, Finland: University of Arts and Design.

Casey, S., Kirman, B., & Rowland, D. (2007). The gopher game: A social, mobile, locative game with user generated content and peer review. In *Proceedings of the International Conference on Advances in Computer Entertainment Technology* (ACE '07, pp. 9–16). New York: ACM.

Chen, S.-J. & Chang, T.-Z. (2003). A descriptive model of online shopping process: Some empirical results. *International Journal of Service Industries Management, 14*, 556–569.

Claypool, M., Le, P., Wased, M., & Brown, D. (2001). Implicit interest indicators. In *Proceedings of the 6th International Conference on Intelligent User Interfaces* (IUI '01, pp. 33–40). New York: ACM.

Cockton, G. (2004). Value-centered HCI. In *Proceedings of the NordiCHI Conference* (pp. 149–160). New York: ACM.

Constantinides, E. (2004). Influencing the online consumer's behaviour: The Web experience. *Internet Research, 14*, 111–126.

Csikszentmihalyi, M. (1990). *The psychology of optimal experience.* New York: Harper Perennial.

Dahlbom, B. (2003). From users to consumers. *Scandinavian Journal of Information Systems, 15*, 105–108.

Dewey, J. (2005). *Art as experience.* London, England: Penguin Books. (Original work published in 1934).

Dieberger, A., Dourish, P., Höök, K., Resnick, P., & Wexelblat, A. (2000). Social navigation: Techniques for building more usable systems, *interactions, 7*, 36–45.

Edvardsson, B., Gustafsson, A., & Roos, I. (2005). Service portraits in service research: A critical review. *International Journal of Service Industry Management, 16*, 107–121.

Forlizzi, J., & Battarbee, K. (2004). Understanding experience in interactive systems. In *Proceedings of the 5th Conference on Designing Interactive Systems: Processes, practices, methods, and techniques* (DIS '05, pp. 261–268). New York: ACM.

Forlizzi, J., & Ford, S. (2000). The building blocks of experience: An early framework for interaction designers. In *Proceedings of Designing Interactive Systems* (DIS2000, pp. 419–423), New York: ACM.

Freyne, J., Farzan, R., Brusilovsky, P., Smyth, B., & Coyle, M. (2007). Collecting community wisdom: Integrating social search & social navigation. In *Proceedings of the 12th International Conference on Intelligent User Interfaces* (IUI '07, pp. 52–61). New York: ACM.

Freytag, G. (1969). *Die Technik des Dramas* [Technique of the drama]. Darmstadt, Germany: Wissenschaftliche Buchgeschäft. (Original work published in 1863).

Gibson, J. (1977). The theory of affordances. In R. E. Shaw & J. Bransford (Eds.), *Perceiving, acting, and knowing* (pp. 67–82). Hillsdale, NJ: Lawrence Erlbaum Associates.

Hassenzahl, M. (2004). The thing and I: Understanding the relationship between users and product. In M. A. Blythe, K. Overbeeke, A. F. Monk, & P. C. Wright (Eds.), *Funology: From usability to enjoyment* (pp. 31–42). Dordrecht, the Netherlands: Kluwer Academic Press.

Hassenzahl, M., & Tractinsky, N. (2006). User experience: A research agenda. *Behaviour and Information Technology, 25,* 91–97.

Hekkert, P. P. M. (2007). Design aesthetics: Principles of pleasure in design. *Psychology Science, 48,* 157–172.

Hoffman, K. D., & Bateson, J. E. G. (1997). *Essentials of service marketing.* Fort Worth, TX: The Dryden Press.

Hoffman, L. J., Lawson-Jenkins, K., & Blum, J. (2006). Trust beyond security: An expanded trust model. *Communications of the ACM, 49,* 94–101.

International Organization for Standardization [ISO]. (1999, June). *Human-centred design processes for interactive systems.* (Standards No. 13407). Geneva, Switzerland: ISO.

Jeppesen, L. B., & Frederiksen, L. (2006). Why do users contribute to firm-hosted user communities? The case of computer-controlled music instruments. *Organization Science, 17,* 45–63.

Jokela, T., Iivari, N., Matero, J., & Karukka, M. (2003). The standard of user-centered design and the standard definition of usability: Analyzing ISO 13407 against ISO 9241-11. In *Proceedings of the Latin American Conference on Human-Computer Interaction* (CLIHC '03, pp. 53–60). New York: ACM.

Jordan, P. E. (2002). *Designing pleasurable products.* London: Taylor and Francis.

Kaasinen, E. (2005). *User acceptance of mobile services: Value, ease of use, trust and ease of adoption.* Espoo, Finland: VTT Publications.

Koskela, T., & Väänänen-Vainio-Mattila, K. (2004). Towards smart home environments: Empirical evaluation of three user interfaces. *Journal of Personal and Ubiquitous Computing, 8,* 234–240.

Kotler, P. (1999). *Marketing management* (the millennium ed.). Upper Saddle River, NJ: Prentice Hall.

Kujala, S. (2003). User involvement: A review of the benefits and challenges. *Behavior & Information Technology, 22,* 1–16.

Kujala, S., Kauppinen, M., Lehtola, L., & Kojo, T. (2005). The role of user involvement in requirements quality and project success. In *IEEE International Requirements Engineering Conference* (RE '05, pp. 75–84). IEEE Computer Society Press.

Lampe, C., Ellison, N., & Steinfield, C. (2006). A Face(book) in the crowd: Social searching vs. social browsing. In *Proceedings of the 20th Anniversary Conference on Computer Supported Cooperative Work* (CSCW '06, pp. 167–170). New York: ACM Press.

Lampe, C., Ellison, N., & Steinfield, C. (2007). A familiar Face(book): Profile elements as signals in an online social network. In *Proceedings of the SIGCHI Conference on Human Factors in Computing Systems* (CHI '07, pp. 435–444). New York: ACM.

Leder, H., Belke, B., Oeberst, A., & Augustin, D. (2004). A model of aesthetic appreciation and aesthetic judgements. *British Journal of Psychology, 95,* 489–508.

Magnusson, P., Matthing, J., & Kristensson, P. (2003). Managing user involvement in service innovation: Experiments with innovating end users. *Journal of Service Research, 6,* 111–124.

Mäkelä, A., & Fulton Suri, J. (2001). Supporting users' creativity: Design to induce pleasurable experiences. In *Proceedings of International Conference on Affective Human Factors Design* (pp. 387–394). Singapore: ASEAN Academic Press.

Mayfield, A. (2007). *What is social media?* E-book by Spannerworks, retrieved on January 20, 2008, from www.spannerworks.com/ebooks.

Moggridge, B. (2006). *Designing interactions.* Cambridge, MA: MIT Press.

Moles, A. (1966). *Information theory and aesthetic perception.* Urbana, IL: University of Illinois Press.

Murthy, S., Maier, D., & Delcambre, L. (2006). Mash-o-matic. *In Proceedings of the 2006 ACM Symposium on Document Engineering,* (DocEng '06, pp. 205–214). Amsterdam: ACM.

Musser, J., O'Reilly, T. & the O'Reilly Radar Team (2006). *O'Reilly Radar: Web 2.0 Principles and Best Practices*. Retrieved February, 15, 2008, from www.oreilly.com/catalog/web2report/chapter/web20_report_excerpt.pdf.

Nielsen, J. (2000). *Designing web usability*. Indianapolis, IN: New Riders Publishing.

Norberg-Schulz, C. (1980). *Genius loci: Towards a phenomenology of architecture*. London: Academy Editions.

Norberg-Shulz, C. (1994). Stedsbruk [Art of place]. *Nordisk arkitekturforskning, 7*, 7–16.

Norman, D. (1988). *The design of everyday things*. London: The MIT Press.

Norman, D. (2003), *Emotional design: Why we love (or hate) everyday things*. New York: Basic Books.

O'Reilly, T. (2005). *What is Web 2.0: Design patterns and business models for the next generation of software*. Retrieved December, 16, 2007, from www.oreillynet.com/pub/a/oreilly/tim/news/2005/09/30/what-is-web-20.html.

Prahalad, C. K., & Ramaswamy, V. (2004a). Co-creating experiences: The next practice in value creation. *Journal of Interactive Marketing, 18*, 5–14.

Prahalad, C. K., & Ramaswamy, V. (2004b). *The future of competition: Co-creating unique value with customers*. Boston: HBS Press.

Preece, J. (2000). *Online communities: Designing usability, supporting sociability*. Chichester, UK: John Wiley & Sons.

Quinn, J. B., Baily, M., Baruch, J., Bikson, T., Carlson, D., Chamot, D., et al. (1994). *Information technology in the service society: A twenty-first century lever*. Washington, DC: National Academy Press.

Rogers, E. (2003). *Diffusion of innovations* (5th ed.). New York: Free Press.

Roto, V. (2006). *Web browsing on mobile phones: Characteristics of user experience* (Doctoral dissertation, Department of Computer Science, Helsinki University of Technology [TKK]). Espoo, Finland: TKK Publications.

Rowley, J. (2006). An analysis of the e-service literature: Towards a research agenda. *Internal Research, 16*, 339–359.

Spool, J. M., Scanlon, T., & Snyder, C. (1997). Product usability: Survival techniques. In *CHI '97 extended abstracts on human factors in computing systems: Looking to the future* (pp. 154–155). New York: ACM.

Väänänen-Vainio-Mattila, K., & Ruuska, S. (2000). Designing mobile phones and communicators for consumers' needs at Nokia. In E. Bergman (Ed.), *Information appliances and beyond: Interaction design for consumer products* (pp. 169–204). San Francisco: Morgan Kaufmann.

Virzi, R. A., Sokolov, J. L., & Karis, D. (1996). Usability problem identification using both low- and high-fidelity prototypes. In *Proceedings of the SIGCHI Conference on Human Factors in Computing Systems: Common ground* (CHI '96, pp. 236–243). New York: ACM.

von Hippel, Initial. (2005). *Democratizing innovation*. Cambridge, MA: MIT Press.

Vredenburg, K., Mao, J.-Y., Smith, P. W., & Carey, T. (2002). A survey of user-centered design practice. In *Proceedings of the SIGCHI Conference on Human Factors in Computing Systems: Changing our world, changing ourselves* (CHI '02, pp. 471–478). New York: ACM.

Vyas, D., & van der Veer, G. C. (2006). Experience as meaning: Some underlying concepts and implications for design. In *Proceedings of the 13th European Conference on Cognitive Ergonomics: Trust and control in complex socio-technical systems* (pp. 81–91). Zurich, Switzerland: ACM.

Wigelius, H., Aula, A., & Markova, M. (2007). Modeling tool for designing usable mobile services. In T. Tiainen, H. Isomäki, M. Korpela, A. Mursu, M.-K. Paakki, & S. Pekkola, (Eds.), *Proceedings of the 30th Information Systems Research Seminar in Scandinavia* (IRIS30; Dept. of Computer Sciences Pub. Series D-2007-9, pp. 512–531). Tampere, Finland: University of Tampere. Retrieved February, 18, 2008, from www.cs.uta.fi/reports/dsarja/D-2007-9.pdf.

Wong, J., & Hong, J. I. (2007). Making mashups with marmite: Towards end-user programming for the Web. In *Proceedings of the SIGCHI Conference on Human Factors in Computing Systems* (CHI '07, pp. 1435–1444). New York: ACM.

Wright, P., & McCarthy, J. (2005). The value of the novel in designing for experience. In A. Pirhonen, P. Saariluoma, H. Isomäki, & C. Roast. (Eds.), *Future interaction design* (pp. 9–30). London: Springer Verlag.

Yanbe, Y., Jatowt, A., Nakamura, S., & Tanaka, K. (2007). Can social bookmarking enhance search in the Web? In *Proceedings of the 2007 Conference on Digital Libraries* (pp. 107–116). New York: ACM.

Yang, F., & Mei, H. (2006). Development of software engineering: Co-operative efforts from academia, government and industry. In *Proceedings of the 28th International Conference on Software Engineering* (ICSE '06, pp. 2–11). New York: ACM.

Zhang, X., & Prybutok, V. R. (2005). A consumer perspective of e-service quality. *IEEE Transactions on Engineering Management, 52*, 461–477.

Precedents for the Design of Locative Media

Dimitris Charitos

Abstract This chapter investigates the emergence of new forms of communication environments, supported by the integration of new mobile and locative media technologies and the impact that the implementation of these systems may have on mediated communication within the urban context. As seen from a user perspective, locative media are considered as spatial communication interfaces. The chapter discusses the technologies supporting such multiuser systems, and suggests a series of precedents that may inform the process of creating location-based collaborative experiences such as hybrid spatial communication interfaces. This investigation ultimately aims to creat a theoretical framework for analyzing the experience of interacting with such systems and for supporting the design of locative media. It is finally suggested that locative media use may lead to revolutionary new ways of social interaction and inhabiting urban space and this possibility certainly calls for reconsidering how to conceive of, and consequently how to design, urban environments in the future.

1 Introduction

Digital media are increasingly becoming a part of one's social life and the context within which this life is taking place. The physical setting of this context consists of everyday environments. At the beginning of the 21st century, these environments are being reordered radically by technological systems and networks. Very recent advances in mobile and wireless communication technologies have begun to transform the potential for social interaction taking place within urban public spaces. More specifically, the convergence of new mobile telecommunication networks, geographical positioning systems, and interactive graphical interfaces on mobile devices, as they are already being utilized in a

D. Charitos (✉)
Laboratory of New Technologies in Communication, Education and the Mass Media,
Department of Communication and Media Studies, National & Kapodistrian
University of Athens, Athens, Greece
e-mail: vedesign@otenet.gr

P. Saariluoma, H. Isomäki (eds.), *Future Interaction Design II*,
DOI 10.1007/978-1-84800-385-9_7, © Springer-Verlag London Limited 2009

series of location-based activities,[1] leads to new forms of interpersonal communication. These forms may significantly alter the relationship of the physical world with the technologically mediated environment experienced by individuals who use these systems and, consequently, alter the way individuals perceive, experience, and conceive of urban public space. Such emerging types of communication may also lead to revolutionary new ways of social interaction and inhabiting urban space. This development certainly calls for reconsidering the way in which urban environments are conceived of and designed, by taking into account the incorporation of these information and communication technology (ICT) systems, since they are inseparably woven into the fabric of everyday life within the urban context.

This chapter aims at investigating the emergence of these forms of communication environments, supported by the integration of new mobile and locative media technologies, as well as the impact that the implementation of these systems may have on mediated communication within the city. The chapter focuses on such systems accessed via interfaces that have a predominantly spatial character and that ultimately afford a hybrid (synthetic and physical) spatial experience in the context of which a novel form of social interaction occurs. For this purpose, the chapter reviews literature discussing the design and implementation of these ICT systems, as well as relevant theoretical approaches that may relate to the use and impact of these systems. It then attempts to synthesize aspects of these approaches in order to outline a series of precedents that may inform the design and implementation of location-based systems and the communication experiences they support. The ultimate aim of this chapter is to inform the process of designing location-based collaborative experiences as hybrid spatial communication interfaces.

2 Relating Space, Communication and Technological Systems: The Case of Locative Media

Architectural design involves communication and thus could be partly considered a communicational activity. Designers may or may not see architectural designs, implicitly, as carriers of information and symbolic content; similarly buildings and urban environments have been perceived and interpreted by many (usually not architects) as cultural texts. At the same time, social and cultural studies have studied buildings and cities as contexts for social and cultural activities and life in general, from their mundane expression of everyday life (Highmore, 2001) to "higher" expressions of artistic creativity.

ICTs relate to both of these levels of scientific inquiry in many ways. Mobile telephony has already restructured the way people socialize and relate to urban space (Plant, 2001). Multiuser virtual environments redefine the meaning of

---

[1] That is, pervasive games, socializing services, commercial applications, and artwork.

mediated communication by immersing communicating participants in a synthetic spatial context. ICTs and new media may also be used for enhancing physical environments in order to communicate meaning and support interpersonal mediated communication among individuals who occupy these spaces. The contemporary urban environment already incorporates various kinds of representations of reality, communicated to citizens via various media and appropriate display systems.[2] These environments may also incorporate systems that capture visual, auditory, and other types of information regarding human activity and, consequently, utilize this input to affect the process of generating digital representations. The most advanced form of such systems is pervasive and ubiquitous computing systems (Weiser, 1991). I can therefore put forward the hypothesis (Charitos, 2005) that the incorporation of ICT systems results in an electronic enhancement of the everyday urban environment and that communication with these environments and with other citizens who exist and act within them is mediated by these systems.

Since 2003, the idea of associating mobile computing, wireless networks, and digital media, and binding them to real locations via location-detection technologies, has led to the concept of *locative media* (Tuters, 2004). These media are considered systems of technologically mediated interpersonal and group communication providing the opportunity to augment traditional urban environments with information and communication spatial experiences that can be accessed through mobile devices.

It is important to stress here that the production of any ICT system is in need of being informed by such disciplines as design studies, architectural and visual design, and social and cultural studies in a quest to create aesthetically pleasing, ergonomically efficient, and functional ICT systems. The need for such an interdisciplinary approach is best articulated by the low quality experienced in a large percentage of online content and applications today. This need is even more urgent when faced with the extremely complex task of designing locative media.

3 Mediated Spaces: Spatial Interfaces as Contexts for Communication

3.1 A Theoretical Framework for Considering Locative Media

This chapter reflects Graham's (2004, pp. 67–68) theoretical approach for analyzing the interrelationships between cities and ICTs as an overall theoretical framework. This approach refers to a series of recombinant perspectives and supports a fully relational view of the links between technology, time,

---

[2] Most of these representations are visual, that is, billboards, video projections, wall paintings, TV closed circuits, touch screens, and so on.

space, and social life. New technologies become interwoven into complex, contingent, and subtle blendings of human actors and technical artifacts to form actor networks that are sociotechnical hybrids. Accordingly, this chapter reflects the view that through such sociotechnical hybrids, social and spatial life becomes subtly and continuously recombined in complex combinations of new sets of spaces and times that are always contingent and impossible to generalize.

This view is anchored around the actor-network theory (ANT)[3] and Haraway's human-technological "cyborg" concept (Haraway, 1991, as cited in Graham, 2004, p. 68). ANT is a constructivist approach known for its insistence on the agency of nonhumans (Diamantaki, Charitos, Tsianos, & Lekkas, 2007). An actor (actant) in ANT is anything that acts, whether human or nonhuman. Humans and nonhumans are treated symmetrically in this theory but, most importantly, they are defined relationally as functors in the same total network. The concept of actants, for instance, denotes human and nonhuman actors, and assumes that the actors in a network take their shape by virtue of their relations with one another. It assumes that nothing lies outside the network of relations. As soon as an actor engages with an actor-network, it too is caught up in the web of relations, and becomes a part of this network of interaction.

This chapter considers ICT users not only as users of technology, but also as active agents who act on the basis of personal, though culturally conditioned, intentionalities and motives and who are perpetually engaged in meaning-production processes. Users themselves appropriate and "construct" the media they use. Therefore, media use must be seen as dependent on the users as well as on the social environment (Diamantaki et al., 2007).

According to ANT, technological artifacts are not simply tools used instrumentally to carry out various tasks; they are media-communicating human experience. The social world is a hybrid technosocial world, consisting of humans and artifacts/tools/technologies. According to the basic axiom of ANT, the social world consists of heterogeneous associations of humans and nonhumans. All human experience is shaped by the artifacts, machines, and sign systems that are used. In this framework, any system of technologically mediated communication (and certainly multiuser locative media are such systems) is assumed to be a type of technologically mediated experience. The importance of this theory is that it sets individuals next to artifacts and objects and emphasizes their mutual relationship (Diamantaki et al., 2007). None of the human actions can be understood without understanding the role of the objects used in daily life and the way these objects are integrated within daily social practice. However, it is understood that tools and machines do not have exactly the same status or role. In any case, this theory is moving away from a purely technological approach by suggesting a renewed emphasis on the

---

[3] ANT was mostly developed by B. Latour (2005) and M. Callon.

communicative and psychosocial dimensions of media use. After all, the axiom that a technological medium becomes a communication environment when it is transformed by a simple tool into a medium of symbolic communication between individuals is hardly ever questioned (Barnes, 2001)

It should also be clarified that I do not suggest in this chapter that the rapid evolution and proliferation of electronically mediated environments and communication networks necessarily have positive effects for everyday life in the urban context. We are daily witnesses to numerous events that reveal how communication via mobile telephony may isolate individuals from the social context within which they act. While taking into account the fact that the dissemination of these technologies and communication practices may undermine social life in the city (Plant, 2001), I attempt here to investigate possible reasons to support the view that it may also contribute to regenerating public space and animating social interactions within it.

3.2 Information Spaces

Spatial metaphors have long been used for aiding navigation within information sets. The term *spatial interfaces* will be used in this chapter to describe human–computer interfaces that utilize space as a context for supporting navigation within information sets. Since humans use spatial organizing principles in their daily lives, they are used to navigating space and communicating easily within space. Therefore, it could be suggested that graphical interactive environments may enhance communication between humans and computers (Dieberger, n.d.). While using information technology is abstract and complex because it lacks affordances (Gibson, 1986), metaphors can create affordances for information technology by mapping affordances from source domains (Kuhn, 1996). Spatialized user interfaces structure the domains of ICT applications through spatial metaphors. One of the first attempts to use a spatial interface as a means of navigation within the hypertextual information space was proposed by Dieberger & Tromp (1993).

It is generally accepted that graphical representations are a good way of communicating relationships among objects (Fairchild, 1993). The use of a graphical, three-dimensional (3D) spatial context for visualizing information may exploit the intrinsic skills that humans have for navigating in 3D space and for detecting visual patterns there. Moreover, it is understood (Fowler, Fowler, & Williams, 1996; Mukherjea & Hara, 1997) that 3D space allows for a more effective arrangement of a large set of informational objects and for visualizing more attributes for each of these objects than a two-dimensional (2D) space does. Accordingly, advances in virtual reality (VR) technology (Robertson, Mackinlay, & Card, 1991) have suggested that interactive visualizations of large information sets in a 3D context may increase the amount of information that people can meaningfully manage.

In order to support these arguments, previous work done on the issue of visualizing information in a 3D spatial context will now be considered. The relevant literature review has revealed three main approaches. The first research approach generally deals with the issue of visualizing large sets of relatively static data. In some cases, this research focuses on visualizing interobject relationships in detail—for example, the SemNet approach (Fairchild, Poltrock, & Furnas, 1988)—or attempts to deal with both interobject and intraobject relationships, such as the SGI FSN 3-D information navigator prototype.[4] Other attempts differ in terms of the way the visualized data are structured. The Xerox PARC cone tree and perspective wall systems (Mackinlay, Robertson, & Card, 1991; Robertson et al., 1991) aim at visualizing hierarchically and linearly structured data, respectively. Also, Benford et al. (1995) have described systems that support collaborative browsing of information and that correspond to differently structured data sets: well-structured and ordered sets, less well-structured without known interrelationships, and hypermedia structures.

Secondly, Benford et al. (1995) have dealt with data sets that are dynamically rearranged in 3D space. VR-VIBE, in particular, supports the positioning of information objects in 3D space according to their relevance to specific concepts called "points of interest" (p. 379–381). Similarly, Fairchild, Serra, Ng, Lee, & Ang (1992) have attempted to arrange objects on the surface of a sphere according to their relationships with a certain object of interest with the VizNet system.

Finally, a series of attempts have been made for visualizing hyperstructures of data. Dieberger & Tromp (1993) have proposed a model for an "information city" metaphor for a 3D interface to navigate hypertext structures. Andrews (1999) has developed the Harmony client for the Hyper-G data model, as a 3D structure map or an interactive 3D visualization of the data structure that may be both hierarchical and hyperlinked. Ingram and Benford (1995) have developed a system called LEgibility for Abstract Data Spaces (LEADS), which improves the legibility of information spaces by automatically creating or enhancing certain legibility features within pre-existing visualized information sets. Finally, Snowdon et al. (1997) have developed a novel browser called WWW3D, which integrates a representation of all Web documents that the user has browsed and history information about the links that the user has visited in the past, within a single 3D display the structure.

3.3 Spatial Communication Interfaces

Communication systems embody and integrate the functions of a communication interface, a series of transmission channels and an organizational infrastructure. Biocca and Delaney (1995) define a *communication interface* as the

---

[4] www.mmrg.ecs.soton.ac.uk/publications/archive/weal1996/html/node41.html.

interaction of physical media, codes, and information with the user's sensor-imotor and perceptual systems. As suggested earlier, an important characteristic of the particular interfaces that this chapter deals with is their environmental character: Users access locative media via multiuser interactive graphical interfaces that display some form of an environmental representation, within which all users of the system are concurrently represented in real time and that could comprise 2D and/or 3D visual content. The interface of other traditional electronic media (radio, TV) could also be considered as having an environmental character, in the sense that these media dominate the space within which they function as well as the mental space of humans who attend to them.

A virtual environment, being a 3D graphical representational context, is an intrinsically spatial type of communication interface. Ellis (1991) has emphasized the role of virtual reality (VR) as a communication technology or a medium of communication. When we experience the daily sense of our presence in the physical environment, we automatically produce a mental model of an external space from the stimuli that our sensory organs receive as input (Loomis, 1992). In this manner, the continuous, constant, and coherent sense of presence is the basic state of our conscience, whereby the user attributes the source of the sensation to the physical environment. When a user experiences a computer-mediated simulation environment, Lombard and Ditton (1997) suggest that the experience is traversed by a common idea: the "perceptual illusion of non-mediation" (p. 24) or what Minsky (1980, as cited in Bracken & Lombard, 2004) has identified[5] as sense of telepresence. The experience of telepresence involves continuous and real-time responses of the perceptual, cognitive, and affective processing systems of the user to objects and entities that are placed within one's environment. The illusion of nonmediation then implies that the user fails, to an extent, to perceive or to identify the existence of a medium, as a cause of this experience and reacts as if this medium were not there (Lombard & Ditton, 1997).

Harvey (1995, p. 376) goes even further, suggesting that VR can be thought of in terms of social presence—and not mere telepresence—thus proposing VR as a culturally important phenomenon and not just a channel of connecting the world. Schroeder (1996) suggests that a single-user virtual environment interface may be defined more accurately as an information technology rather than a communication technology since the concept of information is mostly used to denote what is transferred to a single individual, rather than what is exchanged between two or more individuals.

Virtual environments are not the only types of spatial computer-generated graphical interfaces. Despite their environmental character, the majority of interfaces used in mobile and locative media usually comprise 2D, and not necessarily 3D, graphics displayed to users via relatively small screens. In such

---

[5] Minsky has proposed this term in the context of *teleoperation* technology.

an interactive graphical interface, the experience of telepresence afforded to the user is not as strong as in the case of a VR simulation "world." This is mainly due to the less immersive experience afforded by display devices, as well as the fact that the representational context where interaction occurs may not necessarily be fully 3D. Even in an interactive graphical interface, however, the user may be considered somehow telepresent in the environmental context of interaction, irrespective of the immersiveness or the display quality of the experience. Therefore, this graphical world may still actively engage some of the user's sensorimotor channels, at least up to an extent, by providing a navigable and manipulable spatial context within which communication may take place. Following Biocca and Delaney's (1995) earlier mentioned definition, a single-user interactive graphical interface that is used in the case of locative media could be considered a communication interface. In this sense, the interface could be viewed an advancement in a continuum of communication interface systems, like the radio and the TV. It is an interface that engages the human sensorimotor channels into a vivid communication experience and that also affords an environmental experience. Accordingly, this chapter will use the term *spatial communication interface* to characterize the type of interface experienced by locative media users. Designing such a communication interface implies the design of the way in which interaction occurs among physical media, codes, and information on the one hand and the user's sensorimotor and perceptual systems on the other hand, as well as the appropriate environmental context and representation for this interaction.

4 Introducing Mobility and Multiuser Access to Spatial Communication Interfaces

Consider that graphical interfaces may be accessed by multiple users, concurrently interacting and communicating within this context. These interfaces could, more appropriately than single-user graphical interface platforms, be described as communication media. As Schroeder (1996, p. 146) suggests, "The notion of a communications technology normally implies that two or more people are involved and that the emphasis is placed on the messages that pass between them." Accordingly, the concepts of communication and medium should preferably be used in the framework of multiuser interactive graphics systems. Barnes (2001) argues that a technological medium becomes a communication environment when it is transformed from a tool to a medium of symbolic interaction between people. The term *communication environment* may appropriately correspond to a communication interface, which has an environmental character.

Therefore, the multiuser interactive graphical interfaces discussed here are considered communication environments, which function as systems of interpersonal but computer-mediated communication. Within the context of these environments, communication among remotely located, networked individuals is mediated. Following McQuail's (1997) categorization of different levels of a communication process, these environments function at two different levels:

- At a *personal level* (human–computer communication), information is transmitted to users in various forms.
- At an *interpersonal level* (human–computer–human communication), a multiuser environment may function as the spatial context that accommodates synchronous, interpersonal mediated communication among participants represented within this space by some form of graphical representation.

A series of new technological developments regarding wireless communication networks provide the opportunity for presenting interactive multimedia content via 2D and 3D graphics and video on mobile handsets, thus communicating more information and in a more pleasurable and engaging manner than text-based content. These developments afford the possibility of multisensory communication among remotely positioned and potentially mobile individuals via a graphical human–computer interface (Beardow, 2002).

One very effective type of multimedia with a proven high ability to hold users' attention span is the use of interactive 3D graphics on mobile interfaces. Interactive 3D graphics content adds to the sense of depth and the environmental character of the representation and also affords more possibilities for presenting information on the limited surface of a mobile device display. Moreover, the ability to interact and determine the course of the representation may significantly enhance the engagement of participants with the evolving action (Beardow, 2002). These facts have contributed to the gradual integration of interactive 3D graphics within the interface of mobile devices. This will enable mobileusers to access online 3D games and similar applications that have the potential for creating huge online user communities. In an online game, however, 3D content may be distributed to users playing on the road (on a mobile) but could also be accessed by users at home (on a graphics PC). The introduction of 3D graphics in mobile devices implies the introduction of mobility into interacting with 3D interfaces and the potential afforded to both mobile and home users for participating concurrently in multiuser activities within such mediated spaces. One very good example of artwork affording such a collaborative experience is the revolutionary work of the new media performance group Blast Theory, titled *Uncle Roy All Around You*.[6]

Mobility may also be introduced in more engaging environmental experiences afforded by mixed reality (MR) or augmented reality (AR) simulation

---

[6] "*Uncle Roy All Around You*" was performed during the *Futuresonic* festival in Manchester in 2004. Information about it and other related Blast Theory projects can be found at www.blasttheory.co.uk/

systems.[7] For example, a mobile AR game that takes place in the urban context may place the player in a hybrid kind of space simultaneously comprising the electronically mediated spatial context as well as the surrounding physical settings. A system for playing the popular online video game *Quake* in an urban space, as opposed to with a desktop computer, has been developed at the University of South Australia. A wearable computer was mounted on a backpack and the 3D space of the video game was projected over the real-world landscape through a head-mounted display, while the two projected environments were coordinated with the help of GPS technology (Piekarski & Thomas, 2002).

5 Introducing Context Awareness to Mobile Spatial Communication Interfaces

New types of wireless communication networks enable the detection of a user's position at all times via GPS or related technologies. This information may be utilized by the system for updating the output displayed to users at all times, according to their dynamically changing location at all times. The ability to track the location of users or other potentially mobile entities and the input of information regarding the environmental situation captured by sensors embedded in the physical environment contributes toward creating context-aware systems.

In order to understand the social ramifications of these locative communication media, it is important to investigate the impact the kind of interpersonal communication they support has on our everyday experience within the urban environment. Souza e Silva (2003) was one of the first to suggest the significance of these interactive communication environments, through which virtual worlds immigrate from the Internet to urban spaces. While the Internet allowed physical meeting places to migrate to a virtual spatial context, the introduction of mobile location-based communication networks relates the concept of a "meeting place" to the physical space of an urban environment. Thus, social computing, which was previously restricted to the Internet, is now brought back into the urban realm. Indeed, the emergence of *locativeness* reintroduces the parameter of real location in the activity of mediated communication, thus mapping the virtual mental space of communication to the physical space, inhabited by the real bodies of communicating participants.

In location-based games, for example, the location of each player in the physical world is very important.[8] Thus, the virtual spatial context of the game

---

[7] A *mixed* or *augmented reality system* is a fully interactive system that displays visual output to the user, the source of which is a simultaneous integration of a synthetic 3D computer graphics world and real-time video footage of the surrounding environment.

[8] When the player approaches a location his/her mobile phone notifies him of his/her whereabouts, while at the same time, this location is mapped onto the game's visual representation for all players to view.

is mapped onto the physical world and this hybrid spatial context becomes the arena of the game. Similarly, urban physical space may be enriched with an essentially social quality; the location may become a practical condition of social encounters, offering opportunities for action and interaction. These media may return attention to the social, cultural, and intersubjectively constructed aspects that characterize urban spaces. Most importantly, they afford the possibility for face-to-face interaction and bring back the "compulsion of proximity" (Boden & Molotch, 2004, p. 101) into computer-mediated communication.

Of particular interest to this discussion is the manner in which the spatial context, where situated communication (Suchman, 1987) occurs and is transformed by the introduction of these technologies. Locative media may be called systems of situated, context-aware communication. Location-based mediated environments bring human–computer communication and human–computer–human communication back into the context of the physical world, instead of expecting humans to adapt to the needs of a computer environment. If the Internet is considered a medium and a context, where information and symbolic content are communicated among its users, this information and content do not usually relate to its actual location or to the physical location of its users. Locative media, on the other hand, afford the possibility of relating a part of this content to physical locations and, in a way, promise a kind of *spatialization* of the Internet, whereby a part of its content, and the activities it relates to, are mapped onto physical space.

6 Locative Media Mediating Communication Within the Urban Context

Castells (2004) suggests that space is a fundamental dimension of society, inseparable from the overall process of social organization and social change. Thus the new urban world rises from within the process of formation of a new society, the network society. This chapter, however, does not view the aforementioned novel telecommunications technologies as directly causing urban change because of their intrinsic characteristics as space-transcending and unifying communication channels. As suggested in Section 3.1, this chapter subscribes to a theoretical perspective in which urban places and technological systems are socially constructed in Paralel (Graham, 2004, p. 67) and attempts to investigate possible reasons for supporting the view that mobile and locative media may contribute to regenerating public space and animating social interactions within it. It is therefore useful to ask, at this point, a critical question: Why is public space in need of regeneration?

Auge (1992) appropriately describes the character of urban space in postindustrial highly urbanized societies as a "nonspace" that people perceive, but only in a partially and incoherent manner. The term *space* is more abstract in itself than the term *place*, the usage of which at least refers to an event (which has taken place), a myth (said to have taken place) or a history (high places). Cities today are full of spaces in which the individual feels himself/herself to be a spectator, without paying much attention to the spectacle (Auge, 1992). In these spaces, city dwellers usually navigate without bothering to attempt interaction with others or to relate to the environmental setting; they are mere passersby and rarely find any meaning in these spaces other than merely moving through them, from one point to the other at a topological or geographical level.

The nonspaces experienced in everyday urban contexts are usually not experienced as places. The definition of a place implies a space enriched with meaning, the context within which human interactions and relations take place. For Relph (1976, p. 114), the foundation of the place concept is "existential insideness," the degree to which people feel a part of a place, as opposed to "existential outsideness," which involves feelings of strangeness and separation from a place. A space is subjectively defined and remembered as a place and is thus tightly related to individual actions and intentions. Relph (1976, pp. 42–43) suggests that,

> Places are the contexts or backgrounds of intentionally defined objects or groups of objects or events, or they can be objects of intention in their own right.... Those places are defined largely in terms of the objects and their meanings. As objects in their own right, places are essentially focuses of attention, usually having a fixed location and possessing features which persist in an identifiable form.... They can be at almost any scale depending on the manner in which our intentions are directed and focused.

But why do we need places to dwell in? According to Relph (1976, p. 1), people need to design their environments and to develop frameworks as systems of meaningful places, which give form and structure to the experiences in the real world.

Castells (1996, pp. 441–442) presents a social conception of space as the material support of time-sharing social practices. He argues that society is constructed around "flows": flows of capital, flows of information, flows of technology, flows of people who commute, flows of images, sounds, symbols, and so on, as expressions of processes dominating economic, political, and symbolic life. He then introduces the concept of the "space of flows" as the "material organization of time-sharing social practices that work through flows," supported by information and communication technologies and networks.

Even though the space of flows appears to be the dominant spatial form in the network society, these spaces, and the people acting in them, still exist within the "space of places" of their physical surroundings too. Castells (1996, pp. 441–442) identifies a growing tension and articulation between the space of flows and the space of places. While the space of places organizes experience around the confines of locality, the space of flows links up electronically separate locations into an interactive network that connects activities and people in distinct geographical contexts. Cities do not disappear in the virtual networks of ICTs but are transformed by the interface between electronic communication and physical interaction through this combination of networks and places. At the same time, cities are made up of flows and places and of the relationships among these flows and places. The places of the space of flows are the corridors and halls, usually experienced as nonspaces that connect places around the world. The city dweller of the 21st century is usually mobile and online, moving physically between places, while keeping the network connection at all times. What is quite significant to stress here, therefore, is that "we move physically while staying put in our electronic connection. We carry flows and move across places" (Castells, 2004, p. 88).

As it was suggested in Section 2, everyday urban contexts at the beginning of the 21st century largely consist of electronically enhanced mediated environments. In an attempt to conceive of and analyze the spatial experience of a human inhabiting these spaces, it can be suggested that his/her sense of presence may fluctuate among three different states (Kim & Biocca, 1997):

1. Presence in the physical world: The most natural and nonmediated state of "being here," where the human attributes the source of his/her experience to the stimuli emanating from his/her physical surroundings.
2 Presence in an electronically mediated virtual environment: This could be any synthetic experience with environmental qualities, which is generated by making use of one or more electronic communication media.
3 Presence in an imaginary environment: This sense of presence is dominated by internally generated mental images.

In fact, although a human may experience all three of these states at the same time, usually one of them prevails.

This conception could be related to Hayles' attempt to explain the spatial experience involved in mobile communication: In an interview with Souza e Silva (2003, p. 14), she has suggested that we can conceive of contexts of communication as being "enfolded," so that "there is no longer a homogeneous context for a given spatial area, but rather pockets of different contexts in it." Souza e Silva (2003) further explains this approach: There may be a context that is created by the spatial proximity of people and, inside it, there is another context that is created by the cell phone communicational activity, involving a remotely located interlocutor too. Each new folded context reconfigures reality and the social relationships that take place within one specific area. Each mobile device carries the potential for whole new contexts, ready to fold reality again.

In an attempt to describe the collaborative spatial experience afforded to all participating users of the multiuser locative media discussed in this chapter, it may be suggested that the folded context corresponding to the concurrent flow of content among all users has indeed more of a representational and spatial character, due to the spatial graphical interface of the system. This may result in a kind of hybrid spatial experience, involving the potential coexistence of participants, not only in the space of flows they carry with them, but also in the space of places within which they may experience proximity.

In the context of global cities at the beginning of the 21st century, Castells (2004) argues that public places, as sites of spontaneous social interaction, may again become the communicative devices of society. Could, then, mobile and location-based communication technologies afford highly mobile and indivi-dualistic 21st-century city dwellers the ability to connect to each other, to rediscover the joy of spontaneous social interaction, to become more active, and to recreate communities and bonds of socialization? Could these media contribute towards transforming the devoid-of-meaning nonplaces of contem-porary urban spaces into a socially meaningful network of places for interac-tion? Tuters (2004, p. 1) suggests that locative media may transform the urban space of disconnected flows into a huge "peripatetic computer" of interpersonal contact that is a space full of potentially social places. This may lead to electro-nically enhanced public spaces that can be enjoyed, as they regain life by aiding city dwellers who are virtually strangers to meet in public places and engage together in various activities. In this sense, the urban space, enhanced by the ICT system, partly becomes a spatial communication interface, potentially initiating social interaction among the connected (and possibly unconnected) citizens who inhabit it.

The introduction of mobility into the practice of interacting with spatial inter-faces and the possibility of accessing a virtual environment, afforded concurrently to mobile and fixed users, creates very interesting prospects for collaborative mediated experiences. With the aid of location-based systems, space is being hybridized as the mediated spatial experience that is mapped onto the physical urban environment, allowing for new kinds of collaborative activities and social interaction. Thus, the experience of urban space is augmented by multiple layers of information, potentially accessible by all participating mobile users.

Mobile and locative technologies are seen as supporting novel and revolu-tionary new ways of inhabiting urban spaces. Communication is tied to places and places to communication (Charitos, Diamantaki, Gazi, & Meimaris, 2005). The emergence of locative and mobile communication systems and their potential impact on social interaction in the urban context, however, suggests that new conceptual models regarding the design of such hybrid, dynamically evolving environmental experiences are needed. Locative media may contribute to turning the city into a social arena again. This possibility certainly calls for reconsidering how we conceive of and consequently how we design urban environments that will be inhabited by 21st-century mobile and constantly online city dwellers.

References

Andrews, K. (1999). Visualising cyberspace: Information visualisation in the Harmony Internet browser. In S. K. Card, J. D. Mackinlay, & B. Shneiderman (Eds.), *Readings in information visualization* (pp. 493–502). San Francisco: Morgan Kaufmann.

Auge, M. (1992). *Non-places: Introduction to an anthropology of supermodernity*. London: Verso.

Barnes, S. B. (2001). *Online connections: Internet interpersonal relations*. Cresskill, NJ: Hampton Press.

Beardow, P. (2002). *Enabling wireless interactive 3D*. Retrieved November 1, 2004 from the Superscape site, www.superscape.com.

Benford, S., Bowers, J., Fahlen, L. E., Greenhalgh, C., Mariani, J., & Rodden, T. (1995). Networked virtual reality and cooperative work. *Presence: Teleoperators and Virtual Environments, 4*, 364–386.

Biocca, F., & Delaney, B. (1995). Immersive virtual reality technology. In F. Biocca & M. R. Levy (Eds.), *Communication in the age of virtual reality* (pp. 57–124). Hillsdale, NJ: Lawrence Erlbaum Associates.

Boden D., & Molotch, H. (2004). Cyberspace meets the compulsion of proximity. In S. Graham, (Ed.), *The cybercities reader* [Urban Reader Series, pp. 101–105]. London: Routledge.

Bracken, C. C., & Lombard, M. (2004). Social presence and children: Praise, intrinsic motivation, and learning with computers. *Journal of Communication, 54*, 22–37.

Castells M. (1996). *The rise of the network society* (Vol. 1). Cambridge, MA: Blackwell.

Castells, M. (2004). Space of flows, space of places: Materials for a theory of urbanism in the information age. In S. Graham (Ed.), *The cybercities reader* [Urban Reader Series, pp. [82–93]. London: Routledge.

Charitos, D. (2005). Virtual reality: A new kind of human-computer interface or a new communication medium? *Issues of Communication, 2*, 83–99.

Charitos, D., Diamantaki, K., Gazi. A., & Meimaris, M. (2005, May). *The emergence of new types of hybrid mobile communication environments and their impact on social life within the urban context*. Paper presented at the 3rd International Conference on Communication and Reality, Barcelona, Spain.

Diamantaki, K., Charitos, D., Tsianos, N., & Lekkas Z. (2007, September). Towards investigating the social dimensions of using locative media within the urban context. Paper presented at the 3rd IE International Conference on Intelligent Environments, Ulm University, Germany.

Dieberger, A. (n.d.). *Navigation in textual virtual environments using a city metaphor* [Doctoral dissertation abstract]. Retrieved September 11, 1996, from the Institute for Geoinformation and Cartography [Technical University of Vienna] research group, www.geoinfo.tuwien.ac.at/publications.

Dieberger, A., & Tromp, J. (1993, December). *The Information City Project: A virtual reality user interface for navigation in information spaces*. Paper presented at the Vienna Virtual Reality '93 Conference, Vienna, Austria.

Ellis, S. R. (1991). Nature and origins of virtual environments: A bibliographical essay. *Computing Systems in Engineering, 2*, 321–347.

Fairchild, K. M. (1993). Information management using virtual reality-based visualizations. In A. Wexelblat (Ed.), *Virtual reality applications and explorations* (pp. 45–74). London: Academic Press Professional.

Fairchild, K. M., Poltrock, S. E., & Furnas, G. W. (1988). SemNet: Three-dimensional graphic representations of large knowledge spaces. In R. Guindon (Ed.), *Cognitive science and its applications for human–computer interaction* (pp. 201–233). Hillsdale, NJ: Lawrence Erlbaum Associates.

Fairchild, K. M., Serra, L., Ng, H., Lee, B. H., & Ang, T. L (1992, month). *Dynamic fisheye information visualizations*. Paper presented at the 1st British Computer Society Conference on Virtual Reality.

Fowler, R., Fowler, W. A. L. & Williams, J. L. (1996, October). *3D visualization of WWW semantic content for browsing and query formulation*. Paper presented at the WebNet 96 Conference, San Francisco, CA.

Gibson, J. J. (1986). *The ecological approach to visual perception*. Hillsdale. NJ: Lawrence Erlbaum Associates.

Graham, S. (Ed.). (2004). *The cybercities reader* [Urban Reader Series]. London: Routledge.

Harvey, L. (1995). Communication issues and policy implications. In F. Biocca & M. R. Levy (Eds.), *Communication in the age of virtual reality* (pp. 369–387). Hillsdale, NJ: Lawrence Erlbaum Associates.

Highmore, B. (Ed.). (2001). *The everyday life reader*. London: Routledge.

Ingram, R., & Benford, S. (1995). Improving the legibility of virtual environments. In M. Goebel (Ed.), *Virtual Environments '95* (pp. 211–223). London: Springer.

Kim, T., & Biocca, F. (1997). Telepresence via television: Two dimensions of telepresence may have different connections to memory and persuasion. *Journal of Computer Mediated Communication, 3*(2). Retrieved March 5, 2007, from jcmc.indiana.edu/vol3/issue2/kim.html

Kuhn, W. (1996). Handling data spatially: Spatializating user interfaces. In M. J. Kraak & M. Molenaar (Eds.), *Advances in GIS research II: Proceedings of the 7th International Symposium on Spatial Data Handling.* (Vol. 2, pp. 13B.1–13B.23). Delft, The Netherlands: IGU.

Latour, B. (2005). *Reassembling the social: An introduction to actor-network theory.* New York: Oxford University Press.

Lombard, M., & Ditton, T. (1997). At the heart of it all: The concept of presence. *Journal of Computer-Mediated Communication, 3*(2). Retrieved March 5, 2007, from jcmc.indiana.edu/vol3/issue2/lombard.html

Loomis, J. M. (1992). Distal attribution and presence. *Presence, Teleoperators, and Virtual Environments, 1,* 113–118.

Mackinlay, J. D., Robertson G. G., & Card, S. K. (1991). The perspective wall: Detail and context smoothly integrated. In *Proceedings of the SIGCHI Conference on Human Factors in Computing Systems: Reaching Through Technology* (pp. 173–179). New York: ACM Press.

McQuail, D. (1997). *Mass communication theory: An introduction.* Athens, Greece: Kastaniotis.

Mukherjea, S., & Hara, Y. (1997, April). *Focus + context views of World-Wide Web nodes.* Paper presented at the ACM Hypertext '97 Conference, Southampton, UK.

Piekarski, W., & Thomas, B. (2002). ARQuake: The outdoors augmented reality system. *Communications of the ACM, 45,* 36–38.

Plant, S. (2001). *On the mobile: The effects of mobile telephones on social and individual life.* Study commissioned by Motorola. Retrieved August 2, 2007, from www.motorola.com/mot/doc/0/234_MotDoc.pdf

Relph, E. (1976). *Place and placelessness.* London: Pion.

Robertson, G. G., Mackinlay, J. D., & Card, S. K. (1991). Cone trees: Animated 3D visualizations of hierarchical information. In *CHI '91 Proceedings: Human Factors in Computing Systems* (pp. 189–194). New York: ACM Press.

Schroeder, R. (1996). *Possible worlds: The social dynamic of virtual reality technology.* Boulder, CO: Westview Press.

Snowdon, D., Benford, S., Greenhalgh, C., Ingram, R., Brown, C., Lloyd, D., et al. (1997, April). A 3D collaborative virtual environment for Web browsing. Paper presented at the Virtual Reality Universe '97 conference, Santa Clara, CA. Retrieved August 3, 2007 from www.crg.cs.nott.ac.uk/research/publications/papers/vru97-www3d.pdf.

Souza e Silva, A. (2003). Mobile networks and public spaces: Bringing multi-user environments into the physical space. In R. Ascott (Ed.), *Electronic Proceedings of the 2003 Consciousness Reframed International Conference* [on CD-ROM]. Newport, Wales: University of Wales College, Centre for the Advanced Inquiry into the Interactive Arts.

Suchman, L. (1987). *Plans and situated actions: The problem of human-machine communication.* Cambridge, UK: Cambridge University Press.

Tuters, M. (2004, May). *The locative commons: Situating location-based media in urban public space.* Paper presented at the 2004 Futuresonic Conference. Manchester, UK. Retrieved May 10, 2005, from www.futuresonic.com/futuresonic/pdf/Locative_Commons.pdf

Weiser, M. (1991). The computer for the twenty-first century. *Scientific American, 265*(3), 94–104.

Acceptance or Appropriation? A Design-Oriented Critique of Technology Acceptance Models

Antti Salovaara and Sakari Tamminen

Abstract Technology acceptance models (TAMs) are tools for predicting users' reception of technology by measuring how they rate statements on a questionnaire scale. It has been claimed that these tools help to assess the social acceptance of a final IT product when its development is still under way. However, their use is not without problems. This chapter highlights some of the underlying shortcomings that arise particularly from a simplistic conception of "acceptance" that does not recognize the possibility that users can invent new uses for (i.e., appropriate) technology in many situations. This lack of recognition can easily lead one to assume that users are passive absorbers of technological products, so that every user would adopt the same usages irrespective of the context of use, the differences in work tasks, or the characteristics of interpersonal cooperation. In light of recent research on appropriation, technology use must actually be understood in a more heterogeneous way, as a process through which different users find the product useful in different ways. This chapter maintains that if, in fact, a single technology can be used for multiple purposes, then subscribing to the thinking arising from technology acceptance model research may actually lead one to suboptimal design solutions and thus also compromise user acceptance. This chapter also presents some starting points for designing specifically for easier technology appropriation.

1 Introduction

Understanding and predicting how new technologies will be received by their potential users is one of the central topics both when planning design processes and during the actual design activity. In order to be successful in making predictions, understanding both the users' mindsets and their activity contexts

A. Salovaara (✉)
Helsinki Institute for Information Technology (HIIT), Helsinki University of Technology and University of Helsinki, Helsinki, Finland
e-mail: antti.salovaara@hiit.fi

P. Saariluoma, H. Isomäki (eds.), *Future Interaction Design II*,
DOI 10.1007/978-1-84800-385-9_8, © Springer-Verlag London Limited 2009

have been found to be crucial. As a reaction to these needs, various methods have been devised, borrowing techniques from, for example, ethnography (e.g., Beyer & Holtzblatt, 1998), dramaturgy and theater (Mehto, Kantola, Tiitta, & Kankainen, 2006; Svanæs & Seland, 2004), and, as a third example, the topic of this book chapter, questionnaire-based quantitative studies to assess technology acceptance (Davis, 1989; Davis, Bagozzi, & Warshaw, 1989; Venkatesh & Davis, 2000; Venkatesh, Morris, Davis, & Davis, 2003).

Research on technology acceptance models (TAMs) has had an important impact on recent design thinking. This field has introduced into user-centered design terms like user acceptance, social acceptance, diffusion, and adoption. As a consequence, it is nowadays very common in design meetings to hear discussions on social acceptability and user acceptance and their relevance to the success of the product.

Wrapping the thinking about design processes around this kind of terminology has implications for the actual design practice as well. Naturally, this does not always take place without problems. One caveat is that adoption and acceptability are concepts that refer to masses of users and tend to make one think only about an "average user" who represents the whole user population. This chapter proposes that the various technology acceptance models do not actually address a central characteristic of information technology artifacts: Users' active sense-making processes contribute significantly to the use of the product and its acceptance. Therefore it is not always possible to talk about users as a uniform segment of people, and TAMs are not adept at assessing the real acceptance of technologies.

2 Technology Acceptance Models

TAMs have been developed in response to the need to evaluate users' subjective satisfaction rates, and to use such rates as predictors of a system's success (Davis, 1989; Davis et al., 1989). Different theories and models conceptualize the acceptance in various ways, but a common characteristic is that all of them belong to the research tradition of social cognition, a field that tries to account for human action by applying psychological constructs such as attitudes, values, or norms. For example, Fishbein and Ajzen's (1975) theory of reasoned action (TRA) and theory of planned behavior (TPB) have been used extensively in various information technology attitude measurement scales (see Dillon & Morris, 1996.)

Davis' (1989) TAM is based on Fishbein and Ajzen's (1975) TRA, but it has been streamlined in comparison to the original theory. The main idea of the model is to describe the external factors affecting the internal attitudes and use intentions of the users and, through these, to predict the acceptance and use of the system. The model consists of two attitudinal dimensions: Perceived Usefulness (PU) and Perceived Ease of Use (PEOU). It is postulated that these are directly related to the use of an information system. PU is defined as "the degree to which a person believes that using a particular system would enhance his or her job performance" (Davis, 1989, p. 320). PEOU in turn is defined by user's subjective evaluations on how much cognitive work she or he must expend when using the system.

Building on previous research, Davis et al. (1989, p. 987) postulate that these dimensions are distinct but related constructs. They can be measured individually, therefore, even though PEOU has a direct effect on PU (see Fig. 1). Davis et al. also claim that PU is directly linked to intentions of use (as compared to TRA, which postulates that all intentions are mediated by formation of attitudes). Thus, according to TAM, a user's acceptance of an information system is dependent on two factors: perceived usefulness and perceived ease of use. Together, these factors determine the attitude toward using the technology. This in turn affects the behavioral intentions of use, which then leads to actual use.[1]

Technology acceptance in the model presented by Davis (1989) is measured with 20 questions (10 questions for usefulness, 10 questions for ease of use) that ask the user to rate statements like "Using X in my job would enable me to accomplish tasks more quickly" (see Davis, 1989, p. 340). The result is an estimate of the system's acceptance. Later, different variants of the original TAM and the questionnaire have been presented (for a review, see Dillon & Morris, 1996). Depending on the research questions of each study, questionnaires have been administered at different points in time, ranging from immediate responses after an initial training to arrangements that have covered longer timespans.

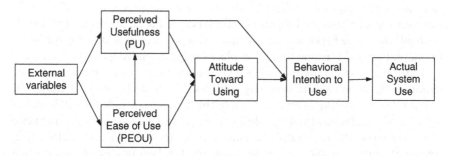

Fig. 1 The original technology acceptance model (TAM) by Davis et al. (1989, p. 985). Reprinted by permission, ©1989 The Institute for Operations Research and the Management Sciences (INFORMS)[1]

---

[1] Reprinted by permission, Fred D. Davis, Richard P. Bagozzi, Paul R. Warshaw. 1989. User acceptance of computer technology: A comparison of two theoretical models, Management Science, volume 35, number 8, August, 1989. Copyright 1989, the Institute for Operations Research and the Management Sciences (INFORMS), 7240 Parkway Drive, Suite 310, Hanover, MD 21076 USA.

3 Scope of the Original Model and Subsequent Criticisms

In his original paper, Davis (1989) claimed that the results obtained through measuring users' subjective ratings in this way can provide trustworthy estimates of acceptance both when the users are very familiar with the technology (e.g., having experience of 6 months of use) and when they have had only a half an hour's experience of using it. To scope this claim, Davis et al. listed some boundary conditions for the applicability of their model. They acknowledged that their primary interest is in workplace settings in which utility is the primary value of user acceptance (1989, p. 986). This was also evident in how the statements in the measurement questionnaire were formulated (see the example statement above). As another boundary condition, their TAM was focused on measuring opinions of individual workers (Davis, 1989, pp. 998–999) and, in doing so, it did not take into consideration the effects of the social organization, such as distribution and delegation of work, different worker roles, or joint work routines at the workplace. Later, more TAMs have been proposed, but they have been based on similar starting points (e.g., see a synthesis of these models by Venkatesh et al., 2003).

However, criticism has started to emerge about such constraints in TAM studies and the research approach in general. One part of the criticism has been directed at the research designs. For instance, based on a review of 101 articles, Lee, Kozar, and Larsen (2003) point out that many studies base their measures on users' self-reported amounts of use and short exposures with the technology in question. Lack of longitudinal studies (i.e., ones containing multiple measurement points) is another issue, also mentioned by Benbasat and Barki (2007). Both Lee et al. and Benbasat and Barki raise the concern that the existing models "do not adequately capture or describe the dynamic interplay that usually occurs between the various user behaviors" (Benbasat & Barki, 2007, p. 215). Longitudinal studies are hypothesized to counter this problem by addressing the issues of adaptation and learning that takes place during extended use.

Naturally, some longitudinal TAM studies have been carried out. For instance, temporality was explicitly addressed in a study by Venkatesh and Davis (2000), resulting in an extension in the model to include four PU-related social influence factors (image, subjective norm, experience, and voluntariness) and three new PEOU-related "cognitive instrumental process" factors (job relevance, output quality, result demonstrability). In four case studies on two mandatory and two voluntary organization-wide workplace systems, the new TAM2 model was found to explain 60% of the variance in judgments of perceived usefulness (Venkatesh & Davis, 2000, p. 198). However, in light of the findings from qualitative studies (as opposed to quantitatively oriented TAM studies) on groupware systems in similar settings, finding such neat correlations should be interpreted with a grain of salt. For example, a study on the Lotus Notes groupware system by Orlikowski and her colleagues showed that a system's use can evolve over time, often in a stepwise manner (Tyre &

Orlikowski, 1994). At many different stages during the years that their study lasted, both the workers and managers perceived both the system and its usefulness in different ways (Orlikowski, 1996). Because Venkatesh and Davis (2000) do not provide much information about the workplace contexts in their studies, the discrepancy between their findings and those of Orlikowski and Tyre is difficult to explain.

The problems related to measuring information system usage have also received much attention. Many researchers have expressed worries about simplistic operationalizations on how systems are used. Schwarz and Chin (2007, p. 232) lament that "most studies to date typically measure usage as extent or frequency of use" and that "IT acceptance is predominantly about predicting a particular mode of use (i.e., degree or amount of use)." Naturally, measuring only the extent of use means that the above-mentioned "dynamic interplay" (Benbasat & Barki, 2007, p. 215) cannot be fully captured in TAM research. To solve this problem, Burton-Jones and Straub (2006) have proposed a two-stage research method that requires the researchers first to define what system usage entails in their study and what are its underlying assumptions. In the second stage, they have to select which measures for each "structural element" of usage—the system, the user, or the task—are to be used. With this methodology, the conceptual imprecision of usage is properly clarified, leading to better explanations of the usage–performance relationship.

Another suggestion for sensitizing TAM research to different types of usage has been proposed by Jasperson, Carter, and Zmud (2005). Their interest is in post-adoptive behaviors, that is, longitudinal observations of use that examine subsequent usage after the user's initial adoption. They suggest lowering the analysis to the level of individual system features, thus increasing sensitivity to changes.

A third criticism has been the insensitivity to different use contexts. The models do not take into account the possibility that a technology may be initially accepted but later abandoned, or vice versa. Nonetheless, they are meant to serve as predictors of the future success of a technology. For example, Davis et al. stated that "in contrast, TAM's U [usefulness] and EOU [ease of use] are postulated a priori, and are meant to be fairly general determinants of user acceptance" (1989, p. 988) and that the contextual variation is included in the model only as an "external variable" (p. 987, see also p. 989). Due to such postulations, TAMs are not sensitive to cases in which the context of use is changing or the relevant aspects of use are somewhat unknown. This complicates comparisons across cases as well as overall generalizations from the results.

In later research, insensitivity to different contexts has been addressed by developing different variations of TAM for different technologies. The goal of developing a family of models is justified by a recent metareview of 63 studies that showed that the type of technology is likely to have a significant moderating effect on acceptance (Schepers & Wetzels, 2007). The authors categorized the various studies into four types of technology: specific software applications (e.g., word processors), Internet-related technologies (e.g., search engines), microcomputers (e.g., PCs), and communications technologies (e.g., e-mail).

However, due to the meta-analysis methodology, they could not compare uses within each type of technology in more detail, and the type of use could only be measured as a unidimensional variable (amount of use).

The final aspect that has been criticized has been directed at the nature of the technology models and how the different models have been improved over the years. Calls have been raised to extend the models backwards, towards identification of the crucial technology qualities that lead users to such belief perceptions as operationalized as PEOU and PU (Benbasat & Barki, 2007, p. 215). The dominance of PEOU and PU as the primary factors contributing to acceptance has also been questioned (Benbasat & Barki, 2007, p. 213). Barki and his colleagues have continued the critique in another article (Barki, Titah, & Boffo, 2007), where they developed a new model (ISURA, or information systems use related activity) that is *not* an extension of the original TAM and attempts to cover a broader spectrum of information on use-related activities, including the actual technology interaction, task–technology adaptation, and individual adaptation. At the time of writing, however, no other articles about ISURA have been published.

Another starting point for questioning the dominance of PEOU and PU has been their utility-oriented objective. Motivated by the difficulties arising from this emphasis, van der Heijden (2004) has presented an alternative model for hedonic information systems, which are characterized not by their instrumental value but with their "fun-aspect," perceived enjoyment, and self-fulfillment value. To prove his point on the need for another model, van der Heijden mentions that technology acceptance studies on the use of the Web have provided conflicting results regarding the relative importance of perceived usefulness versus perceived enjoyment. To reconcile this discrepancy, he suggests that the Web might have actually represented different things to different users. If this is true, he says, the studies have not actually measured the Web acceptance from the same perspectives (van der Heijden, 2004, p. 697). He states as an implication for future research that "progress in user acceptance models can be made by focusing on the nature of system use (whether utilitarian or hedonic), in addition to the inclusion of additional determinants" (p. 699).

We believe van der Heijden's conclusions point to the most crucial issue regarding technology acceptance models that has not been explicated even within the critically aligned articles mentioned above. The fact that users have different orientations toward technology poses a serious weakness in technology acceptance models currently in use. In spite of this weakness, the standard view of technology acceptance retains, year after year, an important position in managerial design thinking, and therefore also in how the design processes are normally carried out. In the following sections, we attempt to explain why different orientations and interpretations of technology use are such a central question, and why disregarding this viewpoint might severely hamper creative, productive design work. We also propose an alternative viewpoint that breaks away from the current limited concept of acceptance in favor of a more heterogeneous view of appropriation.

4 The Problem and Related Evidence of TAMs' Inherent Limitations

Van der Heijden's (2004) remark questions the validity of technology acceptance when measured with questionnaire scales. In fact, it asks whether we know, in the first place, what the scales are measuring when they ask users to assess their perceptions of a particular technology. The conflicting results on Web acceptance point to a possibility that users might actually respond to the questions based on completely different orientations—one group perceiving the Web through its potential utility, another group through its potential for providing enjoyment. In such a case, if the questionnaire does not attempt to account for different orientations, the respondents might in fact be asked wrong questions. One is then unable to tell if the study reveals anything reliable about the real preconditions for user acceptance. Responses that are differentiated based on diverse user orientations should be treated differently in subsequent analysis, but in the standard TAM approach this is impossible since it is assumed that all users subscribe to the same orientation.

Understanding that users may have different perceptions and interpretations of technology reveals also other implicit assumptions in the use of TAMs that prove themselves as problematic. While different users might perceive a certain technology in different ways, it is also possible that a technology can represent multiple purposes even for a single user. For instance, an e-mail program might serve as a way to communicate, but also as a means to store documents (even to an extent that a user might occasionally send e-mails to himself or herself to make some documents more accessible in later situations). In addition, the technology may be perceived in different ways in different situations. These possibilities make discovering the real antecedents of acceptance with the help of predefined questions even more difficult.

As a result, it is unfortunate that the TAM scales do not even have an open-ended text field in which users could describe what they use the technology for, or what purpose of use it represents to them. As stated above ("TAM's U and EOU are postulated a priori"; Davis et al., 1989, p. 988), TAM research is based on a principle that it is the researcher who decides what use is evaluated, even if it is not clear if the users actually represent that kind of use. In reality, the relationships between a system's functionalities and the user's tasks may vary between users and serve completely different ends than expected by the researcher.

This problem can also be investigated on a more fundamental level. As noted above, TAMs are built on the model of attitude formation found in TRA, a model of cognitive processing in which attitudes serve as a basis for cognitive calculation in order to determine the intention to act in a given situation (Fishbein & Ajzen, 1975, pp. 216–287). By emphasizing individual cognitive calculation, TRA ignores the point of view that attitudes (such as perceptions of usefulness and ease of use) are not just individual cognitive processes, but rather are tied to the social contexts of use. This aspect has been the basis of the critique presented by Billig (1987). He points out that humans tend to particularize their attitudes depending on current context. So when talking about a computer program in different contexts, the meanings and evaluations related to that object may differ. Different situations call for different interpretations of a "computer program." This is also why the computer program—as an attitude object—varies across the situations as it is contextually situated within differing evaluative relations. Thus, Billig's (1987) critique of traditional attitude research can be extended also to TAMs. When researchers present propositions to users by referring to the system in a structured form (e.g., by means of a questionnaire), they have no knowledge of contexts in which the users situate and understand these propositions. In fact, the researcher has no way of knowing the meaning of the user's attitude toward the object under evaluation when she or he is replying to the statements.

There is also empirical evidence that such an interpretive heterogeneity actually is very common among users, and therefore the answers given regarding a technology's acceptance really are based on different orientations. This can be the case even if the users themselves are not aware of such heterogeneity. Tamminen (2001) used TAM propositions in open-ended interviews on a team coaching program (Tiimivalmentaja Plus, Team Coach Plus). He interviewed 18 users (about 10% of all the trained users). After the analysis of the responses (the interview material), the program appeared to reflect three very different evaluative objects in the users' speech.

First, the program was evaluated in relation to the tools and the theory it contained. Second, the program was evaluated as an artifact with a constructed interface. Third—and this was a surprising finding—the program was evaluated regarding how well it worked as a vehicle for organizational change. Thus, when the users were talking about the ideas and tools the program contained, they were evaluating how useful it was in relation to their team processes (TAM's PU dimension), and when they talked about the program as an artifact, the users were evaluating the effectiveness of the actual interaction process between themselves and the program interface (TAM's PEOU dimension). But thirdly, distinct from the two prior attitude objects, when the users were talking about the program as a vehicle for organizational change, they were evaluating its effectiveness as a rhetorical tool for changing the prevailing work practices. Users claimed they could use the program to remind or outright argue with managers that, in implementing this program, the managers had also subscribed to a rearrangement of the initial work activity. The TAM propositions of effectiveness were, in this case, situated in relation to the organizational use context of the program—it was evaluated in terms of how well it could be used in organizational persuasion to create novel ways for managing work tasks and reconfiguring power relations between managers and workers. These evaluative situations yielded a quite surprising interpretation of the attitude propositions and of the effectiveness of the program itself. Tamminen (2001, p. 650) i.e. concludes: "The users actually evaluate different things, depending on the context of the proposition. When the different attitude objects are evaluated, the users give differing explanations for their agreement or disagreement with the proposition, depending again on the context."

The possibility that there is no single basis for comparisons between responses can of course be devastating to any research that relies on quantitative measurements. The strength of TAMs in predicting technology acceptance has been claimed to rest on reliable psychographical data. The reason why a more varied and heterogeneous view of computer use has not been embraced in technology acceptance research might lie within the field's positivistic tradition that advocates hypothesis creation and testing rather than a more descriptive approach. The descriptive approach is more common in qualitative research, which does not make a priori assumptions about the similarities between multiple situations (e.g., Silverman, 1993).

Despite the limitations, the use of TAMs for assessing the quality of technology might still be useful in situations in which the system's functionalities provide only very limited opportunities for different uses. Examples of such technologies are automated teller machines (ATMs) that that are used only to draw cash, or interfaces for databases that restrict user tasks to specific queries and inputs only to specified formats. More examples of this kind can be found by looking at, for example, booking systems and logistics applications. In other cases, however, seeing the system use in such a limited way may not be fruitful for good design.

5 Acceptance Models and Design Thinking: An Uneasy Combination

While researchers in management science are probably aware of the inherent limitations (and strengths, of course), as well as the methodological and philosophical commitments, of technology acceptance models, many of the concepts developed in their research field have spread into everyday design discourse. Terms like social acceptability of technology, technology adoption, and technology diffusion all stem from the same thinking about technology acceptance models. This etymology is not always considered when the terms are used beyond the information systems research circles.

As was noted earlier, adopting concepts and terminology from neighboring research fields is not unproblematic . Some of the concepts undergo a translation and are subsequently understood in a different way than their original meaning. Take *social acceptance* as an example. By noticing that acceptance models have been developed with a single-user paradigm in mind, and that social influence is addressed only on the level of the possible effect on the user's attitudes (and not on the level of shared use of digital tools, or negotiation of their use, for example), one can remark that adding *social* in front of *acceptance* extends the original thinking into territories in which the underlying premises are no longer applicable. Seen from an alternative angle, social acceptance is a result of a cultural process that can be studied only with reference to a particular setting and time: What is not socially acceptable in one setting today might be acceptable in the same setting tomorrow. The system itself can also bring about a change in attitudes , as was noted in the study by Tamminen (2001). As a result, the concept of social acceptance is subject to continuous change. Referring to it as a measurable, objective value oversimplifies the understanding of how technology is used in reality and what the contexts of its use are like.

In summary, the concepts arising from TAM research are not always fruitful in design, although they are applicable for evaluation purposes in certain specified work settings, especially if quantitative measures are needed to prove one's point. Although Davis et al. (1989, p. 1000) originally envisioned that TAM could be used in the early stages of product design, ultimately it has been found that the concepts presented do not seem to be able to *drive* design, they can be used only to *verify* it.

6 Appropriation: A Heterogeneous View of Technology Acceptance

As an alternative perspective—one that would serve as a generator of new design—*appropriation* is a concept that can be more useful than user acceptance. Understanding technology acceptance as appropriation means recognizing that a user is an active agent who is able to adapt technology to serve personal or shared goals when needed.

> Appropriation is the way in which technologies are adopted, adapted, and incorporated into working practice. This might involve customization in the traditional sense (that is, the explicit reconfiguration of the technology in order to suit local needs), but it might also simply involve making use of the technology for purposes beyond those for which it was originally designed, or to serve new ends. (Dourish, 2003, p. 467).

For a designer to design for appropriation means developing systems that empower the user with functionalities that enable the accomplishment of tasks that might vary from user to user, and from one setting to another. This also means that a technology used for purposes not envisioned by the designer can be viewed as good design. The rationale behind this thinking is that if the technology is used beyond the scope of its original intent and its users are able to orient to its functionalities in creative ways, then it has succeeded in winning new users and use contexts.

Compared to research published about TAMs, fewer papers have been published about appropriation and evolving use practices. The works that have been published focus primarily on three different lines of research. The first one consists of the attempts to establish a theoretical standpoint for appropriation. Such explorations include presentations of Giddens' structuration theory (DeSanctis & Poole, 1994; Orlikowski, 1992), activity theory (Pargman & Wærn 2003; Petersen, Madsen, & Kjær, 2002), Weick's sensemaking framework (Bansler & Havn, 2006), ethnomethodology (Brown & Perry, 2000; Salovaara, 2007), and phenomenology (Chalmers & Galani, 2004).

The second line of research consists of attempts to capture the necessary properties of appropriable technologies. These papers are focused most directly on making straightforward design-related contributions. Often different qualifiers and adjectives are presented in these papers, including suggestions for design based on openness (Dourish, 1997; Höök, 2006), looking at data from multiple viewpoints (Dourish, 2003), tailorability (MacLean, Carter, Lövstrand, & Moran, 1990), configurational technologies (Williams, Stewart, & Slack, 2005), or technologies as equivoques (Huysman et al., 2003).

The third line of research has presented and analyzed appropriations in particular contexts of use and shown the related design opportunities (e.g., Jacucci, Oulasvirta, Ilmonen, Evans & Salovaara, 2007; Salovaara, 2007; Voida & Mynatt, 2005). In addition, there have been a large number of more general presentations on design implications resulting from open-ended field trials with functional prototypes. Essentially, most of these papers can be seen as reports on appropriations in various settings.

From this large variety of appropriation-related studies the conclusion can only be that a commonly agreed-upon view of appropriation and the implications for how one can design for it are still only emerging. Currently there are only approximate suggestions for understanding the phenomenon theoretically, and similarly only approximate directions for the kinds of designs that are desirable. In addition to this, the body of case studies that considers field trials particularly from the appropriation perspective is only now being built up.

However, there are useful lessons to be learned. Changing the mindset from an all-too-cautious question "What designs will be accepted?" to a more generative and forward-looking question "What designs will be easy to appropriate?" suggests that designs can be improved and made more useful in a larger variety of different contexts.

7 Reconciling the Two Design Mindsets

While the alternative perspective described above might seem promising for a designer, the question still remains regarding how it can be made compatible with the rest of design thinking that sees the quest for user acceptance as the ultimate goal. First and foremost, it is important to note that easily appropriable systems are likely to score high in user acceptance tests as well, even though the users might provide high ratings because of unknown reasons.

A more difficult question is whether the theoretical underpinnings of acceptance and appropriation can be made compatible with each other. At first glance this appears difficult. TAM research does not attempt to take into account users' orientations and interpretations as underlying factors that may affect the scores given by users. In contrast, this is the fundamental starting point in appropriation-oriented design. If open-ended prestudies are arranged in which the actual technology use is first documented and classified, and then used to develop TAM scales individually for each class, there is a possibility that users' different interpretations can be incorporated into the TAM studies with the help of more fine-grained user segmentation. But it is unrealistic to assume that such prestudy activities will become a part of standard TAM methodology. It could also result in an even larger family of competing acceptance models, already considered a problem now (Benbasat & Barki, 2007).

A pragmatic strategy for a designer is to remember the kind of thinking that the original concepts of acceptance, adoption, and diffusion entail, and to defend one's position whenever users' opportunities for creative use are in danger of becoming compromised. However, the ultimate goal of helping users to appropriate should be incorporated into all design process planning. In this case, whenever user-centered design is carried out, achieving appropriability should be one of the key goals of the process. Movement towards this direction has already taken place in, for instance, von Hippel's (1988, 2001) suggestions for fostering appropriation by learning from lead-users and by building user toolkits. The importance of flexible design has also been found in studies on open-source software development and communities (e.g., Tuomi, 2002). However, there is still work to do before these new openings are turned into practical design process characteristics.

8 Designing for Appropriation

How should one design for appropriation? The studies mentioned above provide some starting points for this by highlighting both the overall characteristics (openness, tailorability, configurability, and so on) and context-specific findings. However, the existing literature has not touched the question from the viewpoint of design methods. In the following, we tentatively attempt to describe some properties of design activities that will increase the possibilities for appropriation.

We find it helpful to conceptualize appropriation through the concept of *resource*. Resource is a term in ethnomethodological research used to describe features and properties in a context that provides people with means for action in everyday social interaction. This interpretation can be applied to the analysis of appropriation (Salovaara, 2007) through the notion of *technological resources*. Technological resources are the means for action provided by the system. They are based on the system's functionalities as developed by the designer, either intentionally or unintentionally, and are learned by the user through experiences within different use contexts and tasks. In this light, appropriation can be understood as a transformation process that turns mere system functionalities into personally meaningful technological resources for action.

A system is appropriable if a user can easily learn how the system's functionalities can serve as resources for action. The question of how to design for appropriation thus translates into attempts to help the user flexibly note the potential system functionalities in different contexts, and to understand what resources the functionalities provide for the user once they have been noticed and judged useful. We approach these questions by providing methodological suggestions with respect to three common activities in user-centered design: user research, design activities, and system evaluations.

In early-stage ethnographic user research, attention should be paid to analyzing the users' heterogeneous uses of existing technology. By heterogeneous we mean the mixed use of different systems and technological infrastructures. For instance, users might carry out some tasks with the help of combining e-mail and instant messenger together, or by alternating between different types of access to digital resources (e.g., accessing e-mail via a desktop PC, mobile phone, or Webmail). Such an analysis shows which features in existing systems are relevant to users (i.e., what are the technological resources of each system) and how they are combined together opportunistically. This informs how the new system should be connected with the existing ones. Finally, the observer should pay attention to unexpected uses, and try to find the underlying reasons for such appropriations in order to make similar uses possible in the system to be designed.

With regards to design, the starting point for facilitating appropriation is to build systems that fill their intended use purposes well (a goal which is in line with any design practice),[2] but to not exclude possibilities of other kinds of usages. This is useful in supporting the contemporary knowledge work that is characterized with multitasking, workers' autonomy in deciding how to carry out dedicated work tasks, and immersion in a heterogeneous infrastructure of different mobile, wireless, wired, open, or closed digital resources. In such settings, appropriation can be facilitated by building systems that are portable both physically and digitally, used in different settings, and combined easily with existing technologies. Portability entails also that digital content should be portable between multiple systems. For instance, program code and HTML pages are portable because they can be multiplied and distributed easily. Through portability, many users can benefit from a single user's contribution. The possibility of combining the system with existing technologies is related to the previously mentioned considerations of configurability, open interfaces for the exchange of information, and the possibilities for tailoring and personalization. To make possibilities for appropriation noticeable, available

---

[2] However, this starting point does not hold in cases in which the goal is to invite the user to reflect on and problematize the purpose of the system and, in this way, even force the user to create new interpretations of the system through its nonapparent purpose of use. This approach has been suggested by Gaver, Beaver, and Benford (2003), but specifically in the context of interactive art pieces and digital entertainment. In such cases, purposely complicating the user's tasks is sometimes appropriate.

functionalities of the system should be easily perceivable, so that in different situations the user is able to note how the system is able to interact with and connect to its environment.

When arranging evaluations, assessing the system's support for appropriation requires different metrics than a standard study that often focuses on issues such as speed and accuracy. Existing literature on appropriation does not contain definitions for appropriability metrics, but suitable measures are linked to a system's usefulness in various settings, and its configurability with other systems in the use contexts. Preferably, tests for appropriability should by carried out in realistic or close-to-realistic settings. Appropriation can be assessed, for instance, by asking the user to carry out open-ended tasks and then observing if the switches in interaction between the new system and the existing infrastructure are fluent, or if the user makes use of the system in activities other than those expected in the task instructions.

A short description like this can of course only scratch the surface of the implications that appropriation-oriented thinking might have on design practice. For instance, the description above lacks considerations on how group processes, temporal dynamics (e.g., learning during use and the spread of useful practices), contexts other than knowledge work, and the understanding of human perception and creative problem solving should be integrated into the framework. Such a more focused analysis must be left for future research.

9 Conclusions

This chapter started with an analysis of the concept of technology acceptance as used in management and information systems research, and which since has been adopted into user-centered design discourse as well. It was shown that underlying assumptions of technology acceptance models do not reflect the reality of technology use in many situations. If they are followed and adapted into practice, the design activities might lead to suboptimal design solutions. In particular, it was shown that TAMs do not take into consideration the variation in purposes of use that the users of a technology might have. On the contrary, the models mostly appear to consider all use as equal. This considerably limits their capability to inform design. As a result, (user) acceptance, and related concepts like adoption and diffusion, might actually instantiate a flawed mindset for design.

This chapter has attempted to provide an alternative viewpoint to such a conception on user acceptance, based on the concept of appropriation, that will be more helpful in guiding design . It also provides a better inspiration for design by understanding the user as a creative agent capable of finding different kinds of uses, even unexpected ones, for technologies. In many cases the emergence of creative uses is a sign of successful design. Some initial steps for realizing the appropriation-oriented design in practice were provided in the end of the chapter.

The motivation behind writing this chapter has been to provide a new orientation for design and design management in order to improve user acceptance in ways not previously conceived. It has been pointed out that success in building appropriable systems in this way is not harmful to user acceptance even when understood in its traditional sense. With this in mind, we hope that this chapter contributes fruitfully to forthcoming discussions on the principles and preconditions of good design of information systems.

Acknowledgments Funding for this work was provided by the Finnish Graduate School of User-Centered Information Technology (UCIT).

References

Bansler, J., & Havn, E. (2006). Sensemaking in technology-use mediation: Adapting groupware technology in organizations. *Computer Supported Cooperative Work, 15*, 55–91.

Barki, H., Titah, R., & Boffo, C. (2007). Information system use-related activity: An expanded behavioral conceptualization of individual-level information system use. *Information Systems Research, 18*, 173–192.

Benbasat, I., & Barki, H. (2007). Quo vadis, TAM?. *Journal of the Association for Information Systems, 8*, 211–218.

Beyer, H., & Holtzblatt, K. (1998). *Contextual design: Defining customer-centered systems.* San Francisco: Morgan Kaufmann.

Billig, M. (1987). *Arguing and thinking: A rhetorical approach to social psychology.* London: Routledge.

Brown, B. A., & Perry, M. (2000). Why don't telephones have off switches? Understanding the use of everyday technologies. *Interacting with Computers, 12*, 623–634.

Burton-Jones, A., & Straub, D. W. (2006). Reconceptualizing system usage: An approach and empirical test. *Information Systems Research, 17*, 228–246.

Chalmers, M., & Galani A. (2004). Seamful interweaving: Heterogeneity in the theory and design of interactive systems. In D. Benyon, P. Moody, D. Gruen, & I. McAra-McWilliam (Eds.), *DIS '04: Proceedings of the 2004 Conference on Designing Interactive Systems* (pp. 243–252). New York: ACM Press.

Davis, F. D. (1989). Perceived ease of use, and user acceptance of information technology. *MIS Quarterly, 13*, 319–340.

Davis, F. D., Bagozzi, R. P., & Warshaw, P. R. (1989). User acceptance of computer technology: A comparison of two theoretical constructs. *Management Science, 35*, 982–1003.

DeSanctis, G., & Poole, M. S. (1994). Capturing the complexity in advanced technology use: Adaptive structuration theory. *Organization Science, 5*, 121–147.

Dillon, A., & Morris, M. G. (1996). User acceptance of new information technology: Theories and models. In M. E. Williams (Ed.), *Annual review of information science and technology* (pp. 3–32). Medford, NJ: Information Today.

Dourish, P. (1997). Accounting for system behaviour: Representation, reflection and resourceful action. In M. Kyng & L. Mathiassen (Eds.), *Computers and design in context* (pp. 145–170). Cambridge, MA: The MIT Press.

Dourish, P. (2003). The appropriation of interactive technologies: Some lessons from placeless documents. *Computer Supported Cooperative Work, 12*, 465–490.

Fishbein, M., & Ajzen, I. (1975). *Belief, attitude, intention and behavior: An introduction to theory and research*. Reading, MA: Addison-Wesley.

Gaver, W. W., Beaver, J., & Benford, S. (2003). Ambiguity as a resource for design. In G. Cockton & P. Korhonen (Eds.), *CHI '03: Proceedings of the SIGCHI Conference on Human Factors in Computing Systems* (pp. 233–240). New York: ACM Press.

Höök. K. (2006). Designing familiar open surfaces. In G. Ghosh & D. Svanæs (Eds.), *NordiCHI '06: Proceedings of the 4th Nordic Conference on Human-Computer Interaction* (pp. 242–251). New York: ACM Press.

Huysman, M., Steinfield, C., Jang, C.-Y., David, K., Huis in 't Veld, M., Poot, J. et al. (2003). Virtual teams and the appropriation of communication technology: Exploring the concept of media stickiness. *Computer Supported Cooperative Work, 12*, 411–436.

Jacucci, G., Oulasvirta, A., Ilmonen, T., Evans, J., & Salovaara, A. (2007). CoMedia: Mobile group media for active spectatorship. In M. B. Rosson & D. Gilmore (Eds.), *CHI '07: Proceedings of the SIGCHI Conference on Human Factors in Computing Systems* (pp. 1273–1282). New York: ACM Press.

Jasperson, J., Carter, P. E., & Zmud, R. W. (2005). A comprehensive conceptualization of post-adoptive behaviors associated with information technology enabled work systems. *MIS Quarterly, 29*, 525–557.

Lee, Y., Kozar, K. A., & Larsen, K. R. T. (2003). The technology acceptance model: Past, present, and future. *Communications of the Association for Information Systems, 12*, 752–780.

MacLean, A., Carter, K., Lövstrand, L., & Moran, T. (1990). User-tailorable systems: Pressing the issues with buttons. In J. C. Chew & J. Whiteside (Eds.), *CHI '90: Proceedings of the SIGCHI Conference of Human Factors in Computing Systems* (pp. 175–182). New York: ACM Press.

Mehto, K., Kantola, V., Tiitta, S., & Kankainen, T. (2006). Interacting with user data: Theory and examples of drama and dramaturgy as methods of exploration and evaluation in user-centered design. *Interacting with Computers, 18*, 977–995.

Orlikowski, W. J. (1992). Duality of technology: Rethinking the concept of technology in organizations. *Organization Science, 3*, 398–427.

Orlikowski, W. J. (1996). Improvising organizational transformation over time: A situated change perspective. *Information Systems Research, 7*, 63–92.

Pargman, T. C., & Wærn, Y. (2003). Appropriating the use of a Moo for collaborative writing. *Interacting with Computers, 15*, 759–781.

Petersen, M. G., Madsen, K. H., & Kjær, A. (2002). Usability of everyday technology: Emerging and fading opportunities. *ACM Transactions on Computer-Human Interaction, 9*, 74–105.

Salovaara, A. (2007). Appropriation of a MMS-based comic creator: From system functionalities to resources for action. In M. B. Rosson & D. Gilmore (Eds.), *CHI '07: Proceedings of the SIGCHI Conference on Human Factors in Computing Systems* (pp. 1117–1126). New York: ACM Press.

Schepers, J., & Wetzels, M. (2007). A meta-analysis of the technology acceptance model: Investigating subjective norm and moderation effects. *Information & Management, 44*, 90–103.

Schwarz, A., & Chin, W. (2007). Looking forward: Toward an understanding of the nature and definition of IT acceptance. *Journal of the Association for Information Systems, 8*, 230–243.

Silverman, D. (1993). *Interpreting qualitative data: Methods for analysing talk, text and interaction*. London: SAGE Publications.

Svanæs, D., & Seland, G. (2004). Putting the users center stage: Role playing and low-fi prototyping enable end users to design mobile systems. In E. Dykstra-Erickson & M. Tscheligi (Eds.), *CHI '04: Proceedings of the SIGCHI Conference on Human Factors in Computing Systems* (pp. 479–486). New York: ACM Press.

Tamminen, S. (2001). What do users actually evaluate when evaluating computer programs? Defining the dimensions in HCI by qualitative attitude research. In G. Salvendy

M. J. Smith (Eds.), *HCI International 2001: Proceedings of the 9th International Conference on Human-Computer Interaction* (Vol. 2, pp. 647–651). Mahwah, NJ: Lawrence Erlbaum.

Tuomi, I. (2002). *Networks of innovation: Change and meaning in the age of the Internet.* Oxford, UK: Oxford University Press.

Tyre, M. J., & Orlikowski, W. J. (1994). Windows of opportunity: Temporal patterns of technological adaptation in organizations. *Organization Science, 5,* 98–118.

van der Heijden, H. (2004). User acceptance of hedonic information systems. *MIS Quarterly, 28,* 695–704.

Venkatesh, V., & Davis, F. D. (2000). A theoretical extension of the technology acceptance model: Four longitudinal field studies. *Management Science, 46,* 186–204.

Venkatesh, V., Morris, M. G., Davis, G. B., & Davis, F. D. (2003). User acceptance of information technology: Toward a unified view. *MIS Quarterly, 27,* 425–478.

Voida, A., & Mynatt, E. D. (2005). Six themes of the communicative appropriation of photographic images. In G. C. van der Veer & C. Gale (Eds.), *CHI '05: Proceedings of the SIGCHI Conference on Human Factors in Computing Systems* (pp. 171–180). New York: ACM Press.

von Hippel, E. (1988). *The sources of innovation.* New York: Oxford University Press.

von Hippel, E. (2001). User toolkits for innovation. *The Journal of Product Innovation Management, 18,* 247–257.

Williams, R., Stewart, J., & Slack, R. (2005). *Social learning in technological innovation: Experimenting with information and communication technologies.* Cheltenham, UK: Edgar Elgar Publishing.

The Polysemy of Human–Computer Interaction

Anita Greenhill and Gordon Fletcher

Abstract This chapter provides exemplars of the influence of digital artifacts upon cultural experiences. We argue that the associations between people and artifacts, and specifically digital artifacts, is an increasingly dense, interwoven, and pivotal aspect of everyday cultural experience. Artifacts themselves resist any stability of meaning by being continuously disassembled and reassembled into newly meaningful assemblages. Digital artifacts extend this complexity by accelerating and extending cultural relationships both temporally and geographically, resulting in a wider range of potential and actual relationships in an expansive number of contexts. Through the connections that digital artifacts hold to people, there is a continuously fluid polysemous multivocality that incorporates the multiple and expansive parameters of power, meaning, and cultural knowledge. The human ability to alter and repurpose artifacts to suit immediate and shifting needs prevents any innate definitional quality from making a "table" a table or a "blog" a blog. Purpose and meaning of an artifact is continuously defined and then redefined between individuals and across time, beyond the reach of the original designers or manufacturers.

> *Things have thus become regarded as texts, structured sign systems whose relationship with each other and the social world is to be decoded. In various post-structural approaches to material forms, the metaphors of language, or discourse, and text have remained dominant in an understanding of things. The new emphasis here has been on polysemy, biographical, historical and cultural shifts in meaning, the active role or "agency" of things in constituting rather than reflecting social realities, power/knowledge relations and the poetics and politics of the process of interpretation itself, that we write things rather than somehow passively read off their meanings independently of our social and political location, values and interests.*
>
> (Tilley, 2002. p. 23)

A. Greenhill (✉)
Manchester Business School, University of Manchester, Manchester, England
e-mail: A.Greenhill@manchester.ac.uk

P. Saariluoma, H. Isomäki (eds.), *Future Interaction Design II*,
DOI 10.1007/978-1-84800-385-9_9, © Springer-Verlag London Limited 2009

1 Introduction

Within the polysemy of human interaction, artifacts play a key role in the construction of shared and persistent meaning. The variability of use, form, and purpose of artifacts and the lack of precision that exists in their relationship to individuals ensure that any meanings are necessarily fluid. The associations between people and artifacts, and specifically digital artifacts, is an increasingly dense, interwoven, and pivotal aspect of cultural experience. Artifacts have always made this contribution to cultural logic and knowledge. Digitial artifacts, however, accelerate and extend these relationships both temporally and geographically, resulting in a wider range of relationships in an expansive number of contexts. Through the connections that digital artifacts hold to people, there is a continuously fluid polysemous multivocality that incorporates multiple power, meaning, and cultural knowledges. The human ability to alter and repurpose artifacts to suit immediate and shifting needs prevents any innate definitional quality from making a "table" a table or a "blog" a blog. Purpose and meaning of an artifact are continuously defined and then redefined between individuals and across time, beyond the reach of the original designers and manufacturers.

As the use of information and communications technologies becomes ubiquitous in daily life, increased usage of technology alters how people initiate and engage in everyday social experiences. Premium examples of the influence of digital artifacts on cultural experience can readily be found with the advent of mobile social software, the uptake of YouTube as a mainstream media outlet, the importance of MySpace.com for (re)defining and extending social networks, and what is colloquially described as the "Internet of Things" as a gauge of contemporary technologies' existing social acceptability. Artifacts also resist any stability of meaning by being continuously disassembled and reassembled into newly meaningful assemblages. Our world is constructed by the human ability to alter and repurpose the meaning and understanding of things. We exist in a social soup of polysemous cultural meanings that are framed by objects, feelings, memories, meanings, and understandings. The digital artifact as an artifact and as a continuation of these theoretical understandings, continuously alters human–computer interaction (HCI) and design. Within these relationships of people to things, digital artifacts that are overdesigned at their point of creation decrease the use value of the technology itself and reduce the capability for these artifacts to respond and interactively communicate with those who use them.

2 The Intellectual Heritage of Material Culture

The exploration of artifacts is primarily informed by the intellectual heritage of material culture studies. Contemporary work of authors such as Buchli (2002), Miller (1991), Shanks & Hodder (1997), and Tilley (1989)—who themselves utilize the writings of postmodernists, critical theorists, and feminists, among others—question traditional understanding of objects as inherently meaningful and meaning-stable entities. A consequence of this work is an extensive body of literature that communicates with contemporary debates regarding HCI and design that offers a critical and politically nuanced framework for interpretation.

The perceived lack of, and concern for the lack of, physical presence is a pivotal focus for the critical examination of digital artifacts in terms of their contribution to social and cultural experience. The close association of material culture studies with physical artifacts has also produced an intellectual reluctance to associate this body of work with digital culture. Oldenziel (1996, p. 65) questions the prerequisite of this focus by posing the question, "What is materiality in cyberspace?", to which she answers with another question and the implied claim that "Is it not more or less what semioticians have proposed for some time that things are not existent and meaningless unless a meaning has been ascribed to them through essentially linguistic processes?"

Material culture studies has a lengthy history that is primarily associated with collectors, archaeology, and the modernist project for knowing. Buchli (2002, p. 5) argues that the entire supercategory "material culture" was itself an intellectual invention that

> materializes something entirely new and uniquely Victorian and Western, as modern as the artifacts of industrialism on display at the Great Exposition of 1851 from which our more systematic nineteenth century collection of ethnographic material culture took their inspiration.

However, despite this heritage and the reluctance of researchers, material culture studies is not artifact obsessed, artifact bound, or reduced to the tallying of physical remains. Material culture studies has matured into a discipline that has as its central imperative to interpret cultural practice. This broad remit draws upon a wide-ranging collection of authors from many disciplines in the humanities and social sciences. More critically nuanced studies have introduced a tightly integrated understanding of artifacts in relation to the cultures that produce, consume, interpret (and discard) them (Miller, 1991). The critical turn in material culture studies posits an understanding that the cultural consumption of an artifact is not necessarily bound to its production or its original design purpose. Tilley (2002, p. 27) makes this observation in relation to discussions of gender in a Melanesian context when it was observed that this "is a way of thinking about the relationship between producers and their products centering upon *activity*. It is this that produces meanings and serves to gender both persons and artifacts." Action- or consumption-based perspectives allow material culture studies to break from the simplistic association of artifacts with archaeological provenance. Material culture is capable of examining *any* artifact in the broadest sense. Increased distancing from traditional archaeological contexts also enables the examination of artifacts to move beyond looking at only functional and tool-based items. Ultimately the flexibility provided by existing critical interpretation refutes the assumption that physical presence is the central quality defining an artifact.

3 Digital Artifacts and Everyday Life: Within or Without?

With increased recognition of the ever-presence of the digital artifact, there is a significant and close relationship to mainstream culture. In this context, how a digital artifact is created, and by implication how it is designed becomes an important aspect of everyday and influences wider and wider ranges of individuals. *Digital* has become increasingly synonymous with those social experiences enabled through the mediation of information technology (Thrift, 1996, p. 1464). Popular emphasis upon the technology that enables navigation and access to the hegemonic and celebratory "computer world," however, belies its thoroughly social foundations (Sheridan & Zeltzer, 1997, p. 86). Technology-oriented presentations of the digital world, in the contemporary guise of cyberspace, the Internet, or the World Wide Web, have cast it as a panacea for the problems and experiences of reality (Graham, 1997, p. 41; cf. Stoll, 1995, pp. 10–11). IBM and Microsoft promote their tools as the key to globe-spanning successful commerce. In a similar vein some educational technologists predict the demise of the formal lecture theatre (cf. Stoll, 1995, p. 146). Although these claims solidify the digital world as a definable aspect of cultural practice and as a space for social experience, they do little to clarify any assumed or perceived distinction between "digital" and "human" life. At an immediate and sensory level the digital world is present in a somehow disembodied contrast to the "reality" of physical presence; however, precursors of this form of cultural experience can be identified in radio listening and television viewing (Green, 1997, p. 59) and even the success of the UK's Open University. Disembodiment is the distinctive quality of social experience conducted within a digital provenance. However, and of greater significance for the design and creation of digital artifacts, computer-mediated experience reflects and imitates the practices of real life (Whittle 1997, p. 12).

Regarding the Internet as an environment containing artifacts necessitates a critical and interpretative position regarding the artifact itself, both in cyberspace and in real life. Irrespective of any perceptions of immateriality, the Internet emphasizes artifacts, including those with a digital provenance, as culturally significant (Shanks & Hodder, 1997, p. 8). Artifactual research worldviews are distinct from "everything-as-text"-oriented interpretations. Gottdiener (1995, p. 22) claims

> the issue is not the relationship between the everyday meanings and social practice, but of articulating a philosophy of consciousness independent of social context. Such a position, although challenging to philosophy and the sciences that depend on textual interpretation, has limited value in the analysis of material culture.

If the digital is briefly considered beyond the scope of solely technological definitions, it is most consistently described as a social space without physicality. Thrift (1996, p. 1465) cites a range of conceptualizations of the digital that are all founded upon spatially oriented definitions. Lefebvre's *The Production of Space* (1991) is the starting point for many of these definitions. Lefebvre (1991, pp. 38–39) argues that social space cannot be directly equated with physical space. He also cautions against the "fetishisation" of this space in itself (1991, p. 90). "Itself the outcome of past actions, social space is what permits fresh actions to occur, while suggesting others and prohibiting yet others.... Social space implies a great diversity of knowledge" (Lefebvre, 1991, p. 73). The warning against fetishisation is particularly relevant as it endangers analysis, focusing upon a weak conceptual "wrapper" rather than the relationships of people to things. Wise (1997) reasserts the significance of Lefebvre's triadic conceptualization of space and the privilege of "representational space" within other discussions of social space. Nuanced understandings of social space, Wise (1997, p. 78) claims, prevent the technological contributions to the formation of spatial practice from being disentangled, in any meaningful way, from the symbolic representations of that space. These interrelated mediatory influences prevent discussion of the digital from descending into technological determinist arguments.

Defining the digital world within a critical framework does not discard the technology that mediates these cultural practices, but neither should these approaches be driven by the mere presence of this, or any other, specifically named technology. Technology is intertwined with other cultural phenomena and contributes to the particularity of the provenance in which cultural practices are found and shaped. The emphasis that has been placed upon computing technology should be assessed as a subjective claim that supports particular interest groups and, it could be claimed, particular corporate interests (Bereano, 1997, p. 27). Seeking and finding some form of distinct reality within the digital world attenuates the differences between the space being observed from the space in which the researcher is observing. However, placing primacy on the immediacy of experience in a single space—the fetishisation of space— potentially ignores the ways in which experience and understanding of cultural practices is always multilocational. Everyday life is simultaneously located in many spaces without specific qualification, and it would be a similar methodo- logical nonsense to disentangle the experience(s) of space(s) inside a car parked in a shopping mall in a large city as it is to speak solely of a virtual space as an isolated cultural construction.

A variety of already possible Internet activities show that the experience of the everyday continually reaffirms the reality of the digital environment. These experiences include the significant stages of life such as marriage ceremonies, birth and funereal ceremonies, as well as malicious activities, such as stalking and rape (Silver, 2000, p. 22) and various forms of consumption, including online shopping, gambling, and teaching and learning, as well as more mundane written and spoken communication. Experiences that cross between digital and physical space, by relating sites of cultural engagement to one another, further stress that multiple provenances of experience combine to reconfirm the inter- twined reality of each space. An example of these intersections between digital experience and physical consequence is the early case of the cyberstalking of Jayne Hitchcock, now the president of Working to Halt Online Abuse

(WHOA). During a 2-year period, the stalker spammed, sent e-mail floods, sent unwanted mail-order goods, and had the FBI investigate her. Cynthia Armistead, in another example of cyberstalking, experienced physical stalking, e-mail abuse, and the use of her name and e-mail address for sex services. The significance of these incidents is the manner in which the specific qualities of multiple provenances of cultural practice (Geertz, 1973/1993, p. 22; Marcus, 1995) have been used to maximize the social impact on the victim. The experiences of Hitchcock and Armistead are increasingly mundane, normalized, and routine aspects of everyday life that are regularly reported, ever more briefly, in the media.

Technology and the design of artifacts are ever-present in the discussion of the digital artifact as part of the shifting transitional interface between physical and digital spaces. Information technology, through its constant presence and its observational absence, assists in affirming the reality and purpose of the digital. However, experience of the digital does not directly equate with the experience of any specific technology, software, or hardware, although this does impart distinct qualities onto that particular representation of space (Lefebvre 1991, p. 38).

Analysis of digital artifacts tends to bind analysis to a specific provenance. The abundance of articles that discuss Web pages and Web sites as the meaningful level of study indicates the appeal for this form of analysis (e.g., Cronin, 1998; Rich, 1998; Sclafane, 1998; Smith, 1998). Investigation of specific Web pages risks the disentangling of a digital object from its wider assemblage of cultural and social relations, including other Web pages, for which it is presumed to be a singularly meaningful and interpretable thing. In effect, the analysis of a particular artifact as an isolated object tends towards the effacement of its relationship to the experiences of everyday life and contextualizes it solely as an artifact of technology (Wakeford, 2000, p. 35). One example of overdesign and the obliteration of everyday life from examination of the Web is the insistence on top-down considerations for Web sites that ignore search engines, bookmarks, or even human memory. The object of this seemingly neutral technology is then privileged with the "voice" and powerful hegemonic weight of information technology and the biased status of data. As a consequence the cultural meanings that remain to be interpreted from this object are primarily mediated through the wider metameanings attached to the general technology itself rather than the contextualized and specific mediation of everyday use and experience. While examination of individual objects, such as Web pages, is an important avenue for analysis, it cannot become the focus of all analysis, as the tendency will be towards the overdesign of artifacts or actions with a digital provenance. Such an approach, applied more widely, would necessitate, for example, every discussion of the telephone to be prefaced with a discussion of telephony, and media studies would be required to speculate on the qualities, nature, and meaning of the cathode ray tube and radio frequency propagation.

4 Cultural Artifact—Digital Provenance

The artifact is a culturally meaning-laden "thing." However, discussion of the artifact inevitably conflates it with its physical qualities as an apparently coherent, necessary, and synonymous relationship (Miller, 1991, p. 31). A physical thing that is "meaningful" is always an artifact (cf. Shanks & Hodder, 1997, p. 17). However, discussions that commence with the interpretation of artifactual meanings and design are not bound to any specific material form.

The reference of a digital object to a physical analogy is unnecessary when the Internet has become such a dominant and mainstream site of cultural activity in postindustrial societies (Touraine, 1974, p. 116). Gadamer (1989, pp. 242–254), however, suggests that without a fusion of horizons there can be no communication between parties, in this case among a variety of provenances. For the user undertaking an everyday interpretation of artifacts that is fully immersed in the spaces of the Internet, the awareness and sense of the artifact, and a desire for them, is integral to the current location and environment. The intellectual contradictions between physical and digital artifacts are a political conflict in the broadest sense.

While meaning is generally perceived to shift around the anchorage of an artifact's physical qualities, its various qualities, including its design, provide different forms of meaning-stabilizing anchorages (Miller, 1991, p. 116; Miller & Slater, 2000). However, none of these anchorage points are individually stable entities; they are all, along with the artifact itself, the product of shifting social and cultural forces (cf. Miller, 1991, pp. 126–127). The anchorage of style, in all its indefiniteness, is an important quality for many forms of artifacts (Lemonnier 1993, p. 11). For example, the continually changing form of domestic motor vehicles is tied to a range of qualities including prestige, style, economic imperatives, and, consequently, petrol consumption and engine size.

The tendency to intellectually anchor the artifact to physical qualities emphasizes its original design as the point where particular sets of meanings were made stable (Miller, 1991, p. 3). However, some qualities of the artifact must precede its creation and many others are recrafted after its creation. The tools that aid creation of an artifact also reveal the close interrelationship of artifacts with one another. The very specific utility of woodworking tools, such as planes, shapers, and chisels, is one example of how particular artifacts are not designed in isolation without some understanding of future provenance, desire, or need for the artifacts that they will create. In these tools, qualities such as utility and the raw materials become aspects of the design of the artifact that is created. While there is a need for pre-existing artifacts to craft the indefinite but necessary environment for new artifacts to come into existence, after design and manufacture of an artifact, the relationship of specific qualities to an intended meaning may hold only fleeting association that does not persist through space, time, or across cultures. The further the object is separated from its time and place of original design, the wider the range of potential meanings that will become ascribed to it. Distance, acquired through temporal or spatial separation, is the most effective means of increasing the polysemous qualities of the artifact (Shanks & Hodder, 1997, p. 9).

The increased fluidity of cultural meanings that crafts an artifact's qualities is a hallmark of postindustrial culture (Smart, 1992, pp. 52 & 143; Touraine, 1974). This fluidity is reflected in the relationship of the ideational and physical within contemporary culture as a politically negotiated position. Baudrillard (1981/1994, p. 19) takes this negotiation to an extreme with his claim that, "the impossibility of rediscovering an absolute level of the real is of the same order as the impossibility of staging illusion. Illusion is no longer possible, because the real is no longer possible."

Baudrillard's theorization of the "real" and illusion enable their negotiation to be considered in the postdesign context, and by implication the digital, effectively rendering the physical a nonessential quality of the artifact. Another example, which also suggests that artifacts are not the consequence of any fixed or measured amount of design, comes from archaeology. The materials extracted from archaeological digs again become artifactual through the ascriptions offered of them by archaeologists seen through significant cultural and temporal distance (Hodder, 1989, p. 67). The interpreted artifacts of archaeology possess a complex provenance. The already debatable nature of meaning possessed by artifacts is further problematized by archaeology; the "real" meanings ascribed to the artifact at its creation are distanced from the "imagined" meanings ascribed by archaeologists (Lemonnier, 1993).

Artifacts evoke particular understandings of the culture(s) that they exist within. An artifact can only be designed or understood by being considered in situ and in relation to the other artifacts of that space (Miller, 1991, pp. 109–11; Shanks & Hodder, 1997, p. 11). And even in this context, Aunger (2006, p. 724) observes, "not all social messages are equally attended to or adopted by their receivers." The contextual environment constructs an expectation for the artifact and, in turn, the artifact crafts an expectation for the space. This reciprocation connects artifacts and meanings, creating a normality. The expectation and even desire for normality provides a key anchorage around the meaning of an artifact in this association with a particular meaning or set of meanings.

Everyday artifacts are positioned within existing power structures. The paucity in the range of interpretations that are available is a consequence of their persistence within the mundane. Their interpretation is similarly a consequence of the particular power relations that act upon the artifact. Our claim is that the limited range of interpretations applicable to a fork is closely related to the extent that the fork is bound, through its mundaneness, within a dense system of social and artifactual relationships. With the example of the fork, it is bound to other apparently mundane items with an intensity that almost prohibits conceptualizing it (within contemporary Western culture) without an understanding of a knife. This stable microsystem frames and supports wider parameters of power including, for example, the understanding of dinnertime etiquette. The conflation of physical qualities of the fork with the concept of the artifact called "fork" restricts which artifacts can possess "forkness." The artifact is restricted by these boundaries of meaning but in continually different ways. These limitations are not inherent in the artifact itself but develop through the mediation of contemporary social and cultural relations and the manner by which artifacts are perceived. Tilley (1989, p. 191) says, "an object, any object, has no ultimate or unitary meaning that can be held to exhaust it."

The example of the fork reinforces the deceptiveness of designing and understanding an artifact primarily through its physical qualities. The fork's functional simplicity, as a fork, is a designed simplicity crafted over a lengthy period that reveals the currently received physical forms of the artifact. None of this heritage can be understood, seen, or needs to be seen through direct, uncritical, or untheorized observation. In this way, the fork represents a near-ultimate form in terms of its interface and design.

Defining the artifact as a product of culture that agglomerates various qualities provides the opportunity for understanding future design in HCI. The cautionary aspect of these claims is that the digital artifact is very much a product of its time. Without the influence of debates about cyberspace, the virtual, and the Web, the suggestion that the immaterial and digital can equally be considered artifactual would be seen as esoteric, eccentric, or verging on the theological.

Materiality is one of the qualities particularly ascribed to the artifact, and is sometimes insisted upon as the most significant quality of an artifact (Buchli, 1995, p. 189; Miller, 1991, p. 3). The conflating of the artifact to a particular set of physical qualities can be questioned in the light of a usable and accessible cyberspace that extends beyond the capabilities of unmediated, immediate, and personal exchange. The digital artifact also breaks down the apparent logic for the binarism and separation of symbolism and materiality (Buchli, 1995, p. 186). Seeing the artifact as an artifact allows the textual position to be discarded for an understanding in which the artifact is placed in a direct relationship to human agency (Thomas, 1997, p. 211). This position, with an insistence upon the need for a confirmed and personally affirmed physical reality, leads, potentially, to the argument that, for example, an artifact must be visible (Criado, 1997, p. 198), or touched, to be interpreted. This complexity ensures that there is never, and can never be, a raw articulation or clean sense of meaning (Ricoeur, 1981), but rather a conceptual and experiential polysemous soup filled with related tendencies, possibilities, and oppositions.

Archaeologists infer the presence of absent artifacts from surrounding objects and spatial relationships. The conventional archaeological record, too, only returns a selection of objects through the combined consequences of time and provenance and as a reflection of the relationships of social power in that and subsequent periods of time (Pearson, 1997). Digital artifacts provide denser strata but can only be partially representative of the prevailing social and cultural relations found online. The online journal *Slate* summarizes the representational nature of the Internet by claiming that "to archive the Internet with absolute fidelity would require cloning not only every computer on the Internet, but also every person using every computer" (Barnes, 1997, p. 2). Baudrillard's (1981/1994, pp. 1–2) more general observations regarding simulation extends this point:

> The territory no longer precedes the map, nor does it survive it. It is nevertheless the map that precedes the territory...today it is the territory whose shreds slowly rot across the extent of the map.... But it is no longer a question of either maps or territories. Something has disappeared, the sovereign difference, between one and the other, that constituted the charm of abstraction.

5 Designing Artifacts

Attempting to identify and design an artifact on an interpretative plane within the shifting versions of reality and in relation to contemporary culture is a fraught task. We utilize the term *artifact* in the conventionally received sense as "the product of human action" (Richardson, 1974, pp. 4–5). However, what requires reexamination in light of the significance of HCI and the Web are the acts and actions that are understood to produce the artifact. More widely, it is the interrelationship of artifacts and humans within particular environmental contexts that contribute to each other's definition. It is in the constant reconfiguration and shifting interrelationships between people and artifacts—what is described elsewhere as culture—that produces an understanding of the artifact and an understanding of ourselves. The indefinite, problematic, and variously defined culture assumes a particular reality when it is perceived through artifacts (Soja, 1989, p. 79). Seeking the product of human action on the Web necessitates understanding the artifact as the result of particular intersecting cultural relationships. An artifact is an artifact because humans define it (Hides. 1997, p. 11).

Artifacts move with varying relationships of intensity to the constantly dynamic cycles of social and cultural interpretation and misinterpretation. "Artifactuality," as the collection of an artifact's qualities, operates as a single unified signifier for an arrangement of social relationships (Miller, 1991, p. 13). Most significantly, archaeology deals initially with the qualities of the artifact in order to proceed to an interpretation of the social and cultural conditions in which the artifact was originally ascribed meanings (Buchli, 1995, p. 189; Tilley, 1989, p. 191).

Artifacts are products of human manufacture that have persistence beyond and outside individual subjectivity and are not bound to a specific subject's immediate experience (Richardson, 1974, p. 4). Artifacts have fixed qualities that allow at least minimal interpretation over extended periods of time, irrespective of spatial separation or their alienation from their designer. Miller (1991, pp. 61–62), by drawing upon the intellectual tradition of Munn, identifies the persistence of meaning over significant spatial difference with the canoes of the Kula. What is being portrayed here is a concern with the creation of an object in which social relations are implicated, but which will ultimately be delivered up for the use of other people, by being launched into the Kula Ring. This is an example of the problem of alienation: Certain conditions serve to separate the creators from the object of their creative processes.

It is worth considering the extreme positions in these discussions of the artifact. For the realist, the artifact is "there" telling "us" about the cultural life paths of "others" (Hides, 1997, p. 13). A constructivist position, in contrast, suggests that the artifact tells "us" about "ourselves" through our interpretation of the artifact; it is an act of autobiography revealed by our imparting of particular meanings onto its presence (Baudrillard, 1970/1996, p. 105; Buchli, 1995). The distinction between the interpretations of the anthropologist from the generally more casual observations of the nonanthropologist can be contrasted in a similar manner. To extrapolate cultural life paths from an artifact requires a range of knowledge that cannot be automatically inferred from the examination of an artifact's observable qualities. To achieve this form of interpretation requires the privilege, legitimacy and, probably, training of an anthropologist and the theoretical perspective of the "realist." In contrast, interpreting the artifact as an act of autobiography, in relation to one's own subjectivity, imitates more anticipated everyday processes of interpretation, ascription, and the making of meaning in relation to an artifact. The artifact can be considered by its various qualities, such as utility and aesthetic appeal, the social status it imparts, its value or comparative rarity in relation to the social experiences, and motivations of those who engage with it (Buchli, 1995, p. 190).

6 Spimes and the Internet of Things: An Artifactual Conundrum?

"Spimes" and the Internet of Things are labels for what is currently a primarily conceptual understanding of the evolution of the Internet and of objects more broadly. However, they are significant for this discussion as the consolidation of a series of technological developments and technologist understandings of the contemporary and future artifact-filled world. These things also represent the "next step" in the increasingly blurred distinction between physical and digital artifacts to the point that the need or purpose of the division is effectively effaced.

Spimes are conceptual objects, introduced by Bruce Sterling at SIGGRAPH 2004 and through his book, *Shaping Things* (2005). Spimes are most simply defined as "noisy objects" (Sterling, 2005, p. 11). More specifically, a spime is a physical object that is uniquely identifiable and is aware of its location and current environment. Spimes are conventional everyday objects that are enhanced with the capacity to systematically receive and send data. The spime-object collects and throws out to its surrounding environment vast amounts of data that can be collected and utilized. What is generally implied rather than explicitly defined in Sterling's definition is that the noise of a spime is collected and transmitted in a digital rather than analog format. Sterling can imply this format, as it is clearly the intention in his discussion. This implied assumption leads to the somewhat erroneous belief that the concept of the noisy object is a new and as-yet conceptual thing when it is merely the digital spime that is yet to become available. However, as we have already outlined, the distinction of physical and digital has increasingly become a meaningless and flaccid distinction.

We are already surrounded by albeit less smart and analog spimes in the form of existing physical objects: the fork, the knife, and other mundane objects. The imprecision of the relationship between humans and artifacts is a consequence of the continuously fluid and analog format with which we interact. As straightforward examples of this phenomenon, the multiple meanings conveyed through the printed word provides us with only partial understanding when we read the words on a cereal packet while, similarly, the patina of age on an antique can only partially reflect the environments that it has passed through. Noisy analog data, in the form of conveyed meanings, associations, and context from these old spimes is ever-present but never wholly or permanently captured. More formal analysis and interpretation of the variety of meanings transmitted by analog spimes has been the preserve, as we have already indicated, of material culture studies. The day-to-day interpretation of these same objects is what we do every day. The digital spime does not alter the already-theorized or everyday human relationships with artifacts, although it is possible for suitably specified technology to capture quantitative data from the spime. This transfer of data defers the human relationship with the original spime to become mediated through yet another artifact: digital, physical, or physical with digital capabilities (i.e., another spime). The human–artifact relationship remains firmly positioned as an interpreted mediated negotiation of polysemy through previous human experience and knowledge and the locational, environmental, and relational context of the artifact itself.

7 The Polysemous Soup of Digital Artifacts: Design or Anti-Design?

The Internet of Things provides the technical capacity to make the linkage between physical artifacts (generally well-theorized things) and specific digital artifacts (poorly theorized things). A reflection of the determinism that surrounds the technological bias for this development is the degree with which the Internet of Things has been conducted with little social critique and, instead, has been expressed as a series of capabilities or actions that exist largely *in potentia*. Irrespective of their provenance, things are defined and made meaningful by people. Consequently, designing and defining future artifacts is an act shaped by previous cultural experience, knowledge, and experience with other things. Pivotal to this debate and the relationship of people with artifacts is

Sterling's (2005, p. 11) introduction of the concept of the spime, an object that is entirely trackable during its entire lifetime, which is a concept completely alien to material culture theory and a concept of the object that is readily critiqued.

As elements of the digital impact upon different aspects of everyday life and cultural activity, it becomes increasingly less useful to focus on understanding, and therefore to design around, presumed differences between digital and physical realities. Instead, a more specific mode of analysis is required that reconnects spaces of connected cultural activity. Culturally aware approaches deemphasize technologically determined discussions of contemporary digital spaces in toto and advocate a relative approach in which research is conducted with observation *in* the digital rather than *of* the digital.

The immediate problem for conducting critical digital research is to deliver a position that acknowledges a digital provenance of experience without automatically affirming the simplistic observation that everything digital is not real or physical. The social sciences have expended considerable effort tackling ontological issues regarding reality through works that have entered the sociological canon, such as those of Berger and Luckmann (1966), Arbib and Hesse (1986), and Foucault (1973/1983). These analyses suggest that the assignment of quantities of "reality" to social phenomena is illusory; similarly, the digital world cannot be dismissed or disregarded solely because it lacks corporeality. "Space is social morphology: it is to lived experience what form itself is to the living organism, and just as intimately bound up with function and structure" (Lefebvre. 1991, p. 94). The boundaries to experience in the digital world are the consequence of the complexities of a specific provenance and not because the digital world somehow lacks reality: The virtual is equally capable of producing cultural "truths," meaning, and engagement.

8 Conclusion

Successful artifacts are notorious for resisting the application of design. The "best" artifacts are those that have evolved, been extensively used, and (re)adapted. The example of the fork (or open-source software) is pertinent. Rapid and participatory development and change is preferable to individual design. The individual social understanding offered by a single designer cannot be compared to the collective weight of social understanding that many users provide and increasingly willingly offer. Identifying the key features of an artifact and designing solely for those features present the danger of designing for desire rather than for greater social need or purpose. This approach takes the route of the "best" inventors—Edison's commercial knowledge prevailed over Tesla's ability as an inventor. The result of this example is a Western world left with a commercially successful but inefficient series of artifacts that were willingly adopted and accepted on criteria other than design alone.

The polysemy of human experience and human relationship to artifacts ensures that there is no ultimate or obvious adoption of the best artifacts, whatever that may mean. Designers can adopt and absorb this understanding by becoming part of a participatory process that incorporates feedback loops directly into the design process. The digital artifact is not burdened by the conventional process of manufacture and the ultimate commitment that conventional production implies. Digital artifacts can be created, tried, tested, and discarded within a time frame measured in hours rather than months. However, this flexibility and rapidity must parallel concurrent understanding that some design (and some things) must simply be discarded, as rapidly and as willingly as they can be created.

This is not a position that advocates anarchy or a complete disregard for design. We are making the argument for design processes that develop artifacts within the social and cultural environment where they will be utilized. In other words, designers of digital artifacts need to exploit the participatory, generally adept, and critical environment that Internet and Web technologies have increasingly supported.

References

Arbib, M., & Hesse, M. (1986). *The construction of reality*. Cambridge, UK: Cambridge University Press.

Aunger, R. (2006). Cultural transmission and diffusion. In L. Nadel (Ed.), *Encyclopedia of cognitive science* (p. 724). London: Wiley.

Barnes, B. (1997, February 27). "Nothing But Net", Webhead. *Slate*. Retrieved February 18, 2008, from http://www.slate.com/id/2543/

Baudrillard, J. (1994). *Simulacra and simulation* (S. Glaser, Trans.). Ann Arbor: Michigan University Press. (Original work published 1981).

Baudrillard, J. (1996). *The system of objects* (J. Benedict, Trans.). London, UK: Verso. (Original work published 1970).

Bereano, P. (1997). Technology is a tool of the powerful. In D. Erman, M. Williams, & M. Shauf (Eds.), *Computers, ethics and society* (pp. 26–32). New York: Oxford University Press.

Berger, P., & Luckmann, T. (1966). *The social construction of reality*. New York: Doubleday.

Buchli, V. (1995). Interpreting material culture: The trouble with text. In I. Hodder, M. Shanks, A. Alexandri, V. Buchli, J. Carman, J. Last, & G. Lucas (Eds.), *Interpreting archaeology* (pp. 181–193). London: Routledge.

Buchli, V. (2002). Introduction. In V. Buchli (Ed.), *The material culture reader* (pp. 1–22). Berg: Oxford, UK.

Criado, F. (1997). The visibility of the archaeological record and the interpretation of social reality, In I. Hodder, M. Shanks, A. Alexandri, V. Buchli, J. Carman, J. Last, & G. Lucas (Eds.), *Interpreting archaeology* (pp. 194–204). London: Routledge.

Cronin, M. (1998, May). The travel agents' dilemma. *Fortune, 137*, 163–164.

Foucault, M. (1983). *This is not a pipe* (J. Harkness, Trans.). Berkeley, CA: Quantum Books. (Original work published 1973).

Gadamer, G. (1989). *Truth and method*. New York: Crossroad.

Geertz, C. (1993). *The interpretation of culture: Selected essays*. London: Fontana. (Original work published in 1973).

Gottdiener, M. (1995). *Postmodern semiotics: Material culture and the forms of postmodern life*. Oxford, UK: Blackwell.

Graham, S. (1997). Imagining the real-time city. In S. Westwood & J. Williams (Eds.), *Imagining cities: Scripts, signs and memory* (pp. 31–49). London: Routledge.

Green, N. (1997). Beyond being digital: Representation and virtual corporeality. In D. Holmes (Ed.), *Virtual politics: Identity and community in cyberspace* (pp. 228–241). London: Sage Publications.

Hides, S. (1997). The genealogy of material culture and cultural identity. In S. Pearce (Ed.), *Experiencing material culture in the Western world* (pp. 11–35). London: Leicester University Press.

Hodder, I. (1989). Postmodernism, post-structuralism and post-processual archaeology. In I. Hodder (Ed.), *The meaning of things: Material culture and symbolic expression* (pp. 64–71). Hammersmith, UK: HarperCollins Academic.

Lefebvre, H. (1991). *The production of space*. Oxford, UK: Blackwell.

Lemonnier, P. (1993). Introduction. In P. Lemonnier (Ed.), *Technological choices: Arbitraries in technology from the Neolithic to modern high technology* (pp. 1–35). London: Routledge.

Marcus, G. (1995). Ethnography in/of the world system: The emergence of multi-sited ethnography. *Annual Review of Anthropology, 24* 95–117.

Miller, D. (1991). *Material culture and mass consumption*. Oxford, UK: Blackwell.

Miller, D., & Slater, D. (2000). *The Internet: An ethnographic approach*. Oxford, UK: Berg.

Oldenziel, R. (1996). Object/ions: Technology, culture and gender. In W. Kingery (Ed.), *Learning from things: Method and theory of material culture studies* (pp. 55–69). Washington, DC: Smithsonian Institution Press.

Pearson, M. (1997). Tombs and territories: Material culture and multiple interpretations. In I. Hodder, M. Shanks, A. Alexandri, V. Buchli, J. Carman, J. Last, & G. Lucas (Eds.), *Interpreting archaeology* (pp. 205–209). London: Routledge.

Rich, L. (1998, February 23). Grounding cyberspace. *AdWeek, 8*, 29–30.

Richardson, M. (1974). *The human mirror: Material and spatial images of man*. Baton Rouge: Louisiana State University Press.

Ricoeur, P. (1981). What is a Text? Explanation and understanding. In J. Thompson (Ed.), *Hermeneutics and the human sciences* (pp. 145–164). Cambridge, UK: Cambridge University Press.

Sclafane, S. (1998). Web sites create world wide exposure. *National Underwriter Property & Casualty, 102*(6), 14, 31.

Shanks, M., & Hodder, I. (1997). Processual, postprocessual and interpretative archaeologies. In I. Hodder, M. Shanks, A. Alexandri, V. Buchli, J. Carman, J. Last, & G. Lucas (Eds.), *Interpreting archaeology* (pp. 3–29). London: Routledge.

Sheridan, T., & David S. Zeltzer (1997). "Virtual Reality": Really? In P. Agre & D. Schuler (Eds.), *Reinventing technology, rediscovering community: Critical explorations of computing as a social practice* (pp. 85–94). Greenwich, CT: Ablex Publishing.

Silver, D. (2000). Looking backwards, looking forwards: Cyberculture studies 1990–2000. In D. Gauntlett (Ed.), *Web.studies: Rewiring media studies for the digital age* (pp. 19–30). London: Edward Arnold.

Smart, B. (1992). *Modern conditions, postmodern controversies*. London: Routledge.

Smith, A. (1998). Caught up in the Web. *Progressive Grocer, 77*(3), 32.

Soja, E. (1989). *Postmodern geographies: The assertion of space in critical social theory*. London: Verso.

Sterling, B. (2005). *Shaping things*. Boston, MA: The MIT Press.

Stoll, C. (1995). *Silicon snake oil: Second thoughts on the information highway*. New York: Doubleday.

Thomas, J. (1997). Reconciling symbolic significance with being-in-the-world. In I. Hodder, M. Shanks, A. Alexandri, V. Buchli, J. Carman, J. Last, & G. Lucas (Eds.), *Interpreting archaeology* (pp. 210–211). London: Routledge.

Thrift, N. (1996). New urban eras and old technological fears: Reconfiguring the goodwill of electronic things. *Urban Studies, 33*, 1463–1494.

Tilley, C. (1989). Interpreting material culture. In I. Hodder (Ed.), *The meaning of things: Material culture and symbolic expression* (pp. 23–26). Hammersmith, UK: HarperCollins Academic.

Tilley, C. (2002). Metaphor, materiality and interpretation. In V. Buchli (Ed.), *The material culture reader* (pp. 184–194). Oxford, UK: Berg.

Touraine, A. (1974). *The post-industrial society*. London: Random House.

Wakeford, N. (2000). New media, new methodologies: Studying the Web. In D. Gauntlett (Ed.), *Web.studies: Rewiring media studies for the digital age* (pp. 31–41). London, UK: Edward Arnold.

Whittle, D. (1997). *Cyberspace: The human dimension*. New York: W.H. Freeman.

Wise, J. M. (1997). *Exploring technology and social space*. Thousand Oaks, CA: Sage Publications.

The Human Modes of Being in Investigating User Experience

Hannakaisa Isomäki

Abstract An important challenge for interaction designers is to understand factors that shape user experience, and novel approaches are being developed to establish user experience as a specific field of research. Previous attempts to provide a comprehensive theory of user experience have focused on analyzing sensations and emotions as well as perceptions and behaviors. A holistic view of human experience is still lacking. I argue that a holistic view of the human being is needed to provide the appropriate theoretical foundations for user experience analyses in diverse contexts. In this chapter I introduce a theoretical framework for understanding human experience, and discuss how such a holistic view can reveal how fundamental human modes of being contribute to and shape user experience while people interact with information and communication technologies. Investigating user experience with the help of this framework facilitates interaction designers' understanding of factors that shape a holistic user experience.

1 Introduction

As information and communication technologies (ICTs) have permeated human life and people are seen to carry out their everyday activities with and through ICTs, the ability to recognize, analyze, and design for user experience has become a focal interest within the field of human–computer interaction (HCI) and interaction design. Primary is the human being's experience at the moment experienced rather than the traditional approach of concentrating on analysis of the tasks people carry out with ICTs. User experience is viewed as essential, since product characteristics and functionality are seen to have an impact on usability that, in turn, has an impact on user experience (McNamara & Kirakowski, 2006). In this way, user experience as a research paradigm shifts the focus of

H. Isomäki (✉)
Information Technology Research Institute, University of Jyväskylä, Jyväskylä,
Finland
e-mail: hannakaisa.isomaki@titu.jyu.fi

P. Saariluoma, H. Isomäki (eds.), *Future Interaction Design II*,
DOI 10.1007/978-1-84800-385-9_10, © Springer-Verlag London Limited 2009

interest from functional or instrumental features of HCI to the noninstrumental needs of users, and becomes the ultimate phenomenon indicating the quality of human–ICT interaction.

Despite the current immense interest in user experience, the term has not been unanimously established theoretically and is associated with a variety of meanings. McCarthy and Wright (2004) define experience in terms of culture and, in a subsequent analysis, aim to find varieties of user experience in media-saturated cultures (McCarthy, Wright, Wallace, & Dearden, 2006). Colbert (2005) builds upon an interaction-centered view in defining user experience as users' perceptions of interaction that constitute qualities of use. Forlizzi and Battarbee (2004) also introduce an interaction-centered framework of experience, which typifies user experience as fluent, cognitive, and expressive. Further, Battarbee (2003) emphasizes the social nature of user experience by defining co-experience as created in social interaction. Partala and Surakka (2003), as well as Norman (2004), have highlighted affective and emotional aspects of interaction, whereas cognitive qualities have been seen as a major factor in HCI by several scholars, such as Card, Moran, and Newell (1983) and Rasmussen, Pejtersen, and Goodstein (1994). Finally, Hassenzahl and Tractinsky (2006) summarize recent user experience research by delineating a research agenda incorporating three major perspectives: user experience beyond the instrumental, user experience as affective or emotional aspects of interaction, and an experiential perspective unfolding the situatedness and temporality of the use of ICTs.

These major perspectives include three categories of factors building up user experience: users' internal state, characteristics of the designed system, and the interaction context. Common to the different meanings is that they all aim to find the central elements of human experience in relation to the use of ICTs. Methodologically, these approaches have drawn heavily from either cognitive science and experimental analysis, or a more holistic, phenomenological approach and qualitative analysis (Swallow, Blythe, & Wright, 2006). These previous attempts to provide a comprehensive theory or framework of user experience have been focused on sensations and emotions as well as perceptions and behaviors. Yet a holistic view of human experience is still lacking. A determining factor in selecting an appropriate theoretical definition, and also a research approach, for user experience originates from a notion of the human being: Is he/she a cognitive, emotional, social, or cultural creature? In HCI, humans are seen to interact with ICTs; a central underlying assumption to contemplate should be how the context of use influences user experience?

In this chapter, I argue that a holistic view of the human being is needed to provide the appropriate theoretical foundations for user experience analyses in diverse contexts. In so doing, I introduce a theoretical framework for understanding user experience in terms of human experience. By examining this, it is possible to demonstrate the factors that influence user experience in terms of the fundamental human modes of being. This paper is organized as follows: First I describe a theoretical framework or metamodel for outlining the nature of human experience, and then discuss how the basic human modes of being are intertwined with the use of ICTs while defining knowledge and knowing as elements of user experience. I conclude by discussing the framework in the context of investigating user experience.

2 A Theoretical Account of User Experience

As mentioned above, user experience research has highlighted different qualities in users, but a holistic view of the human being is needed to provide appropriate theoretical foundations for comprehensive user experience analyses in diverse contexts. Further, besides the feasibility of various research approaches in different contexts, an appropriate approach to study user experience depends on the nature of the product for which use is the reference point for the experience under study. As ICT application features are not always controllable or even visible to the user, but often embedded "behind" the actual interface, users' experience while using ICTs emphasizes the inclusion of emergent features of the central functionality issues within those experiences. Therefore, one must first define user experience within a holistic framework that illustrates the nature of the human being and stresses human action as a continuum of an active process with both tacit and explicit dimensions intertwined with the use of ICTs (Isomäki, 2002, 2007). The following framework is noninstrumental because it discloses the genuine nature of the human being, and experiential in that it defines an experience as a combination of various interrelated fundamental modes of being that are present in human–ICT interaction.

2.1 A Noninstrumental Framework for Outlining the Nature of User Experience

User experience concerns an individual's personal experience of using a technological product in a certain context or situation (e.g., Forlizzi & Ford, 2000; McCarthy et al., 2006). A central tendency in user experience research is to find a framework comprehensive enough to entail the whole richness of human experience. A comprehensive explanation for the human being as a self-contained whole is being pursued by researchers in the field of philosophical anthropology. Over the course of time, philosophers have presented several different conceptions or models of the human being (e.g., Laine & Kuhmonen, 1995; Nash, 1968). Generally the various conceptions of the human being can be seen as different combinations of two main elements: the first relates to the number of the human modes of being (Rauhala, 1983), and the second to the basic structure of those modes of being (Wilenius, 1978). These two elements form the grounding dimensions for a conceptual framework for outlining the multiplicity of the human being as a whole.

Rauhala (1983) states that the most common way to regard the first element is to distinguish among the monistic, dualistic, pluralistic, and holistic models of the human being. Monistic conceptions are based on the idea that the human being consists of only one basic mode of being. In general this one mode is matter. Dualistic models consider that, in order to understand the human being, two different modes of being must be presupposed, usually the mind and body. There are big differences within the dualistic conceptions regarding the relationship between mind and body (e.g., Hilgard, 1980). The contrast is sharpest between so called Cartesian dichotomy, which assumes that mind and body are totally detached from each other, and contemporary form of dualism that regards mind and body as two aspects of the same phenomenon. By the ontrast is deep, for example, between Cartesian dualism and modern reductionist aterialism. Different conceptions based on a two-aspectual interpretation of the human being are quite common (Rauhala, 1983), such as analyses of cognitive–emotional aspects of HCI. Vyas and van der Veer (2006), for example, aim at analyzing user experience in a holistic manner, but their analysis focuses on feelings and new understandings in addition to design features and functionalities of the technology involved.

In pluralistic conceptions, it is presupposed that the human is actualized as many kinds of parallel subsystems that have their own structures and thus relative independence (e.g. vision system, central nervous system, memory system, and emotional system). The current multidisciplinary research concerning humans as users of ICTs is based on a pluralistic view. Often research concerning people is focused on certain subsystems in a particular context, for example, human information processing in requirements analysis (Barnard & May, 1993) or development of trust in virtual teams (Järvenpää, Knoll, & Leidner, 1998). A limitation of the pluralistic conception is the difficulty in gathering dissimilarity and stating arguments for the human being as a whole, since the pluralist approach yields results that depict human qualities as separate elements. An attempt has been made to solve this limitation within the holistic conceptions, which assume that the human being is actualized in more than two modes of being and these modes are fundamentally different. Without the simultaneous existence of all of the modes it is not possible to consider a creature as a human being. Therefore, each of the modes presupposes the other in order to exist by itself. Thus, they cannot be reduced from one mode of being to another but need to be understood as a whole (Rauhala, 1983). This definition of a holistic view of the human being as consisting of different, interrelated layers is in line with Husserl's (Keller, 1999) phenomenological notion of human experience.

As Keller (1999, p. 2) points out, Husserl maintains that central to the notion of experience is the concept of intentionality, which illustrates the capacity that human beings possess to direct themselves to objects and to the contextual features of the environment involved in any awareness they have of objects. Various levels of intentionality make up the different levels of human experience. Intentionality reaches down into the most basic forms of perception, or being (Keller, 1999, p. 2). That is to say, human experience as a whole needs to be understood through the different levels of intentionality that compose it. According to Husserl, even the most basic sensory awareness involves a kind of intentionality that is logically distinguishable from perception. Further, intentionality is involved in both individually and socially formed experiences. In Husserlian terms, the experiencing subject is constituted as "we-intentionality," through which persons as groups can be directed at objects, but is always fundamentally based on a prior understanding of objects in the form of "I-intentionality" (Keller, 1999, p. 47). Thus, intentionality concerns human qualities that exist both in individuals and groups of people. In order to understand the qualities of the different but interconnected levels in human experience, a phenomenologically rooted view of the basic structure of the modes of being need to be examined. Therefore, the second element of the framework, the basic structure of the modes of being, refers to the different basic qualities of the human being. With respect to these basic qualities, Wilenius (1978) states that the human being can be seen as a physical system, as an organic system, as a mental–psychical system, and as a social and a cultural creature. These basic qualities cover the basic features of both individuals and groups of people.

2.1.1 The Physical and Organic Modes of Being

The physical system denotes that the structure (e.g., bones and muscular system) and movements of people can be explained, for example, by the laws of mechanics. From this point of view the human being is a mechanism that operates without involving any other human feature in its action. According to the organic (biological–chemical) system, the human being is a living creature whose structure of organic matter and action are prescribed, on the one hand, by heredity and, on the other hand, by the living environment. A special feature of the human biological system is a well-developed central nervous system. A conception that regards humans as biological systems is that of Porra (1996), who applies a systems theoretical point of view and suggests that humans are primarily organic systems that form colonies and co-evolve with ICTs. The co-evolution results in a new species *Compu sapiens* (Porra, 1996, p. 374). Porra's reasoning is based on a naturalistic notion of the human being as a primarily organic being whose social behavior can be reduced to biological features (cf. Laine & Kuhmonen, 1995). This stance has acquired more public acknowledgement through the development of biotechnology. Some researchers even claim that humans have specific genes for different behavior types such as, for example, conformity and resentment (Hirsjärvi, 1982). Further, biotechnological applications are currently being developed in the field of information security, for example, in the biometrical identification of users, which yields a particular user experience in terms of the organic mode of being. The physical and organic mode of being is also highlighted in analyses of haptic user interfaces. Michelitsch, Williams, Osen, Jimenez, and Rapp (2004, p. 1305), for instance, draw on this mode of being when developing a "Haptic Chameleon," an interaction device that conveys information between the users and the system by changing its shape, material feel, and consistency. Reflecting on the empirical implications of the organic mode of being is also the key issue for the design of tangible interfaces (e.g., Sporka, Němec, & Slavík, 2005).

2.1.2 The Mental Mode of Being

The human being as a mental–psychical creature possesses unconsciousness, consciousness, and self-consciousness. A classical way of delineate consciousness activities is to separate thought, emotions, and will. In the same vein, Hilgard (1980) maintains that the classic psychological processes cognition, affection, and conation serve both as a classification of consciousness activities and a reminder that "there is something more" than just cognitive processes in humans. Correspondingly, a common way of conceptualizing humans is to build the underlying definition of the human being upon the basis of consciousness activities. Wilenius (1987) distinguishes between the intellectualistic, emotionalist, and voluntarist conceptions of the human being. Ropo (1985) states that, in the course of different epochs, a common characteristic of human conception has been the appreciation of intellectual abilities, particularly those of knowledge and talent. The modern notion of the human being also frequently emphasizes the intellectual: People are conceived of as primarily perceiving and thinking creatures who plan their actions and circumstances. The majority of usability approaches stress the process view over human cognition (e.g., Barnard & May, 1993), which is also included in usability inspection methods, such as the cognitive walkthrough (Blackmon, Polson, Kitajima, & Lewis, 2002). In user experience research, a cognitive viewpoint usually concerns interactions resulting in user's new knowledge or understanding (Vyas & van der Veer, 2006), or confusion and error if the product does not work as the user expected (Forlizzi & Battarbee, 2004). A particular type of user experience that reflects the cognitive aspect of the mental mode of being is defined in the context of online learning (Griffin & Randolph, 2000). Human attention is also included within the cognitive paradigm, although attention is often expressed as investigation of users' eye movements (e.g., Prendinger, Ma, & Yingzi, 2005). Thus, a connection between the physical–organic and mental modes of being is assumed.

The emotionalist notion of the human being stresses emotions. For example, in the writings of Jean Jacques Rousseau, the idea that feeling should precede thinking is a recurrent statement (Nash, 1968). In recent user experience research, emotions are often regarded as forming the core of human experience (e.g., Hassenzahl & Tractinsky, 2006), and various nuances of emotional experiences are being studied. McCarthy et al. (2006), for example, examine the experience of enchantment as a desire that people may have in their use of ICTs, especially when that use is discretionary. Ståhl, Sundström, and Höök (2005), in turn, assume a connection between the physical–organic and emotional modes of being in investigating users' emotional experiences as both body language and emotional expressions. A rich view of emotional user experience is adopted by Mahlke and Thüring (2007), who study users' perceptions of system quality in terms of emotional reactions involving subjective feelings, facial expressions, and physiological responses. Further, the voluntarist stance regards will as an essential feature (Wilenius, 1987). In current user experience research, the voluntarist stance should evoke ethically sustainable principles, such as good privacy practices and robust informed consent agreements, as it studies the very personal issue of user experience.

2.1.3 The Social Mode of Being

Further, according to Wilenius (1978), the social is also a structure of the human basic modes of being. The human being is seen in a particular relationship to his/her environment. Essential in being a social creature is that the human being is able to develop its specific human qualities (e.g., upright position, language, ways of thinking and behaving) only in a human environment. It is also inherent in individuals to search for community with other people. In other words, sociality is a quality of an individual but the nature of this characteristic leads humans to create diverse interactive human networks and social structures. Since ICTs are often seen as either technical systems with social implications or social systems only technically implemented (Hirschheim, Klein, & Lyytinen, 1995, p. 15), perhaps the most common notion of the human being as a user of ICTs is based on a view of the social dimension of humans, which assumes that individuals are determined by their relationships to their social environment. For instance, users' behaviors in virtual spaces can be socially regulated by particular software routines (Muramatsu, 2003). Regarding the recent study of user experience, Battarbee (2003), for example, defines the concept of co-experience that stresses that user experience is constructed in social interactions, while Müller-Prove (2007), in turn, stresses the importance of user experience in the design of open-source communities.

A more recent theoretical stance on the social mode of being is expressed by postmodernism, which assumes that people are not determined by instincts, laws, needs, or systems. Instead, human behavior is open-ended, changing, and creative. Both human nature and knowledge are being created and laid down in the very acts of human living. This means also that human behavior can only be understood by reading the broader context of life and history within which the behavior occurs. Thereby, the postmodern stance rejects psychodynamic instincts and unconscious minds, behavioristic laws of learning and conditioning, humanistic needs and growth potentials, as well as cognitive structures and processes (Slife & Williams, 1995). Instead, humans become shaped according to their living environments, and in particular through their social relationships. Greenhill and Isomäki (2005) attempt to disclose a postmodern stance applicable in user experience studies by illustrating the incorporation of the self into Web information systems design. In general, the study of sociality offers a wide range of detailed theoretical assumptions that may enrich the understanding of the social mode of being and thus provide means for rich analyses of the social user experience.

2.1.4 The Cultural Mode of Being

The human being defined as a cultural creature emphasizes the creative relationship between people and their material and mental environments. Ever since beginning to use simple tools and make fire, humankind has in a relatively short time created an immensely diverse mental and material culture. According to Wilenius (1978), the cultural features of the human being are truthfulness, ethics, aesthetic awareness and religiosity. Aesthetics has been recognized as an important feature of user experience that clearly contributes to usability as well (Hassenzahl & Tractinsky, 2006). Also McCarthy and Wright (2004) define users' everyday lived experience as primarily aesthetic. Hofstede's (1997) frequently cited definition of the term "culture" is also close to the traditional Western meaning that refers to "refinement of the mind" or "civilization" as signifying the higher spiritual features of humans. These higher spiritual features form also the deep emotional roots of human life in terms of ethics: People do possess a need to do what is regarded as good, truthful, and egalitarian. For example, it is inherent in research work for the researcher to possess a deep motivation to find the truth, and to depict her or his research procedures and results as truthfully as possible. In a same vein, the tradition of human-centered design was originally motivated by principles and methods emphasizing value-sensitive design (e.g., Kumar & Welke, 1984; Mumford, 1983). Recently, Dalsgård and Halskov (2006) have stressed values as important indicators of users' intentions in experience design.

This definition of the cultural mode of being leaves out the social view of the cultural mode of being. Yet these two modes are often seen as intertwined in delineations that apprehend the cultural mode as manifested in social life through symbols, heroes, rituals, and values (Denzin, 1992; Hofstede, 1997). An interlaced sociocultural aspect of user experience is highlighted by Forlizzi and Ford (2000) and McCarthy and Wright (2004), who determine user experience in a way that engages the individual within a particular culture and illustrates user experience as colored by the narratives from a remembered past and anticipated future. This notion of culture exceeds the boundaries of the traditional understanding of culture as rooted in different nationalities, as reflected in cross-cultural design of user interfaces (Marcus, 2001).

To sum up, the above-depicted basic modes of being, together with the structure of those modes of being, form the framework for understanding human experience in a holistic manner (Fig. 1). Thus the human being is seen in accord with the simultaneous existence of physical, organic, mental, social, and cultural modes of being. The framework is theoretical, and when outlining for empirical research the nature of the human being as various combinations of the basic structures and the number of the human modes of being, it should also

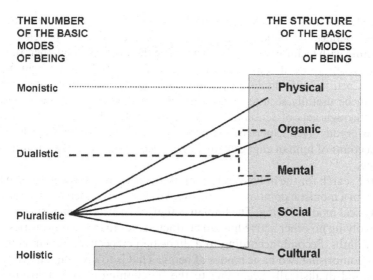

Fig. 1 The theoretical foundation of user experience: the human modes of being

be noted that the nature of the above-mentioned basic structures seems to vary, depending on the origins of the definition of the structure in question. For instance, there are different stances toward the nature of human cognition. In addition, in some cases the relationship between the different structures seems, to some extent, to be hierarchical: The higher structure presupposes the lower, meaning thought presumes brains, emotions presume a central nervous system, and cultural perspectives presuppose a social environment. More specificity on the multifaceted nature of the human being may be gained by considering the basic human modes of being within a particular context. In the following section, the theoretical account of the human basic modes of being is discussed in terms of the user experience within human–ICT interaction.

3 The Holistic User Experience

Since humans are seen to interact with ICTs in HCI, a central underlying assumption to contemplate is how the context of use influences the interplay between people and ICTs. Where the nature of the human being is delineated in the context of user experience, the human being is seen as an actor, influenced by the experience at hand. This is inherent in the term "user experience", which refers to the experience of a human being who uses ICTs.

Since people are acting as whole persons while using ICTs, all the basic human modes of being are understood as active elements in the human being relating to the ICT. According to this active view, the different basic modes of being each contribute to some extent to a processual continuum within which the whole human being is active with the ICT product. This process incorporates the richness of human nature and is the source of user experience: While interacting with technologies, users experience the world through their physical, organic, mental, social, and cultural modes of being. In the same vein, Wright and McCarthy (2005) disclose a phenomenological view in that human experience can be usefully seen as constituted by continuous engagement with the world through acts of sensemaking at many levels. They define the focus of users' everyday lived experience as primarily aesthetic. In this way they focus their account of human engagement with a specific focus on the cultural mode of being.

In the search for the holistic notion of user experience, it is worth noting first that, from a monistic point of view, this active process is understood in regard to the physical mode of being. The human activity is seen as mechanistic functioning, involving no other active human characteristics than the trajectories of the human limbs. Second, according to a dualistic perspective, human activity is seen as comprising two basic modes of being. That is to say, human behavior is understood dualistically according to the functioning of only two modes of being. Third, from a pluralistic viewpoint human activity can be approached from the point of view of various parallel but separate subsystems. The mental mode of being in action may be seen as human information processing that consists of brain functions, attention, perception, and thought activity (Anderson, 2000). In a similar manner, an emotional experience may be seen as a continuum of physical, neural, sensorimotor, affective, and cognitive processes (Izard, 1993). In the same vein, the social mode of being may be seen as action that has interconnected tacit and explicit elements (Nonaka, Toyama, & Konno, 2000; Schön, 1987). The salience of the tacit dimension in the social and cultural modes of being is evident also in the aim of sociological cultural studies, which attempt to unravel the ideological meanings that are coded into the taken-for-granted meanings diffused in everyday life (Denzin, 1992).

This underlines three notable characteristics in human action. First, the hierarchy of the basic human modes of being is also active by nature: Within human action the different modes interact with each other. Second, there are both conscious or explicit and unconscious or tacit dimensions in human action that contribute to human experience. Similarly, Keller (1999, p. 3) highlights that Husserl treats intentionality as an individual's intention to refer to objects that may be either inside or outside of consciousness. Third, the tacit and explicit dimensions are intertwined in the basic human modes of being. This is because people are not conscious of all the aspects of their own experiences within their life situations. For instance, in a social situation where a person meets and recognizes another person, the immediate perception of the other's face is succeeded by recognition of memories—visually and through other senses—connected to the face. Only then can the conscious experience arise (Tranel & Damasio, 1985), and the social situation may be shaped in accord with the meaning that this recognition evokes in the experiencing individual and his or her social relations. Therefore, it seems that in order to understand the active human being as a whole, attention must be paid to both the interacting basic human modes of being and their tacit as well as explicit features in human behavior. This requires a holistic perspective of the human being as an experiencing user of ICTs.

From a holistic point of view the very nature of human action may be seen as the different basic modes of being, each contributing to some extent to a continuum of an active process within which the human being as a whole is actively experiencing ICTs. As mentioned above, this active process may include both tacit and explicit dimensions. This kind of stance may be illustrated with the help of studies that draw on the works of two philosophers, John Dewey and Michel Polanyi. Dewey's notion of the reflective human being is quite generally known as a conception of the human being that attempts to integrate the different consciousness activities and action by synthesizing many of the dualisms of traditional philosophy; the reflective behavior that Dewey argued for is characterized by a synthesis of the dualisms of science and morals, ends and means, thought and action (Nash, 1968). Cook and Brown (1999), in turn, describe human knowledge creation by building on Dewey's concept "productive inquiry." Human knowledge creation is then seen to occur within two intertwined elements: knowledge and knowing, which include the explicit and tacit dimensions of human action. In addition, Cook and Brown (1999) offer conceptual means in transcending the subject–object dualism in regard to the information system–user relationship by defining part of human action involving static human features and another part as consisting of affordances that emerge dynamically in an interaction.

According to Cook and Brown (1999), productive inquiry is that aspect of any activity where humans are deliberately (though not always consciously) seeking what they need, in order to do what they want to do, for instance, with a computer. It is not a haphazard, random search; it is informed or "disciplined" by the use of theories, rules of thumb, concepts, and the like, which Dewey understood as knowledge and as tools for productive inquiry. For example, knowledge may be understood to refer to the goal or purpose of the use of a computer. Using knowledge in productive inquiry gives the inquiry a systematic or disciplined character. In addition, knowledge is one of the possible outcomes of productive inquiry. Another end result of engaging in the situated and dynamic activity of productive inquiry is the production of static knowledge, which then can be used as a tool for further knowing, including knowing in the mode of productive inquiry. Cook and Brown (1999) ascertain that knowledge by itself cannot enable knowing. As a tool, knowledge informs knowing, but does not enable it any more than possession of a hammer enables its skillful use. That is to say, human experience in using ICTs is a dynamic process within which human sensemaking is informed by explicit and tacit knowledge about the factors included in the human–ICT interaction. From the perspective of user experience, the human basic modes of being are in focus.

In other words, when people as whole human beings are engaged in a task, such as the use of computers, they are engaged in a process within which the conscious goal of that task intertwines more or less tacitly with the sensations arising from the basic human modes of being. Similarly, Jones, Failla, and Miller (2007) draw on the work of Polanyi in arguing that the greatest part of knowledge is subservient to one's goals and actions. Thus, the source for the emergent issues of user experience comprises all of the qualities inherent in the basic human modes of being despite the tacitness or explicitness of their nature. These issues are also knowledge that is used as a tool in productive inquiry within users' experiences. Therefore, when people are engaged in using ICTs, the way that they become informed by the technology should be understood in terms of the activity of the intertwining basic human modes of being. Moreover, because the use of ICTs is a recurrent activity, this process of experiencing should be seen as interaction between the human being and ICTs.

Within a holistic framework, when the basic human modes of being are intertwined with each other, a view of human experience may be provided with the help of the concept of affordance. Cook and Brown (1999) define their understanding of the characteristics of interaction with the world, which are at the center of knowing, with the help of the concept of dynamic affordance. Dynamic affordance refers to the sense of affordance that is reflected within the interaction of people and everyday objects, such as ICTs. That is to say, certain properties of everyday objects (e.g., software) arise solely in a certain context of interaction with the world. Likewise, the bits of knowledge that members of a team may possess are a property of that social context, and become facilities or frustrations within interaction. The facilities and frustrations within this dynamic interaction are the dimensions of dynamic affordance. This is particularly true of objects that are the product of human design: What they afford may give rise to the shape and fluidity (facilities) or incoherence and clumsiness (frustrations) of human experience.

However, dynamic affordance is not just a question of perception or tacit sensation gained through one's hands, but of the relationships between the characteristics of the world and the issues of inherent concern to people, such as the basic human modes of being. These modes of being can be understood as static characteristics in that they are inherent in all individuals. Usually, they provide humans with the ability and need to be physical, organic, intellectual, emotional, social, and cultural creatures with their own wills. However, the actual experiential implications of the basic human modes of being emerge in the interaction between humans and ICTs. In other words, there is a sense of affordance that lies beyond the inherently static human characteristics that deserves to be understood within its own right, and in particular with respect to the basic human modes of being. In this way, dynamic affordance also offers a conceptual means to transcend the subject–object dualism in the human–computer relationship. The static characteristics of humans and technology take on a new form within their intertwining activity, which is shaped according to, on the one hand, the affordances and constraints that the human modes of being provide, and, on the other hand, the affordances and constraints embedded in the features of the ICTs.

In a nutshell, dynamic affordance places emphasis on the experience that emerges from the basic human modes of being in the interaction of humans and the world. Because this emerging experience is an implication of the (static) basic human modes of being, it is important to consider them as constituting elements of user experience. This aspect of dynamic affordance is also in accord with the emergent perspective of ICTs: The consequences of the use of ICTs are seen to emerge within the very specific interaction between humans and the system at hand (McNamara & Kirakowski, 2006). From a human-centered perspective, the interaction between humans and ICTs is emerging as fluid and coherent when the system affords users to act in conformity with their basic modes of being. Therefore, understanding human experience requires insight into the different basic human modes of being and their implications within the dynamic affordances that occur between humans and ICTs in different contexts.

4 Conclusions

This chapter describes the preconditions of user experience. First, I introduced a theoretical holistic framework for understanding user experience in terms of the fundamental human experience involving physical, organic, mental (cognitive, emotional, volitive), social, and cultural modes of being. Second, I described how dynamic affordance puts emphasis on the experience that emerges from the basic human modes of being within interaction of humans and ICTs. The static characteristics of humans and technology take on a new form within their intertwining activity, which is shaped according to, on the one hand, the affordances and constraints that the human modes of being provide, and, on the other hand, the affordances and constraints embedded in the features of ICTs. From a holistic point of view, the very nature of human action may be seen as the different basic modes of being each contributing to some extent to a continuum of an active process within which the human as a whole is actively experiencing ICTs. Consequently, recognizing user experience necessitates insight into the human modes of being and their implications within the dynamic affordances that emerge between people and ICTs. This viewpoint is valid in different contexts, since people always experience the world in accord with their fundamental modes of being.

In addition to defining the human experience in a holistic manner, this framework underscores a holistic approach, in that it exceeds the limits of all the three major perspectives in user experience research (Hassenzahl & Tractinsky, 2006): user experience beyond the instrumental, user experience as affective or emotional aspects of interaction, and an experiential perspective. The framework is noninstrumental since it discloses the genuine nature of the human being. Further, it recognizes the emotional mode of being as one of the basic human qualities but also discloses other human basic modes of being for user experience research. It is experiential in that it defines an experience as a combination of various interrelated human modes of being present in human–ICT interaction.

The framework facilitates a comprehensive understanding of the nature of the human experience and of human qualities. This is an overriding concern for user experience research to grasp the genuine nature of human experience arising from the fundamental basic modes of being. Since humans are bound to act as they exist, these human qualities form the basis of an experience emerging within human–ICT interaction. Further, because the interaction between humans and ICTs is fluid and coherent when the application affords users to act in conformity with their basic modes of being, investigating user experience with this holistic framework will help interaction designers understand the factors that shape user experience. I have argued that the study of user experience could benefit from a phenomenology-based holistic framework of the human being for analyses in diverse contexts. An appropriate approach to study user experience is also dependent on the nature of the product for which use is the reference point for the experience under study. Often the nature of an ICT application emphasizes the inclusion of emergent features of user experience. Therefore, the holistic framework developed here can be applied in empirical studies involving both explicit and implicit features of user experience concerning technological products. An empirical application of the framework thus benefits from methods that support the analysis of both implicit and explicit features of experience. Implicit aspects of user experience are often revealed through interpretive methodologies, whereas explicit features are accessible by quantitative methods. In a holistic approach, a mixed-method methodology, such as exploratory research design, may also be needed (Creswell & Plano Clark, 2007).

Finally, regarding multidisciplinary research, this framework could serve as a metatriangulation device, which would facilitate theory building of user experience in terms of multiparadigm inquiry (Lewis & Grimes, 1999). Particularly, when research aims to overcome the problems of pluralist separation of various elements of an experience, a multiparadigm approach could facilitate theory building by serving as the heuristics that may help researchers explore the complexity of user experience and extend the scope, relevance, and creativity of user experience research in terms of various empirical theorizations concerning the human modes of being.

References

Anderson, J. R. (2000). *Cognitive psychology and its implications*. New York: Worth & Freeman.
Barnard, P. J., & May, J. (1993). Cognitive modelling for user requirements. In P. F. Byerley, P. J. Barnard, & J. May (Eds.), *Computers, communication and usability: Design issues, research and methods for integrated services* (pp. 101–146) Amsterdam: Elsevier.

Battarbee, K. (2003). Defining co-experience. In *Proceedings of the 2003 Designing Pleasurable Products and Interfaces* (DPPI) *Conference* (pp. 109–113). New York: ACM Press.

Blackmon, M. H., Polson, P. G., Kitajima, M., & Lewis, C. (2002). Cognitive walkthrough for the Web. In *Proceedings of the SIGCHI Conference on Human Factors in Computing Systems: Changing our world, changing ourselves* (pp. 463–470). New York: ACM Press.

Card, S. K., Moran, T. P., & Newell, A. (1983). *The psychology of human-computer interaction*. Mahwah, NJ: Lawrence Erlbaum Associates.

Colbert, M. (2005). User experience of communication before and during rendezvous: Interim results. *Personal and Ubiquitous Computing, 9*(3), 134–141.

Cook, S. D. N., & Brown, J. S. (1999). Bridging epistemologies: the generative dance between organizational knowledge and organizational knowing. *Organization Science, 10,* 381–400.

Creswell, J. W., & Plano Clark, V. L. (2007). *Designing and conducting mixed methods research*. Thousand Oaks, CA: SAGE Publications.

Dalsgård, P., & Halskov, K. (2006). Real life experiences within experience design. In *Proceedings of the 4th Nordic Conference on Human-Computer Interaction: Changing roles* (pp. 331–340). New York: ACM Press.

Denzin, N. K. (1992). *Symbolic interactionism and cultural studies.* Cambridge, MA: Blackwell.

Forlizzi, J., & Battarbee, K. (2004). Understanding experience in interactive systems. In *Proceedings of the 5th Conference on Designing Interactive Systems: Processes, practices, methods, and techniques* (pp. 261–268). New York: ACM Press.

Forlizzi, J., & Ford, S. (2000). The building blocks of experience: An early framework for interaction designers. In *Proceedings of the 3rd Conference on Designing Interactive Systems: Processes, practices, methods, and techniques* (pp. 419–423). New York: ACM Press.

Greenhill, A., & Isomäki, H. (2005). Incorporating self into web information system design. In A. Pirhonen, H. Isomäki, C. Roast, & P. Saariluoma (Eds.), *Future interaction design* (pp. 53–66). London: Springer-Verlag.

Griffin, J. A., & Randolph, G. B. (2000). Web experience and hypermedia structure in on-line learning. In *Proceedings of the Eighth Annual Consortium on Computing in Small Colleges Rocky Mountain Conference* (pp. 44–53). Chicago: Consortium for Computing Sciences in Colleges.

Hassenzahl, M., & Tractinsky, N. (2006). User experience: A research agenda. *Behaviour and Information Technology, 25*(2), 91–97.

Hilgard, E. R. (1980). Consciousness in contemporary psychology. *Annual Review of Psychology, 31*(1), 1–26.

Hirschheim, R., Klein, H., & Lyytinen, K. (1995). *Information systems development and data modeling: Conceptual and philosophical foundations.* Cambridge, UK: Cambridge University Press.

Hirsjärvi, S. (1982). *Kasvatustieteen käsitteistö* [Concepts in education science]. Keuruu, Finland: Otava.

Hofstede, G. (1997). *Cultures and organizations: Software of the mind.* New York: McGraw-Hill.

Isomäki, H. (2002). The prevailing conceptions of the human being in information systems development: systems designers' reflections (Department of Computer and Information Sciences, Rep. No. A-2002-6). Tampere, Finland: Tampere University Press.

Isomäki, H. (2007). Different levels of information systems designers' forms of thought and potential for human-centred design. *International Journal of Technology and Human Interaction, 3*(1), 30–48.

Izard, C. E. (1993). Four systems of emotion activation: Cognitive and non-cognitive processes. *Psychological Review, 100*(1), 68–90.

Järvenpää, S., Knoll, K., & Leidner, D. (1998). Is anybody out there? Antecedents of trust in global virtual teams. *Journal of Management Information Systems, 14*(4), 29–64.

Jones, B., Failla, A., & Miller, B. (2007). Tacit knowledge in rapidly evolving organizational environments. *International Journal of Technology and Human Interaction, 3*(1), 49–71.

Keller, P. (1999). *Husserl and Heidegger on human experience.* Cambridge, UK: Cambridge University Press.

Kumar, K., & Welke, J. (1984). Implementation failure and system developer values: Assumptions, truisms and empirical evidence. In *Proceedings of the 5th International Conference on Information Systems* (pp. 1–12). Atlanta, GA: Association of Information Systems.

Laine, T., & Kuhmonen, P. (1995). *Filosofinen antropologia: Ihmisen kokonaisuutta etsimässä.* [Philosophical anthropology: In search of the whole of the human being]. Jyväskylä, Finland: Atena.

Lewis, M. W., & Grimes, A. J. (1999). Metatriangulation: Building theory from multiple paradigms. *Academy of Management Review, 24,* 672–690.

Mahlke, S., & Thüring, M. (2007). Studying antecedents of emotional experiences in interactive contexts. In *Proceedings of the SIGCHI Conference on Human Factors in Computing Systems* (pp. 915–918). New York: ACM Press.

Marcus, A. (2001). Cross-cultural user-interface design for work, home, play and on the way. In *Proceedings of the SIGDOC '01Conference* (pp. 91–98). New York: ACM Press.

McCarthy, J., & Wright, P. (2004). *Technology as experience.* Cambridge, MA: MIT Press.

McCarthy, J., Wright, P., Wallace, J., & Dearden, A. (2006). The experience of enchantment in human-computer interaction. *Personal and Ubiquitous Computing 10*(6), 369–378.

McNamara, N., & Kirakowski, J. (2006). Functionality, usability and user experience: Three areas of concern. *interactions, 13*(6), 26–28.

Michelitsch, G., Williams, J., Osen, M., Jimenez, B., & Rapp, S. (2004). Haptic chameleon: A new concept of shape-changing user interface controls with force feedback. In *CHI '04 extended abstracts on human factors in computing systems* (pp. 1305–1308). New York: ACM Press.

Mumford, E. (1983). *Designing human systems: The ETHICS method.* Manchester, UK: Manchester Business School.

Muramatsu, J. (2003). Social regulation in virtual spaces. In *CHI '03 extended abstracts on human factors in computing systems* (pp. 91–98). New York: ACM Press.

Müller-Prove, M. (2007). Community experience at OpenOffice.org. *Interactions, 14*(6), 47–48.

Nash, P. (1968). *Models of man.* New York: John Wiley & Sons.

Nonaka, I., Toyama, R., & Konno, N. (2000). SECI, Ba, and leadership: A unified model of dynamic knowledge creation. *Long Range Planning, 33*(1), 5–34.

Norman, D. A. (2004). *Emotional design: Why we love (or hate) everyday things.* New York: Basic Books.

Partala, T., & Surakka, V. (2003). Pupil size variation as an indication of affective processing. *International Journal of Human-Computer Studies, 59*(1–2), 185–198.

Porra, J. (1996). *Colonial systems, information colonies and punctuated prototyping.* (Doctoral dissertation; Jyväskylä Studies in Computer Science, Economics and Statistics Rep. No. 33). Jyväskylä, Finland: University of Jyväskylä.

Prendinger, H., Ma, C., & Yingzi, J. (2005). Understanding the effect of life-like interface agents through users' eye movements. In *Proceedings of the 7th International Conference on Multimodal Interfaces* (pp. 108–115). New York: ACM Press.

Rasmussen, J., Pejtersen, A. M., & Goodstein, L. P. (1994). *Cognitive systems engineering.* New York: John Wiley & Sons.

Rauhala, L. (1983). *Ihmiskäsitys ihmistyössä* [The conception of the human being in human work]. Helsinki, Finland: Gaudeamus.

Ropo, E. (1985). Erilaisista ihmiskäsityksistä [On different conceptions of the human being]. In *Ihmiskuva ja kasvatuksen haasteet* [Image of the human being and the challenges of education] (Rep. No. 1; pp. 3–17). Helsinki, Finland: Tieteenfilosofinen tutkimusseura ry.

Schön, D. A. (1987). *Educating the reflective practitioner.* San Francisco: Jossey-Bass.

Slife, B. D., & Williams, R. N. (1995). *What's behind the research? Discovering hidden assumptions in behavioural sciences.* Thousand Oaks, CA: Sage Publications.

Sporka, A. J., Nêmec, V., & Slavík, P. (2005). Tangible newspaper for the visually impaired users. In *CHI '05 extended abstracts on human factors in computing systems* (pp. 1809–1812). New York: ACM Press.

Ståhl, A., Sundström, P. & Höök, K. (2005). A foundation for emotional expressivity. In *Proceedings of the 2005 Conference on Designing for User eXperience* (Paper No. 33). New York: American Institute of Graphic Arts.

Swallow, D., Blythe, M., & Wright, P. (2006). Grounding experience: Relating theory and method to evaluate the user experience of smartphones. In *Proceedings of the 2005 Conference on European Association of Cognitive Ergonomics* (pp. 91–98). New York: ACM Press.

Tranel, D., & Damasio, A. R. (1985). Knowledge without awareness: An autonomic index of facial recognition by prosopagnosics. *Science, 228,* 1435–1454.

Wilenius, R. (1978). *Ihminen, luonto ja tekniikka.* [The human being, nature and technology]. Jyväskylä, Finland: Gummerus.

Wilenius, R. (1987). Ihminen filosofisena ongelmana. [The human being as a philosophical problem]. In R. Wilenius, P. Oksala, L. Mehtonen, & M. Juntunen (Eds.), *Johdatus filosofiseen ajatteluun* [Introduction to philosophical thinking]. Jyväskylä, Finland: Atena.

Wright, P., & McCarthy, J. (2005). The value of the novel in designing for experience. In A. Pirhonen, H. Isomäki, C. Roast, & P. Saariluoma (Eds.), *Future interaction design* (9–30). London: Springer-Verlag.

Vyas, D. & van der Veer, G. (2006). Rich evaluations of entertainment experience: bridging the interpretational gap. In *Proceedings of the 13th European Conference on Cognitive Ergonomics: Trust and control in complex socio-technical systems* (pp. 137–144). New York: ACM Press.

Author Index

Subject Index